D101473

This b...

Contemporary Black Men's Fiction and Drama

Contemporary Black Men's Fiction and Drama

Edited by Keith Clark

UNIVERSITY OF ILLINOIS PRESS
Urbana and Chicago

Library of Congress Cataloging-in-Publication Data
Contemporary Black men's fiction and drama / edited by
Keith Clark.
p. cm.
Includes bibliographical references and index.
ISBN 0-252-02676-4
1. American literature—African American authors—History
and criticism. 2. American literature—20th century—History
and criticism. 3. American literature—Male authors—History
and criticism. 4. African American men in literature.
5. African Americans in literature. I. Clark, Keith, 1963– .
PS153.N5C645   2001
810.9'9286'08996073—dc21   2001000518

Contents

Acknowledgments

Several persons contributed to the publication of this volume. I am grateful for the encouragement and guidance of Emily Rogers, a former editor at the University of Illinois Press who took the initiative to contact me about my scholarship and shepherded this volume through its initial stages. Professor Trudier Harris of the University of North Carolina at Chapel Hill generously offered cogent suggestions about the essays as well as much-appreciated encouragement when it looked as though my resolve was waning. Hilary Holladay, a valued colleague and graduate compatriot from Chapel Hill, always graciously agreed to read portions of the manuscript at a moment's notice. I am also indebted to my dear friend F. Myron Dunston, who, unbeknownst to him, served as an unofficial "graduate assistant" as well as an emotional bedrock during this process. I was fortunate to receive the support of two universities—my home institution, George Mason University, and the University of North Carolina at Chapel Hill, which awarded me a postdoctoral fellowship that allowed me to follow through on an idea that had heretofore been confined to my scholarly imagination. Of course, this book exists primarily through the creativity and diligence of the scholars represented here, many of whom responded favorably to my suggestions and revised their essays during some of the most perilous moments of the academic year.

Finally, I am forever grateful to the unflagging support of many families—the Clarks, Wilsons, Lowerys, Malones, and Riches, all of whom offered unconditional love and fervent prayers even when they knew not what I was doing.

◫ ◫ ◫

An earlier version of James W. Coleman's "Clarence Major's *All-Night Visitors:* Calibanic Discourse and Black Male Expression" appeared in *African American Review* 28.1 (Spring 1994): 95–108.

Contemporary Black Men's Fiction and Drama

Introduction

KEITH CLARK

The 1980s and 1990s have marked a proliferation of works written by or about African-American men. If the 1920s represented a kinetic cultural moment in which the "Negro was in vogue," as the poet Langston Hughes said about blacks during the Harlem Renaissance, one might be tempted to extrapolate from the attention currently being devoted to black men that they are experiencing halcyon days. Indeed, the spate of popular and academic books that take black masculine representation as their subject is substantial. *Makes Me Wanna Holler: A Young Black Man in America* (1994), *Brotherman: The Odyssey of Black Men in America* (1995), *Speak My Name: Black Men on Masculinity and the American Dream* (1995), and *Are We Not Men? Masculine Anxiety and the Problem of African-American Identity* (1996) are but a few of the books published in the 1990s alone. Hence, one might conclude that the black male voice is vibrant and omnipresent. The doomsday lexicon surrounding black male "endangerment" in the 1980s would now appear to be a faint memory, a by-product of the reign of the former president on whom the poet-singer Gil-Scott Heron bestowed the derisive sobriquet Ronald "Ray-gun."

Contradictorily, however, the numerous volumes containing or analyzing black men's stories belie a reality in which they are being (ware)housed in what Angela Davis and others have deemed a "prison industrial complex" at an exponential rate. To be sure, black men may be garnering attention as discursive subjects, but the soaring rate of black male suicides, the declining life expectancy of black men under twenty-five because of pandemic violence, the raging modern plague called AIDS, and the near extinction of the black male collegian suggest that they remain in peril and under siege. Whereas Ralph Ellison fictionalized black men's metaphorical and social invisibility in his 1952 magnum opus, that invisibility now takes material, corporeal forms—the black male body is not so much in pain as in absentia. Thus, a contrapuntal narrative emerges: the popularity of black men as social and academic subjects exists in a coterminous relationship with the increasing subjugation or disappearance of actual black men's bodies. Perhaps there is something perversely epitaphic about the explosion of writings on and about African-American men. I am reminded of the last line of Toni Morrison's neo–slave novel *Beloved*, which enigmatically reads, "this is not a story to pass on": indeed, the stories being recorded and told may be elegiac remembrances *about* those who have passed on or ruminations *by* the survivors grieving those passings. In our apocalyptic, millennium-obsessed cultural moment, a moment of post-postmodernism and post-AIDS, the profusion of anthologies and literary exegeses on black men possibly reflects a macabre recuperative gesture—post-blackmale—aimed at keeping alive that which we simultaneously denigrate, celebrate, and, ultimately, commemorate.

So one of my concerns in editing this volume is when and where it enters. The late 1960s and early 1970s represents the starting point for this collection. That period also marked the publication of landmark critical studies such as C. W. E. Bigsby's *The Black American Writer* and Donald Gibson's *Five Black Novelists,* both of which performed invaluable critical service by documenting a tradition of black belles lettres. Unfortunately, though, these works did not explicitly designate their gendered topos and were, therefore, at least benignly myopic: by critical fiat, the designation "black writer" automatically meant "male writer." To invoke and revise the fitting title from a well-known 1981 black feminist anthology, all of the blacks were thought to be men, and none of the writers could have possibly been black women. This form of what Deborah E. McDowell has labeled "disinheritance," where black male writers are installed as the standard bearers of the black literary tradition and women writers rendered invisible, bears witness to some of the limitations of 1960s black nationalist discourse, which was too often poisoned by virulent sexism (and hypermasculinity and its twin scourge, homophobia). Thus, much of the vital work done by black women scholars in the 1970s and 1980s was fueled by two complementary concerns: the need to excavate (think of Alice Walker's "resurrection" of Zora Neale Hurston) the primary texts of heretofore silenced, undiscovered, or undervalued black women writers; and the need to create theoretical matrices for women's writing that were not anchored in tendentiously masculine discourses which, perhaps out of benign neglect at best or out of a Hawthornian antipathy for "damned scribbling women" at worst, amputated the distaff branch of the literary family tree. Hence, my anxiety of scholarly masculinity stems from a fervent desire to avoid perpetuating phallocentric critical practices that have overwhelmingly privileged male writers.

It is my intent that *Contemporary Black Men's Fiction and Drama* will enter a discursive conversation in which issues surrounding black male artistic production are being celebrated and interrogated, as evidenced by publications in the 1990s such as the two-volume edition of the journal *Callaloo* devoted to "Emerging Black Male Writers" and *Representing Black Men,* a hybrid of critical and theoretical pieces on African-American men in disparate media—literature, music, and film primarily. This book is a response to the paucity of studies devoted solely to black men's literary art produced from the 1970s through the 1990s. Though there exist scores of studies on the two writers at the summit of the African-American male literary pantheon, Richard Wright and Ralph Ellison,[1] the relatively sparse number of books on established authors like Ernest J. Gaines and Ishmael Reed, as well as emerging ones like Randall Kenan and neglected authors like the late Georgia-born novelist Raymond Andrews, is disheartening. Indeed, the substantial output of these writers has far outpaced the scholarly energy being expended on their works. In my graduate seminars, I was disappointed that there weren't male counterparts to studies like Majorie Pryse and Hortense Spillers's incisive *Conjuring: Black Women, Fiction, and Literary Traditions* (1985) and Cheryl Wall's seminal *Changing Our Own Words: Essays on Criticism, Theory, and Writing by Black Women* (1989). This is not to suggest that male writers since the 1970s haven't received critical attention: though there remains much work to be done, journals such as *African American Review, Callaloo,* and *College Language Association Journal* regularly publish essays on African-American men's writing alongside the odd piece in *PMLA* and *American Literature.* Thus, I envisioned a volume that covered an amalgam of writers and topics that would speak to scholars in the field but be accessible to undergraduates and even general readers like those in the book clubs that have flourished in the 1990s, where readers devour books like *A Lesson before Dying* and wish to expand their understanding of these texts' multifaceted depictions of black male subjects.

⊡ ⊟ ⊡

In teaching African-American literature, I present to students not only the rich and expansive literary tradition consisting of autobiographies, novels, plays, and poems but also the attendant legacy of black writers aestheticizing and theorizing black art. Just as Robert Stepto accurately claims that black male writers from Booker T. Washington to Ellison have immersed themselves in and responded to Frederick Douglass's 1845 *Narrative* as a master-text of black men's literature, I consider Langston Hughes's proclamatory 1926 essay "The Negro Artist and the Racial Mountain" as a comparable aesthetic manifesto, one that the poet's literary sons and grandsons have critiqued, revised, and inculcated. His artistic exhortations reverberate throughout our critical imaginations as loudly as Douglass's chiasmatic pronouncement, "You have seen how a man was made a slave; you shall see how a slave was made a man": "We younger Negro artists who create now intend to express our individual dark-skinned selves without fear or shame. If white people are pleased we are glad. If they are not, it doesn't matter. We know we are beautiful. And ugly too. The tom-tom cries and the tom-tom laughs. If colored people are pleased we are glad. If they are not, their displeasure doesn't matter either. We build our temples for tomorrow, strong as we know how, and we stand on top of the mountains, free within ourselves" (305). This declaration of artistic independence from the so-called black, derivative Plantation School of Paul Laurence Dunbar and Charles Chesnutt championed the blackness of blackness, a race-consciousness that would be heralded in the works of Hughes, McKay, and other Harlem Renaissance luminaries. Hughes's attempt to give his literary peers an imprimatur for fashioning and articulating an "authentic" black voice presages comparable aesthetic emancipatory proclamations from writers like Clarence Major and Charles Johnson, two of the most prolific novelists since the 1970s in terms of artistic production and aesthetic commentary.

Several critics have noted the post-1960s, post–Black Arts movement sensibilities of black writers who have eschewed prescriptive dictates like the ones Hughes in the 1920s and Larry Neal in the 1960s promulgated. As J. Lee Greene points out,

> Before the 1960s, there were clear parameters that determined whom and what the black novel could center as subject and subject matter. These guidelines contracted and expanded with each generation of novelists and allowed for variety in thematic focus and discursive mode. Yet diversity within these boundaries was limited primarily to issues of color, class, and locale in writing black

subjectivity. . . . Concurrent with cultural, social, and political changes in the nation after the mid-twentieth century, black novelists began to express a greater degree of freedom within (rather than from) the black novelistic tradition's thematic and formalist norms. Certainly, this freedom among novelists is re-defining the tradition by appreciably expanding it. (273–74)

One finds in the writings of Ishmael Reed, Clarence Major, and Charles Johnson the fulfillment of what Greene delineates as the expansion and lib-eration of the black text from the shackles of protest or race-uplift litera-ture, literature with a circumscribing set of critical and artistic imperatives. Major himself uncompromisingly stakes a new direction for his and much post-1960s black writing: "I don't think black writers can be thrown together . . . into some kind of formula. Black writers today should write whatever they want to write and in any way they choose to write it. No style or sub-ject should be alien to them. We have to get away from this rigid notion that there are certain topics and methods reserved for black writers. I'm against all that. I'm against coercion from blacks and whites" (O'Brien 127). Such pronouncements inhere a fundamental irony: just as one detects Ellison's own nuanced, idiosyncratic brand of protest in *Invisible Man* despite his ardent denunciation of Wrightian protest in *Shadow and Act,* one gleans in Ma-jor's and other contemporary writers' "freedom statements" Hughes's re-fusal to be hemmed-in by the popular dictates of his reading public, irrespec-tive of race. So while the parameters have been expanded, the need to fashion and liberate one's artistic voice is, ultimately, not new, the influential anxi-ety being hereditary.

The essays in this volume, like the authors it takes as its subject, are con-ceived with a sensitivity to a tradition of black men's writing while simul-taneously recording how the discursive boundaries have been stretched. While one can certainly find legitimacy in Charles Johnson's claim—accu-sation?—that black men's writing "often seems to be the same story recy-cled or sliced into from different angles, and this is troubling to the degree that one of the legacies of Cultural Nationalism (or the Black Aesthetic) is the agreement among many authors that all blacks have a shared history of oppression, which is admittedly an idea true and necessary to bring blacks together for political action, but in fiction it presents a few prob-lems" (*Being and Race* 74), one can also locate other stories not moored to a dogmatically restrictive "black experience," narratives that go beyond tales of sound and fury bemoaning racial disenfranchisement and social dis-possession.

To be sure, the thematic complexity and technical sophistication displayed

by authors such as John Edgar Wideman, August Wilson, and Johnson himself undercut the latter's claim that black men have metronomically recited
a narrative of black victimization and dysfunction. As the essays gathered
here demonstrate, these writers have engaged disparate and multivalent questions, some from familiar angles, but many from different ones: How have
parochial constructions of masculinity and black male subjectivity been countered and often dismantled? In what ways have black men's relationships to
family and community been reenvisioned, reevaluated, and remapped? How
have writers interrogated representations that assumed black men's allegiance
to a privileged realm of patriarchal masculinity that was inexorably heterosexist and homophobic—not to mention self-abnegating? And how have
contemporary theories of narrative informed stylistic and narratological
concerns—think of the wildly innovative and experimental fictions of Reed
and Major or the theoretical/historical dimensions that undergird Kenan's
narratives. In short, how has black men's literary discourse collided with the
parameters that often confined their art? I would contend that the critical
scope of the essays in this collection bears witness to the existence of what
Johnson deems "experiences of blackness" ("Whole Sight" 2), narratives that
particularize black men's stories and simultaneously liberate black male authors from stifling social and aesthetic mandates. Incontestably, contemporary black men's writing is multivisaged, its countenance doing more than
"facing off" against Anglo-American hegemonic oppression in hopes of erad-
icating the seemingly omnipresent anguish of African-American men.

    Within and beyond the tradition might best encapsulate the scope and
direction of black men's writing since 1970. In recent fictions narrativizing
and thematizing black men's experiences, one indisputably hears echoes of
Douglass and Wright. Indeed, in many writers' critiques of the discursive
limitations of the slave or protest narrative one detects a paradoxical engagement and acknowledgment of these very forms, exemplified in the "prison fictions" that populate Ernest J. Gaines's literary corpus—fictions that
recursively (consciously or not) reinterrogate and "correct" the denouement
of *Native Son* in which an agencyless Bigger Thomas awaits his execution
in an asphyxiating cell. Though she specifies a black women's literary tradition, the black feminist scholar Joanne M. Braxton articulates a notion
of artistic germination and evolution that is germane in terms of black men's
writing: "The current flowering of Black women's writing must be viewed
as part of a cultural continuum and an evolving consciousness, a consciousness that will continue to evolve and unfold" (xxii). Black men, too, create
within the tradition while also interpellating those writers on the continu-

um Braxton specifies. Contemporary African-American men's writing has been tendril-like, rooted in the vineyard of black men's literary creativity while simultaneously spawning new directions for black men's expression and the scholarship it germinates.

In this volume's lead essay, Sheila Smith McKoy contextualizes and scrutinizes a facet of southern African-American men's writing that has been peripheralized or ignored altogether. In "Rescuing the Black Homosexual Lambs: Randall Kenan and the Reconstruction of Southern Gay Masculinity," McKoy explores Kenan's bucolic "Dixie" landscape, where masculinity and homosexuality exist coterminously if not always harmoniously. In her estimation, Kenan's inscriptions of black gay characters are undeniably cultivated from a fertile tradition of southern writers who have addressed the topic of sexual difference, specifically Ernest J. Gaines, Raymond Andrews, and James Baldwin—the latter not technically a "southern" writer but one whose irrepressibly southern sensibilities shape the lives of the transplanted northerners who populate his fiction. McKoy insists that what distinguishes Kenan's portraitures, however, is his remapping of the constricted psychic and geographic regions to which his predecessors consigned African-American gay men. In a radical act of signifying, Kenan rescues gayness and masculinity from the mutually exclusive and excluding spaces to which they have been traditionally bound.

Writing about another southern writer entrenched in and enchanted by the region's mythic character, Trudier Harris examines what she identifies as the "disease of strength" in Raymond Andrews's novel *Appalachee Red* (1978). Andrews created a mythological black folk and vernacular community that hearkens back to Faulkner's Yoknapatawpha; in fact, Andrews's fictive milieu can be read as a response to and corrective of Faulkner's, where blacks stoically "endured" the South's intractably racist mores in narratives that rendered their lives and voices tangential to those of white southerners. In "This Disease Called Strength: The Masculine Manifestation in Raymond Andrews's *Appalachee Red*," Harris dissects what she interprets as a severely flawed portraiture of black masculinity, one rooted in damaging myths surrounding black men's presumed physical superiority. This archetypal narrative of the hyperphysical black male has its roots, Harris argues, in black folkloric heroes such as John Henry, figures who relied on brute strength or violence to achieve society's sanctioned definition of masculinity in a culture committed to their actual or psychic emasculation. Like these mythic folk legends, the novel's protagonist, Big Man Thompson, carves out his prized masculine status through pugilism in lieu of cultivating nurturing relationships with his fellow blacks. As a result, he terrorizes not only those blacks with whom he shares common spatial boundaries but, more ignominiously, his wife Little Bit, a black woman already victimized by a fiercely patriarchal southern culture that sexualizes and commodifies her with impunity.

Employing a similar folkloric framework as the basis for his argument, Raymond E. Janifer traces John Edgar Wideman's artistic evolution. Chronicling Wideman's artistic development from the 1960s, Janifer contends that the author's literary rite of passage has involved an arduous reimmersion into folk and vernacular traditions. While Wideman's earliest novels reflect his inculcation of postmodernist aesthetic values, he has since embarked upon an exhaustive spiritual journey into his family's rich and sustaining rituals of storytelling, a tradition that connects not only generations of Widemans but also African Americans to their diasporic roots that traverse temporal and geographic borders. In correlation with his cultural reconnections, Wideman concurrently has revisited the African-American literary tradition, witnessing how black authors mine folkloric and vernacular tropes and traditions. By "looking Homewood," Janifer demonstrates, Wideman engages heretofore devalued cultural ways of knowing and being; this revisiting of familial and communal roots manifests itself in stories such as "Damballah," which attests to the durability of African-centered folkways and an African-American ethos in oppressive contexts.

The volume's next two essays explore writers who, despite their prodigious output, have yet to receive the critical attention their works merit. James W. Coleman's "Clarence Major's *All-Night Visitors:* Calibanic Discourse and Black Male Expression" takes as its subject an author whose works are so inflected with postmodernist experimental techniques that readers and critics alike have shied away from them. Though perhaps Major's best-known work of fiction to date is *Reflex and Bone Structure* (1975), Coleman focuses his critical gaze on an earlier novel with an unwieldy, elusive narratological style. Refusing to read Major's fiercely idiosyncratic, innovative novel as a seamless, well-made one in the tradition of canonical works like *Native Son* or *Invisible Man,* Coleman posits that the very indeterminacy of *All-Night Visitors,* its resistance to neat but confining literary taxonomies, reifies the knotty issue of black male subjectivity in a culture so ardently committed to denying black men their very personhood. Coleman adduces that the novel's aims are multifarious: he sees it as Major's attempt to claim for black men a linguistic freedom in a culture that silences and erases. Additionally, the essay explores the novel within and against the tradition of black feminist discourse, which sometimes assails black male writers and their protagonists for not articulating a liberating subjectivity that irrefutably opposes confining and constricted Western-based definitions of blackness.

Though more widely known than Major, Ishmael Reed has still not attracted the critical scrutiny his oeuvre warrants. In fact, Reed is probably as much known in some circles as an unflinching literary gadfly who has excoriated white and black feminists alike as he is for a voluminous output of novels, poems, and essays. A. T. Spaulding examines Reed's *Flight to Canada,* a neo–slave novel that represents a much-neglected foray into this subgenre, though Reed infuses it with postmodernist sensibilities. According to Spaulding, Reed constructs a labyrinthine metanarrative that is as much about the contemporary black novelist's own agonizing attempt to locate an authentic artistic voice as it is the nineteenth-century male slave's quest for freedom and voice. Not content to record a slave's emancipation, Reed connects the plight of his slave-protagonist to his own as a twentieth-century black male author: in his purview, the voices of both are consistently mediated, edited, and stifled by the demands of a predominantly white literary hegemony. Spaudling shows how Reed's freewheeling, parodic presentation of slavery, one that is not wedded to historical accuracies, becomes a scathing metacommentary that demonstrates how black men's voices and literary products are constantly packaged for white consumption.

Having received the 1990 National Book award for his neo–slave novel *Middle Passage,* Charles Johnson has established his presence as a path-breaking novelist and an astute critic of the black literary tradition. William R. Nash examines this aesthetic position in "'I Was My Father's Father, and He My Child': The Process of Black Fatherhood and Literary Evolution in Charles Johnson's Fiction," probing how the burdens of race and history often render black men physically, psychologically, and emotionally dislocated. The theme that permeates Johnson's fiction, Nash shows, is the exploration of black male protagonists attempting to negotiate a world where their status as men—fathers and sons—has been imperiled by an array of forces, the most damaging being their inculcation of a victim status that becomes paralyzing and self-destructive. Thus, Johnson's is a storyworld where black men must accept their complicity in their often inert, ineffectual existences. Nash investigates the invaluable role of surrogate fathers in Johnson's work, men who overcome a legacy of oppression and regenerate younger men prostrated by their race and gender. Moreover, the essay explores Johnson's artistic evolution, elucidating the paradoxical position of contemporary writers who at once feel an obligation to preserve a tradition of African-American men's writing alongside the need to redefine the contours of what constitutes black literary art.

Another contemporary author who has wrestled with anxieties over influence is Ernest J. Gaines, who began his distinguished publishing career in the mid-sixties but whose most critically acclaimed writings have appeared since 1970. The Gaines scholar Herman Beavers interrogates the intersections of race, allegory, and religion in "Prodigal Agency: Allegory and Voice in Ernest J. Gaines's *A Lesson before Dying.*" Using the parable of the prodigal as an intertext, Beavers explores the ways in which Gaines imbues this biblical tale with allegorical and political ramifications. Beavers posits that the story of the prodigal is far more complex than a tale of estrangement and reconciliation: it is an irreconcilable story about personal agency and choices and the individual-community nexus. Recalling his literary ancestor James Baldwin, Gaines recasts familiar biblical tales and tropes to complexify blacks' inculcation of traditional Christian principles. As Beavers insists, the spiritual/religious is inextricably bound up with the personal, communal, and political: "Gaines's use of the parable is, in the way of parables, a disruptive act because it is neither neat nor certain; it asserts that the path to redemption is mysterious, unknowable."

Continuing in the vein of Beavers's exploration of the black male writer's religious-spiritual dimensions, Melvin B. Rahming addresses black male identity formation from an Afri-cosmological perspective in two younger writers, Melvin Dixon and Brent Wade, whose innovative works await a wider readership. Critiquing the icons of black men's writing—from Wright to Ellison to Baldwin—Rahming insists that protagonists in these authors' works are paralyzed because they fetishize values that are anathema to African-centered ways of knowing and being. More recent novels such as Dixon's *Trouble the Water* and Wade's *Company Man* represent admirable and, to varying degrees, successful attempts to present protagonists grappling to fill the psychospiritual void left in the wake of black men's self-annihilating acceptance of an alien ethos. Though he sees *Company Man* as a mildly successful departure from the standard male narratives of victimization and cosmological exigency, Rahming interprets *Trouble the Water* as a novel that assiduously reevaluates and reestablishes black men's inherent need for a modus vivendi that locates one's spiritual consciousness as a basic component of black male subjectivity. Rahming imaginatively configures a multidisciplinary model of Afrocentric literary discourse that paves the way for other diasporan approaches to African-American men's writing that encompass the spiritual components of the black male self that are often devalued in Western culture.

If the link between black men's psychological and spiritual health reflects an uncharted space for African-American writers, then sexual difference might be deemed the final frontier. Though the name "Baldwin" quickly falls from the lips of critics and students of black literature whenever the theme of sexual otherness surfaces, there remains a silence around the fluidity of black men's sexuality. Kenyatta Dorey Graves's "Are Love and Literature Political? Black Homopoetics in the 1990s" enters into a conversation that is still in its nascent stages, one surrounding the discursive and hermeneutical issues regarding a distinctly black-centered theory of African-American gay writing. Comparable to Barbara Smith's pioneering lesbi-centric essay "Toward a Black Feminist Criticism" and more recent attempts to configure black gay literary aesthetics by critics such as Charles I. Nero and Kendall Thomas,[2] Graves's essay articulates the political and critical tensions that emerge when black male writers narrativize what Graves defines as "SGL" or "same-gender love." Using the post-Baldwin generation of black gay writers to stimulate his thoughts, Graves explores the narrative choices of both authors and characters to buttress his admittedly controversial critical position: contemporary black gay writing reflects "a period in which two phenomena are occurring simultaneously—the first being the emergence of an identifiable SGL aesthetic and the second being the flourishing of writing by black, gay men that privileges the experience of the larger white, gay community." This foray into often taboo, stigmatized subjects suggests that the "unveiling" of racial issues that Du Bois inaugurated at the fin de siècle may have its analog at the millennium in the uncloseting of black men's sexual desires that do not conform to a heterosexual ideal.

The last essay in the volume looks at another form of difference: alternative configurations of black masculinity that dislodge the circumscribing tenets of patriarchal masculinity. In "Healing the Scars of Masculinity: Reflections on Baseball, Gunshots, and War Wounds in August Wilson's *Fences*," I explore how Wilson invokes the signs and symbols of phallocentric institutions such as the armed services and sports to deconstruct black men's truncated sense of their subjectivity. Though critics often interpret his Pulitzer Prize–winning play as a paean to the "strength" of its protagonist, Troy Maxson, I counter that the play examines the inherent pitfalls of black men confining their sense of wholeness to a hypermasculine Western ideal, one that alternatively renders black men as feral and ill-prepared for the rigors of "masculinity." However, not content to challenge this sanctioned construction of black maleness, the playwright foregrounds alternative countervoices that destabilize Troy's circumscribing beliefs. Like the other essays in this collection, "Healing the Scars" reenvisions the construction of black male identity and black men's writing.

Thus, this collection takes as its subject a wide range of critical, theoretical, cultural, gender, and sexual concerns. Of course, the volume is not and could not be comprehensive: anthologies, like communities, are by definition simultaneously inclusive and exclusive. I would be the first to admit the volume's shortcomings and exclusions: black men's poetry, like African-American poetry generally, does not receive its critical due; the current explosion of biographies by writers as diverse as the journalist Nathan McCall and the literary critic Henry Louis Gates Jr. warrants wider attention; and neglected authors such as the short story writer James Alan McPherson and the dramatist and satirist George C. Wolfe deserve more sustained critical analysis. I hope that this study will perform critical work that will parallel black women's theoretical and critical studies: reintroducing established writers like Ernest J. Gaines and August Wilson, renewing interest in underread ones like Raymond Andrews and Ishmael Reed, and drawing attention to recent literary mavericks like Randall Kenan and Brent Wade. *Contemporary Black Men's Fiction and Drama* demonstrates the extraordinary versatility of contemporary black men's writing, and I anticipate that it will inaugurate further studies of African-American men's literary production.

Notes

1. I deliberately exclude James Baldwin from this "pantheon" because of the dearth of book-length studies on his writing, which reflects a gaping crater in African-American literary scholarship.

2. See Nero's "Towards a Black Gay Aesthetic" and Thomas's "'Ain't Nothin' Like the Real Thing': Black Masculinity, Gay Sexuality, and the Jargon of Authenticity" as recent critical attempts to articulate a uniquely black, gay aesthetic of literature and culture.

Works Cited

Belton, Don, ed. *Speak My Name: Black Men on Masculinity and the American Dream.* Boston: Beacon Press, 1995.

Bigsby, C. W. E., ed. *The Black American Writer.* 2 vols. Baltimore: Penguin Books, 1969.

Blount, Marcellus, and George P. Cunningham, eds. *Representing Black Men.* New York: Routledge, 1996.

Boyd, Herb, and Robert L. Allen, eds. *Brotherman: The Odyssey of Black Men in America—An Anthology.* New York: Ballantine Books, 1996.

Braxton, Joanne M. "Afra-American Culture and the Contemporary Literary Renaissance." In *Wild Women in the Whirlwind: Afra-American Culture and the Contemporary Literary Renaissance.* Ed. Joanne M. Braxton and Andree Nicola McLaughlin. New Brunswick, N.J.: Rutgers University Press, 1990. xxi–xxx.

Gibson, Donald. *Five Black Novelists.* New York: New York University Press, 1970.

Greene, J. Lee. *Blacks in Eden: The African American Novel's First Century.* Charlottesville: University Press of Virginia, 1996.

Harper, Philip Brian. *Are We Not Men? Masculine Anxiety and the Problem of African-American Identity.* New York: Oxford University Press, 1996.

Hughes, Langston. *The Big Sea.* New York: Knopf, 1940.

———. "The Negro Artist and the Racial Mountain" (1926). In *Amistad 1.* Ed. John A. Williams and Charles F. Harris. New York: Vintage, 1970. 301–5.

Johnson, Charles. *Being and Race: Black Writing since 1970.* Bloomington: Indiana University Press, 1988.

———. "Whole Sight: Notes on New Black Fiction." *Callaloo* 7.22 (1984): 1–6.

McCall, Nathan. *Makes Me Wanna Holler: A Young Black Man in America.* New York: Random House, 1994.

McDowell, Deborah E. *"The Changing Same": Black Women's Literature, Criticism, and Theory.* Bloomington: Indiana University Press, 1995.

Nero, Charles I. "Towards a Black Gay Aesthetic." In *Brother to Brother: New Writings by Black Gay Men.* Ed. Essex Hemphill. Boston: Alyson, 1991. 229–52.

O'Brien, John, ed. *Interviews with Black Writers.* New York: Liveright, 1973.

Pryse, Marjorie, and Hortense J. Spillers, eds. *Conjuring: Black Women, Fiction, and Literary Traditions.* Bloomington: Indiana University Press, 1985.

Thomas, Kendall. "'Ain't Nothin' Like the Real Thing': Black Masculinity, Gay Sexuality, and the Jargon of Authenticity." In *Representing Black Men.* Ed. Marcellus Blount and George P. Cunningham. New York: Routledge, 1996. 55–69.

Wall, Cheryl, ed. *Changing Our Own Words: Essays on Criticism, Theory, and Writing by Black Women.* New Brunswick, N.J.: Rutgers University Press, 1989.

1

Rescuing the Black Homosexual Lambs: Randall Kenan and the Reconstruction of Southern Gay Masculinity

Sheila Smith McKoy

> But remember, black boy, you heard it here first: You're a
> faggot.... You're a faggot.
> —Randall Kenan, *A Visitation of Spirits*

> And then there are the sexual standards we black men must
> meet—because we are not permitted to be men anywhere else,
> we must at least be men in the bedroom.
> —Darieck Scott, "This City of Men"

In *A Visitation of Spirits,* Randall Kenan allows readers to glimpse the rural southern landscapes—and lifescapes—of eastern North Carolina, a space wherein lives read through a nexus of sin, sexuality, and race provide an intriguing examination of the ways in which both heteronormative and gay identities are shaped. Having been born in New York and raised in Chinquapin, North Carolina, a tiny hamlet in the southeast region of the state, Kenan's personal and creative histories "revise" the familiar urban and northern histories of the life and oeuvre of James Baldwin who, though born in the transplanted "southern" community of Harlem, came of age and came *out* in New York. According to Robert McRuer in his study of the reinvention of gay and lesbian identity, *The*

Queer Renaissance, Kenan's project is vitally significant in the process of exposing how gay fiction, particularly coming out narratives, subordinates "racial identity to an unmarked (white) gay identity" (47). Positioned within both of the contesting identities figured in the opening epigraphs—specifically the desire for and to be black men—Randall Kenan's exploration of blackness and homosexuality posits that both identities are indeed simultaneously possible.

Kenan's depiction of the black gay subject as both black and "manly" struggles against a peculiar history, one that was shaped by a quagmire of literally historic proportions. The oppressive histories of the concomitant religious, race-based, and cultural marginalization that people of color have faced, though certainly potentially devastating, only contribute to the problem. People who dare to identify as both black and gay also face a range of homophobic responses within cultures of color. The Afrocentric disavowals of homosexuality that permeate the range of political, social, and religious discourses are renowned.[1] In the political forum, various national debates characterize homosexuality as being outside of the African cultural experience. And, because they have struggled with the well-founded fear associated with being perpetually defined outside of the normative, Africans in the Americas and the Caribbean share a particularly virulent history of homophobia. Charles Rowell describes this shared experience in terms of its terrorism:

> In the Caribbean, South America, and Africa, very few individuals are brave enough to sign or identify themselves gay to the public. The consequences of doing so are grave: They result from state-sponsored homohatred or from anti-gay cultural practices, which threaten the life of the individual. This terrorism has been underscored by certain political and cultural activities on the African continent and in the Caribbean. The homophobic pronouncements of Zimbabwe's President Robert Mugabe, and the recording of anti-gay lyrics by popular Caribbean musicians, such as Buju Banton and Shabba Ranks, are ample testaments confirming the terrorism to which gay men and women are subjected. (339)

The controversial release of gospel duo Angie and Debbie Winans's "Not Natural" is only one of the many titles we might add to the list of songs with anti-gay lyrics. The song's release and the duo's performance of it at the Million Woman March in 1997 sparked a national debate. The sentiments the Winans express in "Not Natural" represent the black church's public view of homosexuality although, within the private histories of most black churches, black lesbians and gay men have been continually and typically present. In short, due to a number of social and cultural pressures, homophobia is legendary in Africa and the African Diaspora despite the fact that black gay men and women have been a continual and popular presence in these communities. This is especially true of African-American culture in which black gay men from Little Richard to Sylvester to RuPaul perform racial as well as sexual tricks for a wider and whiter public audience.[2]

This homophobic quagmire seems to entrap even its advocates, especially when one notes that Zimbabwe's former president, Canaan Banana, was charged with sodomy in May 1998. Ironically, it was during Banana's presidency that homosexuality and sodomy were criminalized in Zimbabwe. The Winans have also been victims of their own homophobia: in response to the anti-gay "Not Natural," black gay rights organizations have sponsored successful boycotts of the duo's performances. Yet, despite the "queer" backlash, these homophobic pronouncements persist. By locating homosexuality outside of the parameters of black identity, this phobia aligns homosexuality with whiteness and with what Phillip Brian Harper terms "failed manhood" (50). In other words, black gay identity is erroneously connected to what is not masculine and not black. This misalignment is precisely what Kenan's fiction witnesses against.

While black gay portraits have focused on the political and aesthetic concerns of northern and urban gay identity since Claude McKay published *Home to Harlem* in 1929, these portraits have relied upon black gay identity to read the racial, sexual, and gendered experiences of characters who are often neither black nor gay. Baldwin's *Giovanni's Room,* for instance, broke new ground in black gay literature when it was published in 1956; however, the novel is exclusively populated with white characters. Even in his first best-seller, *Another Country* (1962), Baldwin refuses to fully articulate the struggle for wholeness in which his black gay character, Rufus Scott, is embroiled. Despite the fact that he chooses to contrast Rufus's problematic and violent relationship with a southern white woman against his comforting alignments with white men, Baldwin stops short of identifying Rufus as gay. Instead, as I shall fully delineate, the novel's surviving characters—whether white or black, straight or gay—each play with gay identity as they seek sexual salvation from Rufus's white, southern lover, Eric. In *Another Country,* Baldwin seems to suggest that black gay relationships will always be defined by whiteness and therefore representative of a wholly alien and (an)other culture. Kenan counters this message, however, insisting that homosexual desire can transform culture and that it can open a space wherein black men can embrace a gay identity, even in the rural South.

In a curious or queer sense, then, Kenan's portrait of the brilliant and tortured Horace Cross in *A Visitation of Spirits* (1989) is as much about the politics of coming out as a black man as it is a coming out narrative about the rural South. It is with these racial and spatial outings in mind that I consider Randall Kenan's response to the portraiture of black gay men in the African-American literary tradition in general and in southern black literature in particular. My objective is to explore the ways in which *A Visitation of Spirits* and Kenan's related short stories comment on the representations of black homosexuality prevalent in works written by or about black gay men. Further, I want to explore the ways in which Kenan transforms the image of black gay desire in southern black literature.

A Visitation of Spirits: Rescuing Baldwin's Sacrificial Lambs

The genius of James Baldwin provided American literature with its first gay glimpse of the ways in which American society menaces both the racial and the sexual other. Through his novels and essays, Baldwin consistently out-ed America's misconduct towards African Americans and towards any sexual identity that deviates from the heterosexual "norm." Set primarily in the urban centers of the North, Baldwin's works reflect the tenacity with which he attacked the lack of civil and sexual rights in America; the two oppressions are intimately related in his work. Situated in communities that critique homosexuality and homoerotic desire literally to death, these narratives render the imagined lives of his black gay characters as corollary to the politics of race and gender in the communities that comprise what we claim as American culture.

Kenan, who would likely count Baldwin among his literary forefathers, is also primarily concerned with the relationships between the racially and sexually marked other and the community.[3] McRuer rightly connects the two writers in his insistence that Kenan's *A Visitation of Spirits* revises the text of Baldwin's *Go Tell It on the Mountain:*

> Kenan's novel is a complex signification on James Baldwin's 1953 *Go Tell It on the Mountain.* The story of a young boy torn between sin and the church, after all, has been told before. Through *A Visitation of Spirits,* Kenan rewrites Baldwin's story of John Grimes, bringing it—if you will—out of the closet. . . . *A Visitation of Spirits* in general reads like an openly gay version of *Go Tell It on the Mountain,* and it is Kenan's more general signification on Baldwin that suggests the church and community in *A Visitation of Spirits,* not Horace, are in need of transformation. (80)

As accurate as McRuer's comparison is here, the novel world of *A Visitation of Spirits,* despite its rural landscape, is a closer commentary on *Another Country* than *Go Tell It on the Mountain,* especially when one considers the culminating effects of the suicides of Rufus Scott and Horace Cross. Kenan links these characters further by playing on the biblical history that the names Rufus and Horace Cross share.[4] The New Testament Rufus was the son of Simon of Cyrene, who was compelled to carry Christ's cross; Kenan's Horace Cross bears his own and thus assumes a pivotal position in black gay portraiture. Through these two protagonists, Baldwin and Kenan dramatize the devastating congress of racist and sexist oppression and its impact on two young men who, though black and gay, struggle to reside within the parameters of normalcy in their respective communities.

From the beginning of *Another Country,* Baldwin focuses on the sexual anxiety of Rufus Scott, indicating that his discomfort is as much a commentary on American society as it is on his splintered psyche. The same is true of Kenan's portrait of Horace Cross, whose story chronologically, though not structurally, begins *A Visitation of Spirits.* Both protagonists ponder the ways in which their environments shape the possibilities of defining themselves as both black and gay. Moreover, Baldwin makes it clear that these questions arise out of a historical connection between race, sex, and desire in American culture itself. In his failed search for black gay manhood—for Rufus is ultimately unable to view himself as both a man and gay—Rufus makes this startling connection in the bathroom of a bar while holding the "most despised part of himself," the symbol of his status as a black man in America and of his uncomfortably shifting sexuality: "It smelled of thousands of travelers, oceans of piss, tons of bile and vomit and shit. He added his stream to the ocean, holding that most despised part of himself loosely between two fingers of one hand. . . . He looked at the horrible history splashed furiously on the walls—telephone numbers, cocks, breasts, balls, cunts, etched into these walls with hatred. *Suck my cock. I like to get whipped. I want a hot stiff prick up my ass. Down with Jews. Kill the niggers. I suck cocks"* (74). The history that Baldwin inscribes here is peculiarly American. It is one that marks sexual and racial difference as disruptive, "niggerizing" both. It is also a history that Rufus can escape only in death, making his dying act a ritual sacrifice for the racial and sexual awakenings of the other characters. Baldwin structures Rufus's passion—and I use the term "passion" to invoke what it connotes of desire, suffering, and death—so that it becomes an act of sacrifice through which those *un*marked by the twin demons of race and homosexual desire are vicariously transformed in their understandings of race, sexuality, and normalcy.

In his portrait of Horace, Kenan reenacts the ritual of self-sacrifice; however, this sacrifice transforms the entire community rather than the individuals whose lives Horace intimately touches. Kenan makes this objective clear from the opening passages of the novel, during which Horace decides that his transformation must enable him to remain connected to the small community of his birth, Tims Creek. He notes this connection in his description of Horace's struggle to transform himself:

> At first Horace was sure he would turn himself into a rabbit. But then, no. Though they were swift as pebbles skipping across a pond, they were vulnerable, liable to be snatched up. . . . More than anything else, he wanted to have grace. If he was going to the trouble of transforming himself, he might as well get exactly that. Butterflies were too frail, victims to wind. Cats had a physical freedom he loved to watch, the svelte, smooth, sliding motion of the great cats of Africa, but he could not see transforming himself into anything that would not fit the swampy woodlands of Southeastern North Carolina. He had to stay here. (11)

Even as he contemplates the end of his existence as he knows it, Horace remains intimately connected to his community. This is particularly pertinent given the fact that, like Horace, each of the characters who populate the novel confesses to some kind of sexual misconduct. Horace's grandfather, Zeke, and his great-aunt, Ruth, both confess—though not publicly—to extramarital entanglements. His cousin, Jimmy, who is both his minister and the witness to his suicide, confesses to the "true sin" of living a double life filled with "freshman debauchery" and his ministry (174). Jimmy remembers his wife, Anne, in beatific terms; however, Anne is unable to commit completely to him, and she cuckolds him without regret. The legacy of sexual debauchery seems to touch even the minor characters in the novel. In short, there is no moral authority in Tims Creek, with its numerous and "fleshy affairs" (221). In delineating the fact that everyone in Tims Creek has committed secret sexual sins, Kenan refuses to characterize Horace's death as a necessary sacrifice for the moral integrity of the community.

Kenan insists, moreover, that Horace is integral to the moral life of Tims Creek; in fact, he shapes the narrative so that Horace's passion is tenacious enough to impact the community forever. Kenan's selection of the name, Horace, which literally means one who marks time, speaks of this continuity. The novel's structure also supports Horace's temporal permanence.

Horace reaches back through time to gain the ancient knowledge he needs to summon a demon whose power will enable him to change from the unnamed "thing" he is into something else.[5] Both date and time mark the chapters that depict Horace's descent into the demonology through which he attempts to transform himself. Kenan also sets time in the novel over three specific days—April 29 and April 30, 1984, and December 8, 1985—as well as within the advent season, giving credence to the fact that Horace's story is truly a passion narrative. Further, Kenan constructs the novel world so that it moves back and forth between these temporal moments. By doing so he counterposes Horace's struggle against the moral questions articulated by the surviving inhabitants of Tims Creek. The reader is forced not only to remember Horace but also to remember the ways in which he and the other members of the community are "bound by the necessity, the responsibility, the humanity . . . to remember" (257).

While their passion stories offer quite different possibilities for the black gay men they create, Baldwin and Kenan also focus on the rural South as the locus of homoerotic desire, racial identity, and emergent manhood. Baldwin repeatedly images the southern roots of Rufus's first male lover, Eric. Eric's sexual coming of age is a part of the fabric of the Alabama of his memory, where "cold white people" were balanced by "warm, black people" who "smelled like good things in the oven" (165–66). Through these memories and remembered sensations, Baldwin makes it clear that there is a relationship between racial and sexual oppression in American culture; in fact, Baldwin sees Eric's struggle against "the flesh" in both racial and sexual terms. Eric's initiation into homoerotic experience is with Leroy, a black gay teenager Eric claims as "*his* colored boy," yet denies the fact that he is "a nigger" (172): "He was frightened and in pain and the boy who held him so relentlessly was suddenly a stranger; and yet this stranger worked in Eric an eternal, a healing transformation. Many years would pass before he could begin to accept what he, that day, in those arms, with the stream whispering in his ear, discovered; and yet that day was the beginning of his life as a man" (176). Their encounter takes place in a tree-lined haven located just beyond the town's railroad tracks, the physical boundary that still marks the racial dividing line of most southern cities. Baldwin thus situates this moment as a denial of the normative categories of "whiteness" and heterosexuality.[6] In this moment of sexual exploration, Baldwin arms Leroy with the means to slip the yoke of ownership and race. And it is in the arms of a black man that Eric—white, southern, and rich—denies each of these identities to claim his gay self.

Of course, Horace crosses the line into sexual experience in the South as well. In his description of Horace's first homoerotic experience, Kenan also notes that the experience marks his transition into manhood. Horace's first sexual encounter is with Gideon Stone, a brilliant and beautiful young man who has always embraced his homosexuality. It is toward Gideon's manhood that Horace is drawn; his desire is awakened by a "transformed" Gideon who, in the summer before his freshman year in high school, emerges as "something solid and decidedly manly" (146). Kenan brings the openly gay Gideon and the closeted Horace together in the novel when they are forced to work together on a science project. The project itself, a study of plant tropism, also suggests that Horace's sexual outing is necessary, a recognition of the "orientation of [the] organism" (155). Gideon's presence, like the stimuli that excite growth in the plants they study, exposes the nature of Horace's desire and leads him to ask, "What if I'm the queer . . . ?" (152).

The similarities between the two novels certainly suggest that Kenan is purposefully revising Baldwin's text, paying particular attention to the ways in which homosexual desire both threatens and promises to change the social fabric of the rural South, which he particularizes as Tims Creek. As McRuer indicates, there is something about Horace's story that suggests that it could not have taken place elsewhere (77). It seems that in *A Visitation of Spirits* Kenan weaves a story of tragic consequences that arise, in part, from its southern roots. As much as the South is necessary for Horace, it is integral to Kenan's writing, for as much as he is a black gay writer, Kenan is also a southern writer. As he reveals in a 1997 interview, "To me it's silly to assume that I can be anything other than a Southern, black writer." He further notes precisely what these designations mean:

> Even if I wrote science fiction I would be a "Southern" "black" writer. The question becomes, then, if I am a writer of the South and about the South, or a writer of blackness? I hope these notions are borne out in my work. Am I only a "black" writer? Am I only a "Southern" writer? I think that some people believe that a writer is limited by these labels, and in some cases their narrowing gazes become true. However, I can never take them seriously. Which is to say that I am a human being first, a writer second, and black always. I'm still trying to figure out the Southern part; but I think all Southerners after 1863 are trying to do the same. (White)

Writing out of the complex identity that includes "southern," "black," and "gay," Kenan provokes his readers to explore America's discomfort with race and sexuality. There are few writers who can claim this triple legacy, although "black" "southern" writers have provided substantive explorations

of the rural South through their portraits of black gay men. Kenan specifically critiques these portraits, challenging the prevailing image of black gay
men in the works of black southern writers who precede him.

Southern Discomfort: Kenan's Critique of Ernest J. Gaines and Raymond Andrews

To begin at the beginning of black gay male portraiture in southern African-American literature is somewhat difficult since, as Charles I. Nero indicates, publication and cultural politics have attempted to erase the image
of the black gay subject in African-American literature.[7] The writers of the
Harlem Renaissance, both gay and straight, offered the most open portraits
of black gay men up to the contemporary period. Of these writers, only
Langston Hughes focused on the rural South. Hughes, however, is remembered more for his focus on the racial other rather than on black gay masculinity. In the contemporary period, two black southern writers, Ernest J.
Gaines and Raymond Andrews, have examined the ways in which "faggots,"
"punks," and "sweet boys" transform the racial and sexual inappropriate-
ness of the rural South. Gaines creates three distinct black gay men in his
novel *Of Love and Dust* (1967) and in his short story "Three Men" (1968).
Raymond Andrews presents a fully developed black gay character, Darling
Pullman—whose name is deliberately provocative—in two of his three novels, *Appalachee Red* (1978) and *Baby Sweets* (1983). Gaines and Andrews
position their gay characters to play on various definitions of black manhood; nevertheless, they remain outside of normative experience. In *A Visitation of Spirits* and in several related short stories, Kenan counters these
images of southern manhood by constructing his narratives around black
gay protagonists whose lives and deaths shape a communal and an individual response to the questions that arise when both blackness and sexuality
inform identity.

   Like Randall Kenan's writings, Ernest J. Gaines's fiction is informed by
his identification with the rural South. Born in Oscar, Louisiana, a generation before Kenan, Gaines has written a substantial literary corpus. All of
his fiction is marked by a fundamental concern for black male empowerment. Despite the fact that he may be best known for his endearing portrait
of a centenarian civil rights advocate in *The Autobiography of Miss Jane
Pittman* (1971), his literary canon is dominated by his vision of black masculinity that he has consistently developed since he published his first novel, *Catherine Carmier,* in 1964. Always cognizant of the role race plays in

America's image of black men, Gaines peoples his novels with blacks, whites, and Cajuns, all of whom are bound in uneasy alliances. Unlike most writers of his generation, Gaines dares to explore a range of sexual taboos by confronting America's discomfort with interracial and homosexual desire. Rather than opening a space for black gay subjectivity through his portraits of gay men, Gaines uses them to comment on the lessons in life and morality that his heterosexual protagonists learn as they define what it means to be black men. In his focus on gay men in *Of Love and Dust* and "Three Men," however, Gaines actually negates the socially transformative power of homoerotic desire by validating heterosexual desire and heterosexist moral authority.

In *Of Love and Dust,* Gaines introduces two black gay characters, John and Freddie, whose relationship is accepted and acknowledged by the community. Employed as sharecroppers on a plantation built upon the racial and sexual oppression of the South, Gaines suggests that their presence—and, perhaps, their sexual orientation—is as natural as the landscape. Unlike Kenan's Horace Cross, these men find acceptance in the full range of community life, including the black church.[8] Gaines notes this cultural belongingness from the moment they are introduced in the novel:

> John and Freddie were two punks. John was the big punk, Freddie was the little one. Together they pulled more corn than any other two men I had ever seen; in church on Sunday they shouted more than any two women. The funny thing about it, John and Freddie were ushers in church and they were supposed to look after the women when the women started shouting. But it always ended up with everybody else looking after John and Freddie. A couple of good-sized women could hold down Freddie when he started shouting, but it always took seven or eight men to hold down big John. (25)

I quote at length from the novel because the details Gaines includes here are critically important. He immediately identifies John and Freddie for what they are: as "punks," their sexual proclivities are not the secret sins that typically bedevil tales of homosexual desire in most southern fiction.[9] Further, Gaines makes us immediately aware of the sexual roles that each man plays in the their relationship. These very intimate details—which even Kenan is reluctant to reveal in his novel published over twenty years later—reveal that the community is not only aware of their homosexuality but intimately acquainted with it. Equally important, however, is the fact that Gaines persuades the reader that it is impossible to be both a "punk" and a "man." He describes both men as being betwixt and between gender roles in a literal limbo of sexual identity. This portrait is most clear in Gaines's description of John and Freddie on their way to work in the fields. Despite the fact that they wear "khakis and big straw hats and brogans," they could easily be "two little perfumed gals going to the dance" (33). And, although they are capable of outworking most men—indeed, they "work" the novel's principal character, Marcus, until he learns to be a man—Gaines's portrait of them suggests that it is almost impossible to define gay manhood. Gaines also reveals that this impossibility extends to the definition of heterosexual manhood. In his fiction, heterosexual manhood is difficult to define because it is only made visible in relation to what he has refused to define: homosexual manhood.[10]

Of Love and Dust, however, is a complex novel about dangerous things. Marcus is jailed for accidentally killing a man in a fight over a woman. His quest for manhood is fulfilled when he dies while trying to flee to the North with his lover, the blond wife of the plantation's Cajun overseer, Bonbon. Bonbon, despite his name, is far from being "good." He is a murderer, a blackmailer, a thief, and an adulterer in love with a black woman. Like Kenan's *A Visitation of Spirits,* Gaines's novel is filled with people who violate sexual and social taboos. These portraits are all countered by a single, sustaining and faithful relationship: the homosexual union that John and Freddie share. In effect, they become the moral exemplars of the community. However, once they teach Marcus how to *be* a man, they fade from the pages of the novel. Gaines supplants the image of manhood that John and Freddie symbolize with the more acceptable, though still racially transgressive, heteronormative manhood that Marcus represents. This narrative strategy, as I shall explore further, allows Gaines to deny any possibility that there can exist any mutuality between "real" manhood and homosexual identity.

Gaines defines Marcus's emergent manhood with a great deal of attention to sexual and social avarice. He returns to this same image of emergent heterosexual manhood in his short story, "Three Men." Published in *Bloodline,* "Three Men" is a captive narrative, taking place in a rural jailhouse in the midst of a plantation community. The protagonist of the story, Procter Lewis, like Marcus, kills accidentally in a moment of passion. Gaines situates him between the two men with whom he is initially jailed: Munford, a lifetime criminal, and Hattie, a black gay man jailed for committing fellatio in a movie theater. Based on the public nature of his "crime," it is also clear that Gaines highlights the fact that Hattie's sexual orientation is a matter of public knowledge and that there is something deeply vicarious about its cultural impress. Despite these negative and personally negating aspects of his portrayal of Hattie, Gaines initially suggests that his is the voice of moral authority. It is Hattie who offers compassion to his cellmates; it is Hattie who refuses the advances of Munford when he propositions him, responding that he would never "sink so low" (139); and, finally, it is Hattie who forces Procter to accept the fact that he is "a merciless killer" (151). Interestingly, it is only after recognizing the validity of Hattie's moral indictment of him that Procter is able to become a man.

Gaines's portrait of Hattie is characteristic of his practice of validating heterosexual manhood by destabilizing the moral and masculine image of his black gay characters. Gaines obviously feminizes Hattie, identifying him as a "freak" and a "bitch." He is active in Procter's transformation to manhood when a fourteen-year-old boy, badly beaten and in need of comfort, is jailed with them. Gaines positions this boy at a critical moment between childhood and manhood during which he needs to be nurtured. Hattie's reaction is to embrace the crying child, and it is Hattie's comforting embrace that literally propels Procter into acting out his manhood. He physically attacks Hattie, displacing him both in the narrative and in his role as nurturer. Procter washes the boy, symbolically and physically cleansing him of any residue of his association with Hattie. And, as is true of his black gay characters in *Of Love and Dust,* Hattie remains silent in the narrative from the moment Procter becomes the masculine and moral authority in the narrative. Procter's manhood, then, becomes visible only when Hattie's is denied. Certainly, these portraits suggest that Gaines sees gay and heterosexual manhood as mutually exclusive and competing categories. Gaines's image of manhood is equated with worldly knowledge, especially with the knowledge that a "freak" can never be a *real* man.

If the image of black gay manhood seems impotent in Gaines's fiction, it is certainly comically so in the southern Georgian landscape that Raymond Andrews creates in his trilogy, which includes *Appalachee Red* (1978), *Rosiebelle Lee Wildcat Tennessee* (1980), and *Baby Sweets* (1983). Andrews, a Georgia native, was awarded the James Baldwin Prize for *Appalachee Red,* through which readers become acquainted with Muskhogean County, a fictive county located in northeastern Georgia. Andrews, like Kenan, writes about "rural black folks in the South." In his preface to *Appalachee Red* he notes: "sadly, because of television and the cinema, most people now regard Afro-Americans chiefly in terms of the inner-city ghettos with their crime, drugs, and poverty. Such a world exists, but it is one I never knew. I could not write honestly about it even if I wanted. My American roots (like those of most Afro-Americans) are southern rural. This particular land and the individuals who have lived and died on it are what my books are about" (viii). It is the rural South that lives in Andrews's Muskhogean County, which is populated by black people, by white people, and by those dangerous few who are both black and white. The principal character of the trilogy, Appalachee Red, the son of the county's wealthiest and most powerful white man and his black maid, embodies the range of social, sexual, and racial taboos by virtue of his very existence. Each of the novels revolves around Red, his absences and presences, and the reactions of men and women who fear and love him. Among the people whose lives are affected by Appalachee Red, Andrews offers a comical but troubling portrait of Darling Pullman, who is arguably the most sexually objectified character in black southern literature.

For Andrews, Darling represents one of the "characters" who populate the rural South. He is, in fact, "sissified" to the extreme. In *Appalachee Red,* Darling proves to be an enigma: the only male heir in his family, he is a lover of ladies who is permanently alienated from the menfolk in his native community, which Andrews tellingly names Burnt Bottom. Andrews invariably describes Darling, who is affectionately known as Doll, in sexual and objectifying terms. This is readily apparent from his description of Darling's walk:

> But it was his walk which caused the community to buzz . . . as well as causing nearly every young female in the Bottoms at the time to copy it. The older heads claimed the young man was incapable of walking a straight furrow, much less plow one, as each step he took proved a production in itself. When he walked, or strutted, along, after each one of his tiny, ever-so-slow and delicate footfalls his entire weight would shift all the way from the other side of the road and gently across the back, bottom part of his baby-fat body, coming to a quivering rest directly north of the calf of the just-implanted leg. And with the next dainty step the process would be repeated, ending atop the other leg, back over on that side of the road. No, Burnt Bottom's menfolk agreed, this sort of stride of Darling's sure as hell wouldn't get much plowing done. (155)

In light of Andrews's description of Darling, it is appropriate to note that Andrews sees a difference between the definitions of "sissy" and "punk." At this point in his portrait, Darling is merely a sissy, "a boy who likes doing girl things such as cooking" (162). As a "sissy," Darling has a social identity that does nothing to destabilize Muskhogean County's social customs. However, Andrews makes it clear that there is no acceptable social place for anyone who acts on his homoerotic desires. In fact, should Darling act out his sexual identity, he will be what Andrews calls a "punk," a word—and an identity—that Andrews indicates even sounds "nasty" (162).

Given the homophobic associations that are apparent in these definitions, it is obvious that Andrews denies that an authentic black gay experience is possible. Note the way in which Andrews furthers his problematic characterization of homosexual desire in *Baby Sweets*, asserting that "there are those men who are so intimidated by the pussy that they hate it. Hate it to the point of fear . . . or envy. Fearful of being swallowed up alive, kicking and screaming, by the formidable pussy, these men retreat to the safety of their own kind, where they have created their own version of the pussy, a purely functional, artless . . . barren . . . cavity" (92–95). Given this troubled and troubling definition of gay desire as "pussy envy," it is not surprising that Darling is never able to define himself as a gay man. True to Andrews's association of homosexuality with fear, Darling literally runs from heterosexual entanglements, though he does not run to gay ones. There are no other homosexual men in the novel because there is no place for gay desire in Andrews's novel world.[11] The author completes his sexual objectification of Darling in the culminating scene of *Baby Sweets*. In that novel, Red's Café has been transformed into a brothel where white clients are served by black prostitutes upstairs, and black clients are served in the back by the Third Whore, a "white" prostitute. Everything is in its sexually proper place until two lesbians enter the scene. True to Andrews's comic and tragic vision, these "sisters" are pursued by identical twin men who plan to celebrate their twenty-first birthday by losing their respective virginities. Andrews selects this unlikely moment for Darling to assert his gay identity. Excited by one of the virginal twins, Darling leaves the brothel in the company of the twins, the lesbians, and Mary Mae, Darling's kitchen helper who has acted out her twenty-year crush on him by chasing Darling home every day. To say the least, it is quite a novel ending. Darling manages to sissify himself, for there will certainly be no opportunity for him to claim his gay identity given the company he is keeping at the end of the novel. What Andrews achieves here is a very complex signification on gay identity, especially when one notes that the Third Whore—who is not white and no whore—sings the "Signifying Monkey" as the scene unfolds. Foreclosing the possibility of authentic gay desire, Andrews makes it clear that there is no space for Darling in this heterosexist community.

Writing in opposition to these portraits, Kenan insists that gay identity and homosexual desire are not out of place, even in the rural South. He rejects Gaines's notion that heterosexual masculinity naturally subsumes black gay masculinity and Andrews's assertion that homosexual desire is grounded in fear. Consistently, his fiction is a commentary on both of these problematic constructions of black gay identity. Kenan's black gay subjects revise the portraits that Gaines and Andrews offer by insisting that there should be a space where men can be black and gay without being dominated by heterosexism. In *A Visitation of Spirits,* Tims Creek becomes the representative rural and southern space, and, appropriately, it is to Tims Creek that Kenan repeatedly returns to shape the narratives of all of his black gay characters. His depictions of black gay men are theoretical and critical explorations of the ways in which place, race, and sexuality shape both the public and private constructions of the self. It should already be clear that *A Visitation of Spirits* accomplishes this goal. Kenan's vision of black gay subjectivity is further solidified in four short stories about black gay identity: "Clarence *and* the Dead," "The Foundations of the Earth," and "Wash Me," each of which suggests something about the role of the community in the formation of identity; and "Run, Mourner, Run," in which Kenan creates his most fully developed portrait of black gay masculinity.

In "Clarence *and* the Dead," a story about the debilitating effects of homophobia, the reader is introduced to young Clarence, a five-year-old who is capable of speaking to the dead and with animals but who is incapable of reacting to homosexual desire with more than indifference. Clarence is born on what becomes remembered as a remarkable day, the day that the town's only talking hog utters its first words. Reared in the home of his grandparents, Eunice and George Edward, Clarence's short life is remembered by the Tims Creek townsfolk as a series of "strange thises and thats" (3). Clarence has a peculiar knowledge about adult matters, including the hidden sins and unacknowledged desires of his Tims Creek neighbors, all of which is revealed to him by the dead. Clarence's unusual knowledge made the townsfolk, even those who accepted the talking hog into church, regard him as something akin to evil. Indeed, "Clarence *and* the Dead" is an extremely dense narrative in which Kenan explores the rather indistinct boundaries between life and death, abnormal and normal desire, and reality and fantasy. Kenan quite masterfully blurs all of these distinctions, and he is most myopic in his view of the relationship between homoerotic and heterosexual desire in the story when Clarence carries a message to one of Tims Creek's most eccentric inhabitants, Ellsworth Batts, from his deceased wife, Mildred. The message is about love, and Ellsworth transfers all of the love he has to Clarence. Kenan tells the story thusly:

Every day for a week Ellsworth showed up to see Clarence and every day Miss
Eunice and Mr. George Edward would exchange weary glances and shrugs,
while one would stand guard over what begun to look more and more like
courting and sparking. Ellsworth brought candy and then flowers, which Miss
Eunice took from Clarence straightaway and finally said to Mr. George Edward:
"This has just got to stop." And Mr. George Edward said: "I know. I know. I'll
talk to him."

Nothing like talk of crimes against nature gets people all riled up and speculating and conjecturing and postulating the way they did when word got out
about Ellsworth Batts's "unnatural affection" for Clarence Pickett. The likeli-
hood of him conversing with his dead Mildred through the boy paled next to
the idea of him fermenting depraved intentions for young and tender boys. (19)

While the community is wary of the "unnaturalness" of homosexual desire,
it is incapable of seeing the naturalness of Ellsworth's attraction to his dead
wife's spirit that Clarence happens to embody. However, amidst the homophobic reaction of the Tims Creek community, Kenan unfolds a classic
love tragedy. Like their Shakespearean counterparts, Clarence and Ellsworth
are lovers who are kept apart by societal restrictions. And, like the star-
crossed lovers Kenan casts them to be, Ellsworth and Clarence die when they
are kept apart. Kenan crafts "Clarence *and* the Dead" as a story about
misdefinitions of morality because the community is unable to distinguish
between natural and unnatural desires.

Indeed, "Clarence *and* the Dead" is a story about the fine line between
natural and unnatural desire; however, it is also an indictment of Tims
Creek's blind commitment to homophobia. The community's response to
Ellsworth's desire for Clarence centers on the unnaturalness of homosexual desire rather than on the fact that the otherworldly knowledge Clarence
accesses reveals secrets that impugn the morality of the very people who
judge Clarence in the narrative. The dead speak to Clarence about incidents
of incest, adultery, avarice, and betrayal in the lives of the moral exemplars
in Tims Creek; in fact, they speak about the kinds of secret sexual sins that
Kenan juxtaposes against homosexual desire in *A Visitation of Spirits*. Kenan
indicts their blindness in his description of the community's "queer" reaction to Clarence's death. Rather than considering "something our imaginations were too timid to draw up," no one speaks about Clarence (22). What
Kenan suggests about their silence, however, is that life in Tims Creek does
change; folks are forced, even in their silence, to confront the fact that heterosexuality and homosexuality are uncomfortably and indisputably linked.
As is true of Tims Creek at the time of Horace Cross's death, those who

witness Clarence's life and death are forced to remember that unspeakable desire, even in this rural southern community. The prevailing image of the existence of supportive gay communities in large, urban centers, especially outside of the South, suggests that Kenan's southern alternative should offer no respite from heterosexism. In each of these short stories, however, Kenan dares to suggest otherwise.

In "The Foundations of the Earth," Kenan revisits the theme of migration. The story has a moral: gay migration affects a community's ability to dismantle long-standing racial, religious, and sexual oppressions. In this story, the black gay character, Edward, is deceased, but his grandmother, Miss Maggie, dares to speak about the nature of his desire. She forces herself to understand what it is like to be "black," "gay," and "southern"; and the only person who can help her understand how her grandson embraced this difficult identity is his white, northern-bred lover, Gabriel. True to his ability to use the Bible to validate gay identity, Kenan revises the image of this angel of the Lord, sending him south with Edward's body and with a body of knowledge in his position as the "interpreter for the dead" (22). Perhaps more importantly for Kenan's revisionist project, Gabriel is an interpreter for the living. He shares a dangerous knowledge with Maggie: that to be black and gay is not only hard, but it is normal. Kenan recognizes the role of the community in the shaping of black gay identity in this story, for Maggie's understanding of black gay experience is witnessed by all of those who matter in the Tims Creek community, including the preacher and the church gossip. Kenan reinforces the notion that homoerotic desire can transform society in "Wash Me," in which he continues his portrait of Gideon Stone. As we learned in *A Visitation of Spirits,* Gideon was awarded a prestigious academic scholarship to attend the University of North Carolina at Chapel Hill. In this story, set in the heat and dirt of a tobacco harvest, Gideon struggles with the fact that he is trapped in a complicated web defined by his rural roots, his educational achievements, and his sexual orientation. Kenan makes it clear, however, that Gideon is a product of this community that he cannot reject and that cannot reject him. The fact that Gideon is able to explore his place in the community while participating in the ritual of the tobacco harvest suggests that, even at the moment in which Gideon embraces his sexuality, he manages to be black, gay, and a man outside of an urban center where, as Charles Rowell suggests, black gay men can best find respite from the "immediate dangers of the homohatred of heterosexists" (342). In fact, in every portrait of Gideon Stone, Kenan insists that there is a place for black gay desire in the rural southern landscape.

Kenan's text speaks to the ways in which identity and community are mutually affective categories. Working to demonstrate this relationship, he presents his most fully developed black gay portrait in his characterization of Raymond Brown in "Run, Mourner, Run." As the title implies, the story plays with the idea of sin. Mourners are a part of the ritual of salvation in the rural church. During revivals, the mourner's bench is reserved for those who come for salvation, a process that requires that they testify and confess their sins before members of the community. What Kenan testifies and confesses to in his portrait of Raymond Brown is that fully realized black gay subjectivity is possible.

Unlike Horace Cross and Gideon Stone, Raymond Brown has already survived his sexual coming of age; he is, therefore, both sexually and socially threatening. Brown is wealthy, educated, married, and gay. As if these identities were not problematic enough for a black man in Tims Creek, he also owns the one plot of land that the wealthiest white man in Tims Creek, Percy Terrell, desires. The site is the homeplace of the Brown family, linked to both their slavery and their freedom, but according to Terrell, it is land that "Niggers shouldn't own" (166). And it is in his desire to objectify Brown both racially and sexually that Terrell hires Dean Williams, described as "poor white trash: a sweet-faced, dark-haired faggot," to seduce Brown (166). As Terrell's camera catches Brown in his sin, Kenan calls Terrell rather than Brown to the mourner's bench. Empowered by his sexuality, Brown refuses to be "caught." Even as he attempts to subjugate Brown, Percy is forced to testify to and validate Brown's manhood:

> Percy's face turned a strawberry color. He stood motionless. . . . Slowly he began to nod his head up and down, and to smile. He put his hands on his hips and took two steps back.

> —Now, boys, I want you to look-a-here. I respect this man. I do. I really do. How many men do you know, black or white, could bluff, cool as a cucumber, caught butt-naked in bed with a damn whore? (180–81)

Not only does Brown refuse to have his responses dictated by Percy's homohatred, but Kenan ultimately insists that Raymond Brown, rather than Percy Terrell, controls the series of seductions in the story. In Kenan's description of Dean's memory of "that night," he reveals Brown's maxim: "Some things you just let happen" (172). The meaning of the maxim becomes clear by the narrative's conclusion. Months pass before Brown decides to sell the "homeplace" to Terrell. And, rather than profiting from his part in the affair, Dean is left penniless, clinging to the memories of the intimate moments he shared with Brown. Just as Dean is forced to proclaim Brown's manhood, Percy is unable to avoid acknowledging the truth of Brown's maxim. It becomes the explanation for his own spiritual and literal bankruptcy at the narrative's conclusion. Kenan structures the plot so that white males proclaim Brown's manhood as well as his place in the community, which is secure despite the fact that he is a black gay man. In essence, Kenan refuses to "punk" Brown. Instead, he subverts heterosexual privilege in the narrative by allowing Brown to "punk" the two conspirators. In this refusal to be affected by the limited and socially limiting definitions of black masculinity and gay manhood, Raymond Brown is Kenan's most fully realized portrait of black gay manhood.

Randall Kenan reconstructs the image of black gay manhood in his fiction by requiring his readers to understand the kind of "queer knowledge" that his protagonists profess about homosexual desire and about being black men. It is the knowledge that he imparts in his image of black gay men who refuse to assimilate to a society that refuses to validate their experiences. And theirs is the uncomfortable knowledge that homosexual desire and heterosexual desire are intimately interwoven into the fabric of every community everywhere. Kenan reconciles what had been previously irreconcilable in black southern literature: that it is possible to define black gay manhood. What, essentially, is a man, when whiteness and heterosexual desire are not the expected or normative parts of the definition? This is precisely the question Kenan requires his readers to confront by creating provocative images of men who are unapologetically black and gay. His characters refuse to continually validate their right to simply be who and as they are. Thus, the author revises black gay representations by challenging the queer definitions of manhood that have prevailed in American culture, where it has always been equated with whiteness and heterosexuality.

What is endearing about Kenan's work is that he asks readers to believe in the remarkable diversity of people who populate Tims Creek by sharing all of their stories with us. And, if we can believe that in Tims Creek there was once a hog that could talk, there was once a demon summoned, and— at least once—the dead rose, then we ought to believe that black men can desire to be men and be loved by other men. By insisting that gay men are as impacted by their communities as their communities are impacted by them, Kenan promises to transform our understanding of sexual orientation and desire. It cannot be displaced by virtue of its relationship to the Mason-Dixon line or the urbane. Kenan's oeuvre revises the image of black gay portraitures in southern literature, in African-American literature, and in gay literature. Writing across and within each of these genres, he manages to disturb our understanding of what the labels "black," "gay," and "man" mean. Through the black gay portraits he offers in his novel and short stories, Randall Kenan examines the range of possibilities that exist when it is no longer a privilege to be able to define oneself as all three.

Notes

1. For further reference see Frances Cress Welsing, "The Politics behind Black Male Passivity, Effeminization, Bisexuality, and Homosexuality"; Ekwueme Michael Thelwell, "A Profit Is Not without Honor"; and Nathan Hare and Julia Hare, *The Endangered Black Family: Coping with the Unisexualization and Coming Extinction of the Black Race.*

2. While my argument is also applicable to black lesbian experience in these cultures, I have purposely narrowed my focus here; however, it is not in an effort to devalue or exclude black lesbian experience. I have limited my discussion to the ways in which these oppressions shape the black gay male experience in order to comment on the specific experience that Kenan explores in his fiction.

3. See Kenan's *James Baldwin,* a biography that is part of a young adult series on the lives of notable gay men and lesbians.

4. See Mark 15:21.

5. Kenan identifies Horace with Baldwin's Rufus even in his decision to become a red-tailed hawk. Rufus means red-haired; the tail of the red-tailed hawk is most accurately described as being rufous-colored.

6. Cora Kaplan also makes an interesting connection between same-sex relationships and race in *Another Country* in "'A Cavern Opened in My Mind': The Poetics of Homosexuality and the Politics of Masculinity in James Baldwin."

7. See Charles I. Nero, "Towards a Black Gay Aesthetic."

8. It is worth noting that the contemporary black gay writer most concerned with reforming Christian doctrine and church policies concerning homosexuality is E. Lynn Harris. Harris, whose works are as much gay romance novels as they are novels about Christian morals, is a best-selling author. All except one of his black gay characters, Basil Henderson, are committed homosexuals and Christians. His novels, then, work to develop a Christian theology that validates gay desire. To date, Harris has published six novels: *Invisible Life* (1991), *Just as I Am* (1995), *And This, Too, Shall Pass* (1996), *If This World Were Mine* (1997), *Abide with Me* (1999), and *Not a Day Goes By* (2000).

9. Southern writers, accustomed to the cultural otherness of the South, have complicated their images of gay sexuality by creating protagonists whose identities are moored in other unresolved cultural questions, especially that of race. This shift likely accounts for the predominance of interracial gay coupling and social problems in such narratives. Tennessee Williams's short stories "Desire and the Black Masseur" and "The Killer Chicken and the Closet Queen" are certainly examples of this par-

adigm. Flannery O'Connor couples the idea of homosexuality with sexual violence in *The Violent Bear It Away* (1960) by creating a gay male character whose desire for violence is as central to his identity as is his sexuality. Perhaps the most extreme and the most amusing example of this paradigm occurs in Charles Harvey's story "When Dogs Bark" (1996), in which the "gay" protagonist is only able to act on his erotic desires in New York City where his barking, growling, and interracial homosexual lust are all equally acknowledgeable as long as he is north of the Mason-Dixon line.

10. I thank Helen R. Houston for making this connection for me.

11. This point is particularly ironic given the fact that Andrews was awarded the first James Baldwin Prize for *Appalachee Red* in 1979.

Works Cited

Andrews, Raymond. *Appalachee Red.* 1978; rpt., Athens: University of Georgia Press, 1987.

———. *Baby Sweets.* Athens: University of Georgia Press, 1983.

———. *Rosiebelle Lee Wildcat Tennessee.* Athens: University of Georgia Press, 1980.

Baldwin, James. *Another Country.* New York: Dell, 1962.

Gaines, Ernest J. *Catherine Carmier.* New York: Vintage Contemporaries, 1964.

———. *Of Love and Dust.* New York: Vintage Contemporaries, 1967.

———. "Three Men" (1968). In *Bloodline.* New York: W. W. Norton, 1976. 121–55.

Hare, Nathan, and Julia Hare. *The Endangered Black Family: Coping with the Unisexualization and Coming Extinction of the Black Race.* San Francisco: Black Think Tank, 1984.

Harper, Phillip Brian. *Are We Not Men?: Masculine Anxiety and the Problem of African-American Identity.* New York: Oxford University Press, 1996.

Harris, E. Lynn. *Abide with Me.* New York: Doubleday, 1999.

———. *If This World Were Mine.* New York: Doubleday, 1998.

———. *Invisible Life.* New York: Anchor, 1994.

———. *Just as I Am.* New York: Anchor, 1995.

———. *This, Too, Shall Pass.* New York: Anchor, 1996.

Harvey, Charles. "When Dogs Bark." In *Shade: An Anthology of Fiction by Gay Men of African Descent.* Ed. Bruce Morrow and Charles H. Rowell. New York: Avon Books, 1996. 290–302.

Kaplan, Cora. "'A Cavern Opened in My Mind': The Poetics of Homosexuality and the Politics of Masculinity in James Baldwin." In *Representing Black Men.* Ed. Marcellus Blount and George P. Cunningham. New York: Routledge, 1996. 27–54.

Kenan, Randall. "Clarence *and* the Dead." In *Let the Dead Bury Their Dead and Other Stories.* New York: Harcourt Brace and Co., 1992. 1–23.

———. "The Foundations of the Earth." In *Let the Dead Bury Their Dead and Other Stories.* New York: Harcourt Brace and Co., 1992. 49–72.

————. *James Baldwin*. New York: Chelsea House, 1994

————. "Run, Mourner, Run." In *Let the Dead Bury Their Dead and Other Stories*. New York: Harcourt Brace and Co., 1992. 163–91.

————. *A Visitation of Spirits*. New York: Anchor, 1989.

————. "Wash Me." In *Shade: An Anthology of Fiction by Gay Men of African Descent*. Ed. Bruce Morrow and Charles H. Rowell. New York: Avon Books, 1996. 260–72.

McRuer, Robert. *The Queer Renaissance: Contemporary American Literature and the Reinvention of Lesbian and Gay Identities*. New York: New York University Press, 1997.

Morrow, Bruce, and Charles H. Rowell, eds. *Shade: An Anthology of Fiction by Gay Men of African Descent*. New York: Avon Books, 1996.

Nero, Charles I. "Towards a Black Gay Aesthetic." In *Brother to Brother: New Writings by Black Gay Men*. Ed. Essex Hemphill. Boston: Alyson, 1991. 229–52.

O'Connor, Flannery. *The Violent Bear It Away*. New York: Farrar, Straus, 1960.

Rowell, Charles H. "Signing Yourself: An Afterword." In *Shade: An Anthology of Fiction by Gay Men of African Descent*. Ed. Bruce Morrow and Charles H. Rowell. New York: Avon Books, 1996. 335–43.

Scott, Darieck. "This City of Men." In *Shade: An Anthology of Fiction by Gay Men of African Descent*. Ed. Bruce Morrow and Charles H. Rowell. New York: Avon Books, 1996. 117–40.

Thelwell, Ekwueme Michael. "A Profit Is Not without Honor." *Transition* 58 (1991): 90–113.

Welsing, Frances Cress. "The Politics behind Black Male Passivity, Effeminization, Bisexuality, and Homosexuality." In *The Isis Papers*. Chicago: Third World Press, 1991. 81–92.

White, Linda Peal. "Randall Kenan Is 1997 Grisham Writer in Residence." *Southern Register* (Fall 1997). <http://www.olemiss.edu/depts/south/register/97/fall/kenan.html>.

Williams, Tennessee. "Desire and the Black Masseur." In *Collected Stories*. New York: New Directions, 1985. 205–12.

————. "The Killer Chicken and the Closet Queen." In *Collected Stories*. New York: New Directions, 1985. 552–70.

2

This Disease Called Strength: The Masculine Manifestation in Raymond Andrews's *Appalachee Red*

TRUDIER HARRIS

The John Henry Syndrome

The creators of the tale, legend, and ballad of John Henry not only perpetuated a hero who has permeated the African-American as well as the larger American folk cultural imagination, but one who has saturated African-American literary texts.[1] While it would obviously be erroneous to make John Henry the sole—or even the primary—basis for black strong male heroes, the point of intersection at the site of strength is nonetheless noteworthy.[2] Strong black men in African-American literature frequently extrapolate the trait of physical prowess from the tradition of John Henry, but they pervert it in that unleashed power is not matched by the larger moral, communal, or cultural imperative that guides John Henry's use of strength. These characters thus break through the mold of creative strength[3] that John Henry offers and instead fit into the pattern of the "John Henry syndrome"; this is especially true in the case of the character of Big Man Thompson in Raymond Andrews's 1978 novel *Appalachee Red*.

The John Henry syndrome, as defined by the epidemiologist Sherman James, is a condition that exists at large in the black American male population.[4] Many black men, who have been taught to rely on their own bodies more than anything else, have simultaneously been taught—through history, popular culture, and their own communities—that their bodies are physically superior to those of the frail, "puny" white men who enslaved them. This superior physical strength therefore enables them to endure—and withstand—extreme physical duress. They can carry more weight (think of black men's historical work on levees or in cotton fields or other physically demanding situations), fight harder (boxing, physical contests during slavery), run longer (escape from slavery), jump higher (sports), and withstand more (war, prison)—or so they believe. Their belief in their bodies is so resolute, in fact, that they conclude that they can withstand disease. Consequently, a black man who gets a cough or who experiences an occasional stomach or heart pain is much more likely to "tough it out" or ignore it longer than his non-black counterpart. He will ignore such discomfort, asserts James, to the point where it becomes irreversibly detrimental. Thus many more black men die from curable ailments because their belief in their bodies and their strength (certainly combined with economic factors in some cases) leads them to delay doctor visits for longer periods, ignore clear warning signals of the onset of disease, and die in a culturally defined drama that will value how they are "laid to rest" just as enthusiastically as they valued the strength that led to their deaths.

As James outlines this pathology, therefore, strength itself can become a disease in some African-American males. Their very attempts to define their manhood paradoxically lead them to destroy the thing they esteem most—and themselves in the process. Literary portraits of these black men of "tombstone disposition, graveyard mind" range from Charles W. Chesnutt's Josh Green in *The Marrow of Tradition* (1901), to Chester Himes's Bob Jones in *If He Hollers Let Him Go* (1945), to John A. Williams's title character in *Captain Blackman* (1972), in which strength literally gets metamorphosed into reincarnation. Himes's Bob Jones feels that his body is his most potent weapon against the racism of the 1940s. While his mood will eventually change, his attitude toward his body when he moves from Cleveland to California is nonetheless noteworthy: "When I came out to Los Angeles in the fall of '41, I felt fine about everything. Taller than the average man, six feet two, broad-shouldered, and conceited. I hadn't a worry. I knew I'd get along. If it had come down to a point where I had to hit a paddy I'd have hit him without any thought. I'd have busted him wide open because he was a paddy and needed busting" (3). A fictional predecessor of Bob Jones, Chesnutt's Josh Green embodies a similar invincibility that inspires him to walk through the bullets that the white supremacist Major McBane fires at him and choke the man to death before his inevitable demise. Similarly, a pattern of seemingly death-defying invincibility fits Andrews's Big Man Thompson, a contemporary fictive incarnation of Jones and Josh. Described as "230 pounds of compact muscle on a frame rising well beyond six feet" (11), Big Man is designated "the young Hercules." Big Man's war with the racist Clyde "Boots" White, a white lawman in Appalachee, Georgia, may lead to his death, but, more important, it leads to his immortalization in the town's folklore.[5] To the black population of Appalachee, Big Man Thompson is a man's man, idealistically worthy of emulation precisely because he gave his life in what they believe is a noble cause.

Appalachee Red is one of a trilogy of novels that Raymond Andrews completed about the mythical territory of Muskhogean County, with the small town of Appalachee as the county seat, located fictionally in the northeastern part of Georgia. The first narrative in the series, *Appalachee Red* precedes *Rosiebelle Lee Wildcat Tennessee* (1980) and *Baby Sweets* (1983); all three volumes chronicle the history and narratives of black and white inhabitants of Andrews's fictional town and county. *Appalachee Red* introduces us to the forebears of the title character and records their stories. Big Man Thompson is Red's stepfather, though by no choice of his own. Appalachee Red's activities, especially the mind games he plays with Boots, who has become chief of police by the time Red returns, are therefore set against the backdrop of Big Man Thompson and his interactions with a younger version of this same lawman. Big Man Thompson is the legend that always taps Appalachee Red on the shoulder in one of those "Hey Boy, are you living up to the hype?" kind of gestures. In the John Henry syndrome, the star *always* lives up to the hype.

The Badman Hero

John Henry is certainly not a Stagolee kind of badman hero, but he is *ba-ad* in the sense that he overcomes a tremendous physical obstacle and, in spite of his death, serves as an idealistic example for other black men.[6] Big Man Thompson is only a few years removed from the actual tale of John Henry, and Raymond Andrews could have easily had this mythic narrative in mind when he imagined his character. Like John Henry, Big Man Thompson is a laborer, a sawmiller. A big lug of a man, he embodies the innocence usually identified with such characters. His nickname is more descriptive of size than legend at this point, as he is a young man who is simply rather large for his age. He works hard and minds his own business. He rather naively believes, as John Henry does, that right will win

simply because it is right. When he is falsely accused of making illegal
whiskey and sent to prison, he resembles the country bumpkin who has
been in the wrong place at the wrong time.

The circumstances surrounding his arrest and imprisonment abound with
irony. One week after his marriage to Little Bit in 1918, the twenty-one-year-
old and strikingly honest Big Man mistakenly goes to the site of a whiskey
still to collect a debt a friend owes him. Finding no one present, he decides
to wait and falls asleep while doing so. The still is raided, and this "devout
teetotaler" (6) is arrested and sent to Yankee Town, the local prison. In his
absence, eighteen-year-old Little Bit seeks work at the home of young John
Morgan, who makes sex a condition of her job, "thus launching another
white-man-and-black-woman love affair, a then prevalent Southern pastime"
(7). The business-minded Little Bit, still very much in love with Big Man,
concludes that she might as well take practical advantage of her situation
and profit from the relationship with Morgan. She persuades him to give
her a small lot and build a two-story house on it, which becomes known as
the White House. When a baby arrives "'as red as a green blackberry'" (9),
Little Bit sends the "red baby" to Chicago to live with her sister. That baby
will grow up to become the infamous Appalachee Red, who will follow in
the footsteps of the legendary Big Man Thompson. The incident of the baby's birth foreshadows the series of events that will illustrate clearly the
pathologically destructive nature of the strength identified with Big Man.
The pathology can be viewed from the perspective of Big Man himself; his
adversary, Boots White; his wife, Little Bit; the townspeople, who are voyeurs more than anything else; Raymond Andrews, as creator of the narrative; and the readers. Each perspective sheds light on the function and impetus to strength, why it is manipulated as it is, and the consequences it
engenders. Big Man's response to his wife's sexual violation goes in only one
direction—toward his wife. He can respond to the rape that John Morgan
has essentially perpetrated against him only by using his body, his strength,
against the black woman who has already been victimized. Thus the first
diseased component of his strength is that he intends to *re*victimize her.
Initially, Big Man threatens his wife via the message system between the town
and the prison; he declares, "'no red baby had better be sucking on my
woman's black tits'" (9) when he reaches home. In a pattern documented
throughout African-American history, Big Man finds himself unable or
unwilling to confront John Morgan, the perpetrator of his manly and hus-
bandly discomfort. Instead, he transfers his anger to the black woman in
his life.[7] Upon returning home after a year in prison, Big Man "gave unto

his wife the whipping of her young life" (11), but he is not otherwise perturbed by her involvement in the "southern pastime"—at least not until she insists that they live in the White House. Thus begins their legendary status, for their fights become known throughout the community; the previously nondrinking Big Man takes to drink, and Little Bit takes to "specializing" in cussing him out and to carving up his face with a razor: "Such commotion along the back street did these battles create that the town's blacks soon began telling the bit about the family Blackshear, owners of the undertaking parlor sitting directly across the dirt street from the White House, each evening stuffing cotton into the ears of their dead so that they wouldn't be kept awake nights by the brawling couple and have to appear 'tetchy' at their funerals" (12). Even at this early stage of his commentary on their violent encounters, Andrews is already overlaying the pathology with a legendary quality—tall tales—that the townspeople will shortly interpret as acceptable if not downright romantic. By transforming violence into legend, Andrews begins the process of establishing Big Man and Little Bit as mythic characters. Interestingly, however, Little Bit will later suffer a mental breakdown and thereby have her mythic status compromised. Big Man, however, dies, like John Henry, and it is his death that ensures his mythic status.

The legendary fights between Big Man and Little Bit eventually end only when Sam Wallace, a stranger to Appalachee, buys the White House and Big Man and Little Bit return to a smaller place in Dark Town, the local black ghetto. It is not until the Depression, in 1935, when Little Bit returns to work for John Morgan—who immediately reinaugurates the sexual "southern pastime"—that the couple resumes their battles. Ultimately, out-of-work Big Man, unable to influence his wife's actions, simply broods in Sam's Café, the local gathering place, until his fateful encounter in 1936 with Boots White. Big Man's positioning in the tale to this point, however, makes clear the options for black men in rural southern communities. The concept of manhood can only be manifested in the black domestic or communal arena, either in bed, beating one's wife, or beating one's neighbors. The black man must finally accept his wife's degradation and lament that he cannot persuade her to abandon a position that he knows supports them both. Yet what is fascinating about Andrews's treatment of Big Man is that he makes him larger than life nonetheless. Alarmingly, in elevating Big Man to legendary status, the author de-emphasizes or erases altogether Big Man's violence against Little Bit, or it gets subsumed by the author's mythmaking process. This backgrounding and peripheralizing of sexual violence bespeaks

the women's devalued positions throughout the narrative. In the predominantly male world of Sam's Café, as well as in the streets where he and Little Bit spar, Big Man Thompson achieves an omnipotence that is reinforced
by the author's unwillingness to counter his protagonist's distorted conception of strength and masculinity.

Crowned the "King of Dark Town," with Sam's Café as his "throneroom,"
Big Man is also king of the "poolboard" (checkers); he spends his days
during the Depression enticing people to challenge him. He is also king
because the Hard Labor Holers, the hardcore roughnecks who make their
weekly trek from peach-picking into town looking for drink, gambling, and
"female in-between-legs" (22) entertainment, and who would cut a person
as soon as look at him or her, have learned not to "mess with" Big Man
Thompson. To be sure, his reputation as a fighter extends far beyond his
escapades with his wife: "he was the biggest and respected as the toughest
black in the area and all without having to carry a knife. Over the years his
big stone-like fists had broken enough of other people's bones to convince
those who had seen him in action that he, Big Man Thompson, did not need
a blade" (37). A particularly dramatic encounter with two of the locals, who
are fighting in Big Man's throneroom, makes this clear:

> The two fighters suddenly and accidentally kicked over the table holding the
> poolboard. Watching the board, the bottle caps used for the pool pieces, and
> his chance for a great come-from-behind victory all go flying across the grimy
> floor of the café shook Big Man by the roots of his temper. With nostrils flar-
> ing and blood in his eyes the big fellow jumped up and grabbed both of the
> scrappers, one under each arm, and threw them bodily out of the front door
> into the street, missing the porch altogether. And from that time onward none
> of the Hole or Town Nigger toughs ever started scrapping in Sam's while Big
> Man sat playing pool. (37)

This incident signals to the townspeople one of the "rules" by which Big Man
operates in the café. He thus sets the precedent for defending his throneroom
against any assault upon his poolboard, a precedent that is central to his
confrontation with Boots White.

Locating Big Man and Little Bit in Appalachee is central to Andrews's
creation of legendary characters, for their interactions confirm that the
townspeople applaud such "entertainment" even if they eventually summon
the law to intervene. It also confirms the atmosphere of violence and potential violence that captures the imaginations of Dark Town's inhabitants.
Big Man's and Little Bit's antics further demonstrate that black people's

reactions to exploitation might be self-destructive, but they earn admiration from others who are equally oppressed (a part of Big Man's reaction to his wife's relationship with John Morgan is that there are few secrets—black, white, or otherwise—in Appalachee; everybody knows everybody's business, which means that pride is the only response available).

The physical violence in which Big Man and Little Bit openly engage is matched only by their violent lovemaking; in fact, the former often precedes the latter. Its source of inspiration and its place of execution are further evidence of the pathological nature of what the townspeople consider mythical:

> The first time one of these near-nightly chases [Big Man chasing Little Bit after she has razored him while he is sleeping] took place between the loving couple, one of the naive residents of Dark Town seeing the giant thundering along after the screaming, yet speedy little woman, quickly ran from his own house, clad only in a pair of long winter underwear, all the way up to the police station in the heart of town and brought back the law in an attempt to prevent what looked to him a sure murder. Speeding to Dark Town with guns drawn, the law, arriving at the scene, found the murderer and murdered lying together in a clump of bushes next to the fertilizer plant fucking at a feverish pitch. (12)

The humor of this scene and the neighbor's embarrassment illustrate the sacrificial as well as the entertainment function of legend making. Big Man and Little Bit are exposed, but they could not care less as far as their textual audience is concerned. Yet their very exposure, given the racial and gender ramifications of this episode, calls the legend-making process into question. Nonetheless, Big Man's sexual prowess echoes the sexual appeal of John Henry and the numerous accounts of wives and girlfriends who are bowed with grief when they learn of his death. Indeed, Little Bit asserts that her liaison with John Morgan is purely financial, for "despite evidence of his own satisfaction with the relationship, in bed he was no Big Man" (7). Thus sexual and physical adeptness, indispensable in terms of black male immortality, remains the yardstick for measuring "true manhood."

This scene is also important in legitimizing the voyeuristic approach to heroic creation. The lawmen and the concerned neighbor are equally embarrassed when they find the oblivious couple, but they look nonetheless (and the neighbor suffers more grief the next day when Little Bit gives him a thirty-minute sampling of her legendary sass and invective). Spectators throughout the text are the creators of legend, and even the narrator suffers from this voyeuristic posturing. The narrator and the neighbors are waiting for the good show, the bloodletting or sexual escapades that will give them a respite from their mundane lives and help stave off future incidences of boredom. Unfailingly, Big Man and Little Bit deliver the spectacle that the spectators crave—in this particular instance, desire fulfills desire.

The testing of black manhood continues when physical prowess takes on a racial dimension. Inevitably, Boots White, whose father Ezra is a notorious KKK leader, has a run-in with Big Man Thompson, the "King of Dark Town." Boots has acquired his own legendary status within the community, which he never allows the black residents to forget. Every Saturday night, he announces his arrival at Sam's Café by crunching his boots against the gravel outside, then kicking the door open and walking into the middle of the room: "Standing here, he would glare around at the sea of black faces until one by one their white eyes would shift floorward. After staring everyone down to his satisfaction, Boots would then spit in the middle of the floor, wheel around, and stomp out of the café with the sound from those steel-plated black boots reverberating off the walls" (43). Annoyed that Big Man never seems perturbed by his floor-spitting ritual and equally piqued by the fact that the current chief of police complains about young Boots locking up so many blacks every Saturday night, Boots strides into Sam's Café on Easter Sunday, 1936, and instigates a confrontation with Big Man by declaring that "'ain' no checkah play'n 'lowed in heah on Sunday!'" (48). Big Man's playing partner quickly disappears, but Big Man still ignores Boots:

> Big Man continued to sit and stare down at the poolboard as if he was contemplating his next move and hadn't heard the words of the Man, or even noticed that he was now playing the game alone. (That was the way it seemed to the seven or eight people who were in the café that day, including Sam, though to anyone who listened to all the later versions of the story it must have seemed that at least half the blacks in the county had been present.) Big Man kept looking at the board, then proceeded to move one of his pieces. (48)

The narrator's self-consciousness about the legend-making process layers the present with the future, the event in the act of being created with the narratives that will be told about it. Thus the act of legend formation is just as legendary as the character about whom the legend is being formed. Such a seemingly small thing as daring to move a lone checker piece is enough to instigate the confrontation with Boots from which Big Man can no longer escape. And escape is certainly not the issue at this point, for the communal expectation that "something is going to happen," and the tension surrounding that expectation, make it impossible for Big Man Thompson to do anything but live up to his reputation. Directly challenged in a kind of cowboy do-or-die fashion, he must rise to the occasion.

His defiance in turn leads to Boots's committing the unforgivable sin by using one of his black shiny boots to kick over the checkerboard: "nobody went around mistreating Big Man's poolboard . . . not even the white Man. The next thing everyone in the place knew was that Boots was lying flat out on his ass on the floor up near the front door, where Big Man had sent him flying with one blow from the back of his big fist" (49). Unfortunately, the moment of decision for Big Man is the moment of death, for, in this case, to react is to die. That decision to step into immortality, to transition permanently into folk hero, only inspires the textual audience and the narrator. The narrator's awareness of the insider/outsider nature of what he is witnessing—that is, recounting it even as he is aware that others will recount it differently—continues to layer the pathology as well as the legend. Looking, observing, recording—those are the traits of the narrator; he never applies an informed moral analysis or places a value judgment on what he observes:

> Then things began happening even faster. So fast in fact that it seemed no one present (or absent) on that day was ever able to tell the straight of things. There were those who said that after getting up from his chair, Big Man started walking towards the fallen Man, lying with face red with surprise, fear, and blood, to reach the front door at the policeman's back and get out of the café. And then there were those who swore that Big Man was walking up to the downed Man with the intentions of stomping the living shit out of him, for if this had not been the case, these believers contended, then Dark Town's King never would have gone and left his poolboard lying there on the floor where somebody was liable to step on it. However, no one was to ever learn the King's real intentions, because the moment the frightened Boots looked up and saw the giant approaching him, he was somehow able from where he lay to whip out his pistol and pump six bullets into Big Man's wide body. But even carrying all of this lead, the King, like a big bear, continued advancing towards Boots, who after firing his last shot somehow managed to scramble up and reach the front door just ahead of Big Man. (49)

This passage documents the community's insatiable need for legends, no matter the personal costs to those of legendary status; they would even rewrite escape into the story, when that obviously could not have occurred under the circumstances. Big Man has done, as with the denizens of Ralph Ellison's Golden Day, what the neophyte invisible man (in this case the townspeople) dares not do. Their vicarious identifications with Big Man fulfill their desires for status and power. The passage also emphasizes the extranatural strength of the hero. These factors, combined with the equation of human characteristics and bestial ones, all serve to underscore why Big Man would be elevated to legendary status in spite of the pathology associated with that elevation. In this brief instance, his defiance of white patriarchal oppression is as expressive and defiant as Robin Hood stealing jewels from under the nose of the Sheriff of Nottingham.

Despite the romantic aura that envelops this scene, it also exposes the pathological interracial interaction between Boots White and Big Man that privileges brute strength. It could be argued that Big Man's strength *belongs* to Boots White; because Boots controls Big Man's violence, he controls Big Man's strength. Boots White is the force that contains that strength or sets it in motion. Consider the John Henry myth as an analog. It is a white man who makes the bet that his steam drill can beat John Henry, and it is a white boss who supervises John Henry's involvement in the bet. John Henry pits his flesh against metal at the spoken word of the white man. John Henry is merely the box that contains the energy. Similarly, Big Man's "230 pounds of compact muscle" sit idle until the white man speaks and thereby "acts" it into motion. Big Man then pits his body against the "blue steel" of Boots White's gun, a confrontation he can only lose. But the fact that his string has been pulled, his energy unleashed in Boots White's sadistic ritual of racial repression, raises questions as to whether he controls his own strength, his own body. Consider, too, that John Morgan also "acts" Big Man's strength into being when he impregnates Little Bit. If Big Man is therefore merely a responder to stimuli, a rat in a maze of violent racist behaviors, then his strength is further compromised out of legend and into pathology.

Boots White has some unhealthy intentions in this scene as well. By reenacting his ritual of racial repression—the stomping, staring, and spitting—he seeks to control the monsters he perceives Big Man and other blacks to be. Keeping them on a leash, so to speak, letting them know every Saturday night that he is boss, he replicates the authority/submission dynamics his ancestors enacted during slavery. Every Saturday night he makes clear that there is only one *man* in Sam's Café (not coincidentally, he is referred to as "the Man," meaning the law—the one with the power and the gun as well as the white skin). Clearly, the gun emblematizes psychosexual dynamics in this manhood/race/sexuality triad. Put another way, Boots can thus claim manhood in his hands if he cannot claim it in his pants. As the law, however, he can create his own hegemony in legal, gendered, and racial terms, and he seeks to ensure that no black male will challenge his sovereignty. He thus enters the local lore as a "ba-ad cracker," and the voyeurs watch him as closely as they watch Big Man.

While the townspeople might have second thoughts about Boots White, no such second-guessing enters their elevation of Big Man to heroic statue. The same is true with Little Bit. As this legend-making process develops, the black woman also has her role to play in the mythologizing of her man. Little Bit thwarts Boots White's attempt to seize her body, her curses, and her razor.[8] When she realizes that her husband is dying, "with one swipe of her razor the southpaw-swinging Little Bit carved a streak down the right side of the policeman's face, beginning just above the eyebrow and extending downward to the middle of his smooth pink cheek" (50). For her effort, she is pistol-whipped, kicked, unattended at the hospital (the doctor is trying to save Boots's eye), and comatose for a week shortly after giving birth to a true black baby fathered by Big Man. Only Boots's empty gun prevents her death. But she serves her part in mythologizing Big Man, for even as she is being stomped, and even as he finally succumbs to the fusillade of bullets that have entered his body, he still tries to reach Little Bit, the love of his life. The black woman serves, then, to bolster the legendary potential of her man; her role is always secondary. Still, she maintains an indisputable significance in Big Man's folkloric and mythic ascendance.

The King of Dark Town's exit from the narrative creates more presence than absence, for he becomes the measure of how larger-than-life characters can act toward the law when the confrontation is a matter of saving one's dignity and one's reputation in the community. None of the legend makers seems to mind that Big Man would not fight white folks for his wife; what matters, ultimately, is that he fights for himself. This incongruity does not in any way lessen their admiration for Big Man, but it does highlight the deeply flawed nature of mythmaking when this kind of strength is the primary characteristic. Big Man's becomes the life and the tale to overcome, the touchstone against which other would-be badmen, especially a couple of youngsters from Hard Labor Hole, are measured. And he provides the standard for heroic emulation against which Appalachee Red will also be measured and whose pattern Red will expand and exceed.

But no bet is won; no rain falls; no release comes to the community. There are, however, negative consequences. His nose broken by Big Man and his right eye lost to Little Bit, Boots becomes meaner than ever (the eye patch he must wear will later earn him a new nickname—"ol' One-Eyed"—but it does not replace "Boots"). It is not enough that Big Man dies or that Little

Bit loses her mind; Boots must still heap punishment upon the family. His father, Ezra, sends members of the Ku Klux Klan to burn down the home of Little Bit's parents, with them and two of her younger siblings inside. This is the nadir of black/white relations in Appalachee, for Boots's "one-man law" is institutionalized, blacks are terrorized, and there is no one strong or crazy enough to stand up to him in an effort to change things. That is the state of affairs from 1936 to 1945, by which time Boots has become chief of police. It is left to Appalachee Red to even the score.

By imbuing his characters with such mythic, larger-than-life traits, Andrews is clearly entertained by the scenarios he creates. He uses humor to express his admiration for southern customs, speech, and folkways as well as to laugh at his characters. He manipulates them as much for his own voyeuristic pleasure as for that of the textual audience or readers. Preferring to tell a good joke or story in lieu of developing his characters, Andrews seems less committed to depicting them as full-bodied creations. Using them, instead, as grist for his own laughter mill, he watches their antics from a lofty, superior perch. His choices, therefore, raise questions that a more centralized bestowal of authorial sympathies would perhaps have eliminated.

The Legacy of the Badman Hero

The "Big Man" appellation that was mere description during his younger years becomes *Big Man* of legend and derring-do in Big Man's later life and especially after his death. The events that lead questioning readers to locate his exploits in the realm of strength as disease simultaneously lead the townspeople to view him as heroic. John Roberts's comments on the nature of heroism are relevant in sorting through this conundrum: "We often use the term 'hero' as if it denoted a universally recognized character type, and the concept of 'heroism' as if it referred to a generally accepted behavioral category. In reality, figures (both real and mythic) and actions dubbed heroic in one context or by one group of people may be viewed as ordinary or even criminal in another context or by other groups, or even by the same ones at different times" (1). I posit a similar gap between Andrews's textual audience and members of his reading audience. Big Man's community might view his actions as heroic—if not worthy of emulation—but we can see without legendary blinders the destructive consequences of his actions (and even Roberts suggests that heroic actions are problematic if they lead to destructive consequences for the community, which Big Man's encounter with Boots White certainly brings).

The strength that leads Big Man to challenge Boots White also leads him to fight with Little Bit, which is the arena where sexuality and strength converge in the portrait of the diseased "strong" black male. The same climate in the early twentieth century that would applaud a black man for challenging a "nigger-stomping" white lawman also allows him to take his fists to a black woman, then make passionate love to her. These conspicuous and potentially dangerous connections between violence and sexuality cannot be overlooked when evaluating the so-called strong black male hero. Indeed, they harbor images of the sexual perversion inherent in lynching and the beatings of enslaved persons as documented by Walter White, James E. Cutler, Arthur F. Raper, Harriet Jacobs, Frederick Douglass, and others.[9] Compartmentalizing violent actions is especially problematic when the victims are members of one's own race and community—indeed, one's own family. Instead, societally sanctioned notions of violence and sexuality inform Andrews's black male protagonist—a portraiture in which a black man is afflicted with a cancerous conception of masculinity and selfhood.

The inability to distinguish between oppressor and oppressed, as Richard Wright so eloquently illustrated in *Native Son* (1940), leads the embattled, oppressed black man to commit assaults against black people that are as egregious—if not more so—than the ones he commits against whites. Recall, specifically, Bigger Thomas's killing of his black girlfriend, Bessie Mears—a crime eclipsed by his slaying of the white and wealthy Mary Dalton. Similarly, in the world in which Big Man Thompson lives, no such distinction is made, and Little Bit becomes as much a victim of Big Man as she does of Boots White. Unable to create space for a sympathetic response to her victimization—indeed, by making her a victimizer as well—Andrews trivializes the issue of black male brutality against black females. Their violent episodes, so the narrator of the text would have us believe, constitute an elaborate mating ritual. Therefore, Andrews squanders the potential for a more complex portrait—and one possibly more empathetic of Little Bit's abuse—in favor of the legendary portrait in which both characters transcend their toxic interactions and become the stuff of the townspeople's gossip and lore.

In the spaces and pauses within those stories, however, are some serious implications. First, Andrews suggests that violence against black women is acceptable—as long as they fight back. Of particular interest is the fact that he does not make any exception for the pregnant black woman; indeed, Little Bit is three months pregnant with Blue the last time Big Man knocks her "flat on her ass." Second, violence is acceptable if it cements a "romantic" relationship between husband and wife. Third, violence is condoned if it can be defined as sexual foreplay. Fourth, violence in the defense of black man-hood—even though it leads to death—is of crucial importance; black mar-tyrdom is preferable to white humiliation, especially in a public space. With greater consequences, the situation might be compared to those in which youngsters playing the dozens *must* fight or suffer the humiliation that wit-nesses to their degradation will heap upon them if they do not. In fact, the narrator comments that Big Man would walk away from Boots White if he could: "Now anyone who knew Big Man could've called Boots aside and told him in a nice sort of way that the black King of Dark Town didn't mind being cussed at a little, or even being called nigger from time to time, just so long as he felt no harm was meant" (49). However, he categorically will not allow his poolboard to be disturbed. The public challenge, as in the dozens, must be met.

Thus, this portrait of sanctioned violence dramatizes the cramped space into which Big Man Thompson and Little Bit have been slotted historical-ly, socially, and artistically. Big Man is moved about by the forces of the law in Appalachee like one of Baby Suggs's checker-piece children in Toni Mor-rison's *Beloved* (1987). When he most thinks that he is in charge of his fate, he is least so. The reactionary nature of his heroism thus calls its validity further into question. He believes he is acting out of his own volition when he is really responding to someone else's notion of what a strong, violent black man should be and do. In playing that role, Big Man is complicit in his own degradation, acquiescing through his own corrosive response to the world.

The loner stance from which Big Man defines his so-called heroic response to white racism is another indication of its diseased roots. In the John Henry syndrome, black men do not consult other black men about their problems or seek their advice; they keep their ailments to themselves or mention them only in humorous passing references. Big Man sits and broods, hulking over the checkers, sometimes just as frightening to the members of the black community as he might appear to be to those outside. He refuses to share his emotional state or introspections (if he has any) even with his wife; in-deed, they are separated on many occasions when we see him in Sam's Café. Thus he is *of* the community but not completely *in* it, already set apart in the hero-making process, for all heroes by their nature must be larger than the mere fallible mortals around them. As Andrews writes of Big Man, "solely an individual, Big Man was known to jump anyone, regardless of their origins, who he felt had wronged him" (36–37). An important caveat here might be: with the exception of a powerful white man who impregnates his wife.

The ultimate consequence of Big Man's so-called heroic action might be called the Solomon response. Big Man makes an individualistic choice, just as Milkman does in Morrison's *Song of Solomon* (1977), and flies on off and leaves a body. The body he leaves is Little Bit, who goes insane after her encounter with Boots; she is left socially, financially, and psychically compromised for life (Red ends up providing for her, but Big Man certainly had no assurance that any such benefactor would materialize when he made his choice). Because he would not distinguish between constructive and destructive uses of strength and violence, Big Man also leaves the body of his community in the throes of Boots White's aggressively racist authority for a decade. While he certainly gains immortality within this community's conception of that status, he is finally just as diseased as the black man who beats his wife on Saturday night just because he can.

Notes

1. The ballad of John Henry can be briefly told. In a contest with a steam drill at the Big Bend Tunnel in West Virginia in the 1870s, John Henry agreed to match his physical prowess with a steel-driving hammer against the mechanical ability of the steam drill. John Henry won, but the exertion cost him his life. The story has been told and retold in a variety of media, from scholarly treatments to children's books to film. For coverage of early scholarly treatments, see Richard M. Dorson, "The Career of 'John Henry.'" John Henry has been used to teach values in young children and to support larger American cultural values such as honesty and hard work.

2. Sexual expertise is the other feat most frequently emphasized about John Henry, but it is obviously one that is usually downplayed in the pristine versions of the legend presented to American school children. In some of the literary portraits of strong black men, however, this feature is reincorporated.

3. John Henry's strength has been interpreted alternatively as supporting the status quo—a black man using his strength to earn money and advantages for a white man—but the prevailing interpretation is usually positive.

4. Professor James was on the faculty at the University of North Carolina at Chapel Hill in the early 1980s when he conducted this research. He is now on the faculty at the University of Michigan at Ann Arbor.

5. Boots White has acquired his name from his "nigger stomping" boots, which he uses to terrorize the black residents of Appalachee. In one memorable instance, he literally and viciously stomps a drunken black man into hospitalization for accidentally bumping into him and ripping buttons from his uniform. His penchant for violence, combined with his general racism, makes him a formidable adversary for Big Man Thompson as well as for Appalachee Red, though Red will initially choose

to handle the situation through means other than direct confrontation. Boots ritualistically strides into Sam's Café every Saturday night and glares at the black cus-
tomers just to remind them that he is in charge; Big Man Thompson consistently
ignores him, which adds tension to their relationship.

6. Stagolee is a badman hero in part because he uses a gun to achieve his objec-
tives. He defies and kills members of the black community, and he even challenges
the law and the courts. In some versions of the long narrative poems about him called
toasts, he arrives in hell, takes over, and kills the Devil. Mrs. Devil then gives him a
light so that he can go off and start a hell of his own. He epitomizes the badman
heroic tradition in its positively negative manifestation. For representative selections,
see Roger D. Abrahams, *Deep Down in the Jungle: Negro Narrative Folklore from
the Streets of Philadelphia*.

7. Consider similar literary patterns in Cholly Breedlove blaming Darlene for the
sexual discomfort he feels in the presence of two armed white men in Morrison's
The Bluest Eye (1970), or the black men's displacing of their guilt onto Deborah in
James Baldwin's *Go Tell It on the Mountain* (1953) after she has been gang-raped
by white men. In both instances, it is easier for the black men to assuage their guilt
by blaming black women for their victimization than to face directly the psychic
castration that results from their inability to contest white patriarchy. While Big Man
will eventually square off against Boots White, the overarching literary pattern is
nonetheless noteworthy here.

8. I think of how razors are stereotypically and historically associated with black
violence, which Marlon Riggs chronicles in his 1989 documentary *Ethnic Notions*.
While black men are portrayed as the ones who usually wield razors, Little Bit's
strength almost masculinizes her. Think as well of the knife- and razor-wielding black
women described in Zora Neale Hurston's *Mules and Men* (1935).

9. See Walter White, *Rope and Faggot: A Biography of Judge Lynch* (1929);
James E. Cutler, *Lynch-Law: An Investigation into the History of Lynching in the
United States* (1905); Arthur F. Raper, *The Tragedy of Lynching* (1933); Harriet
E. Jacobs, *Incidents in the Life of a Slave Girl, Written by Herself* (1861); Freder-
ick Douglass, *Narrative of the Life of Frederick Douglass: An American Slave*
(1845).

Works Cited

Abrahams, Roger D. *Deep Down in the Jungle: Negro Narrative Folklore from the
Streets of Philadelphia*. Chicago: Aldine, 1970.

Andrews, Raymond. *Appalachee Red*. 1978; rpt., Athens: University of Georgia
Press, 1987.

Chesnutt, Charles W. *The Marrow of Tradition*. Boston: Houghton Mifflin, 1901.

Dorson, Richard M. "The Career of 'John Henry.'" In *Mother Wit from the Laughing Barrel: Readings in the Interpretation of Afro-American Folklore*. Ed. Alan
Dundes. Oxford: University of Mississippi Press, 1990. 568–77.

Himes, Chester. *If He Hollers Let Him Go.* 1945; rpt., New York: Thunder's Mouth Press, 1986.

Roberts, John W. *From Trickster to Badman: The Black Folk Hero in Slavery and Freedom.* Philadelphia: University of Pennsylvania Press, 1989.

Williams, John A. *Captain Blackman.* New York: Thunder's Mouth Press, 1972.

3

Looking Homewood: The Evolution of John Edgar Wideman's Folk Imagination

RAYMOND E. JANIFER

Readers of black fiction produced in the last few years sooner or later come to realize the quasi-biographical intention of many Afro-American authors who believe that one service they can—in fact *must*—perform is telling stories about black people who have been written out of history. Their hope, as is the case with John Edgar Wideman's *Sent for You Yesterday* (1983), a triptych of narratives about the black residents of Homewood, is to honor their predecessors in stories that break stereotypes and portray a piece of their lives. It is an effort to keep them alive, perhaps even to enshrine the meaning of their lives (as the author sees it) in the theater of a story, poem, or novel. . . . Much of black writing in the last decade or so is a meditation on remembrance. Praisesongs from writers who feel themselves to be keepers—or transmitters—of the past for the sake, as with Wideman, of future generations.

—Charles Johnson, *Being and Race*

Past lives live in us, through us. Each of us harbors the spirits of people who walked the earth before we did, and those spirits depend on our continuing existence, just as we depend on their presence to live our lives to the fullest.

—John Edgar Wideman, *Sent for You Yesterday*

In his Homewood Trilogy, the novelist and essayist John Edgar Wideman unquestionably situates the overall perspective of his work within the black and African diasporan cultural experience. He accomplishes this by de-emphasizing tropes from European literary traditions such as modernism and existentialism and, more importantly, by utilizing African and African-American folkloric traditions, embracing what Wideman has called "black English vernacular." In the three novels that comprise his Homewood Trilogy—*Damballah* (1981), *Hiding Place* (1981), and *Sent for You Yesterday* (1983)—he begins to write fiction that is able to withstand the criticism that his previous work does not reflect "authentic" portrayals of African Americans and cultural nuances. In this series of interconnected stories about the Pittsburgh, Pennsylvania, Homewood ghetto in which Wideman was reared, the novelist's black characters, speaking primarily in black English vernacular, regularly draw upon their folklore and traditions as empowering and sustaining forces. In these works, a communal ethos begins to take center stage in his literary universe, and he continues this trend in all of his successive works.

In the Homewood Trilogy, existentialism and modernism still maintain important positions, but Wideman begins to minimize their influence by adding Afrocentrism and black postmodernism to his literary repertoire. By drawing upon Afrocentrism, he acknowledges Molefi Asante's belief in the centrality of Africans in postmodern history (Asante 6). Furthermore, Wideman acknowledges Asante's position that African Americans are only able to draw on these contributions of their African ancestors by placing African ideals at the center of any analysis that involves African culture and behavior. Asante argues in *Afrocentricity* (1988) that the non-Afrocentric African American operates in a manner that is negatively predictable because his or her images, symbols, lifestyles, and manners are contradictory. He says that because of this contradiction they do not know their African ancestors, and they are unable to call upon their power (1).

Utilizing the idea of Afrocentricity to his creative advantage in his Homewood Trilogy, Wideman connects the African-American folklore and traditions of his family in Homewood, Pennsylvania, to a prehistory in Africa. By embracing postmodernism, he is rejecting canonicity, master narratives, and the hierarchy in American literature between the written tradition of "Standard Received English" and "Black Vernacular English" (Giroux 347). Matthew Wilson notes that Wideman's Homewood Trilogy "reflects a symbiotic fusion of multiple traditions both European and African-American" (244). Indeed, in this collection Wideman begins to tap the imaginative potential of diverse literary philosophies and his own iconoclastic imagination.

By the time Wideman completes this collection of works, he skillfully melds existentialism, modernism, postmodernism, Afrocentrism, and the black English vernacular in a manner that serves his eclectic intellectual tastes. Despite indulging these diverse intellectual interests, however, Wideman foremost bases these works on African-American folkloric and cultural traditions with an implicit prehistory in Africa. According to James W. Coleman in *Blackness and Modernism: The Literary Career of John Edgar Wideman,* this diverse mix of literary tropes satisfied his previous critics, who had questioned Wideman's credentials as a legitimate black writer (98). As I will explore in a discussion of the trilogy's first novel, *Damballah,* Wideman overcomes such criticism by carefully placing his black characters in a sentient, mythical environment. In this milieu, neither the characters' nor the author's worldview is shaped predominantly by European cultural and literary traditions. Instead, the characters' perspectives evolve within their own extended African-American family circle in the fabled community of Homewood, as well as within an African-centered cultural ethos.

Wideman explains the poetic license he utilizes with the people, places, and geography of the mythical community he constructs for his African-American Homewood residents in an interview with Jessica Lustig: "There is a neighborhood in Pittsburgh called Homewood. It was there before I was born, and probably when I'm dead it will still be called that. It's considered a number of streets, houses, and population changes—people get old and die. It's a real place in that sense. The distinction I want to make is that once I started to write about Homewood, I was creating a place based partly on memories of the actual place I lived in, and partly on the exigencies or needs of the fiction I was creating" (Lustig 453). Thus, his Homewood Trilogy provides him with the sustaining myth he had been searching for during his hiatus from publishing during the 1970s in Laramie, Wyoming, and systematically facilitates the continued growth and development of his fiction and his own identity. This series of works marks his coming-of-age as an African-American intellectual who plays a constructive role in the black community and garners him even wider recognition than he gained from his earlier novels, *A Glance Away* (1967), *Hurry Home* (1973), and *The Lynchers* (1973).

Although Wideman did not publish any fiction during the eight-year period preceding the publication of the Homewood Trilogy, he shared with the critic Wilfred Samuels that he had spent this time doing his homework on the African-American literary tradition. He also asserts that much of his research involved remembering and refamiliarizing himself with the folk-lore and traditions of his extended family in Pittsburgh. The other major part of this homework, he said, was spent reading and studying historical, sociological, and literary texts by various black authors. He explained that although he did not publish any fiction during his hiatus at the University of Wyoming, he had been constantly "woodshedding"—learning and experimenting. He concludes that throughout this self-imposed exile, he had been trying to identify and apply the voice of the black English vernacular in his fiction projects:

> I was trying to learn a different voice; I was doing a lot of studying and catching up. I was constantly writing and I produced a lot of manuscripts, none of which were satisfactory. Some of them were sent out, and people either didn't like them or wanted more, or liked them and didn't want to publish them. I was engaged in that kind of business constantly, but as far as having a finished manuscript, for about six or seven years, I did not. Just bits and pieces. I was learning a new language to talk about my experience and my blackness. (Samuels 45)

Further, he revealed that after his first three books, he was also beginning to attempt to write for an African-American reading audience: "I wanted to write books my brother, aunts, sisters, cousins, mother, and father would read. . . . Their feelings, thoughts, intelligence—all have been tested and refined—so it wasn't a question of writing down to a less educated set of readers but rather to expand my own frame of reference" (44). Ironically, focusing specifically on African-American folkloric and vernacular culture enabled Wideman to give his fiction even more of the universal appeal of great classical literature, which he had sought to do in his first three novels.

Before coming upon the ideas and voices that would eventually become the Homewood Trilogy, Wideman continuously scanned the African-American literary tradition, encountering the poetry of Wheatley, Hammon, Dunbar, and Hughes, and the fiction of Chesnutt and Toomer. He read slave narratives and works by contemporary novelists such as Ishmael Reed, Charles Johnson, Toni Morrison, Ernest J. Gaines, Gayl Jones, and Gloria Naylor. He also began publishing scholarly articles on the African-American literary tradition, concentrating especially on the theoretical concept of the utilization of black English vernacular in American literature.

Reading and analyzing the diverse authors of the black literary tradition more and more carefully, Wideman became preoccupied with defining the black voice in American literature. He sought to identify how African-Amer-

ican writers express this black voice in their fiction. Part of his scholarly in-
vestigations resulted in articles entitled "Frame and Dialect: The Evolution
of the Black Voice in American Literature" and "Defining the Black Voice in
Fiction," where he concludes that the black English vernacular tradition had
historically been incorporated into the literary or written frame of American literature as a substandard dialect. Wideman contends that, dating from
precolonial times, a hierarchical relationship existed between the black English vernacular and standard received English in American literature: "The
Black English Vernacular expressed as Negro dialect in the frame of American literature always announces and signifies the presence of an entire value
system—white superiority and black inferiority. Against this background one
can view the evolution of the black voice in American literature as the attempts of various writers to free them from a frame which devalues black
speech" ("Frame and Dialect" 45).

He continues his analysis of the intersections between black vernacular
and literary traditions in "Charles Chesnutt: *The Marrow of Tradition,*" by
looking at the ways that Chesnutt tries to invert the traditional chain of
command in American literature between the frame of standard received
English and the dialect of black English vernacular. Wideman argues that
as a fiction writer, Chesnutt achieved his greatest accomplishment by placing the black English vernacular on equal intellectual and literary footing
with standard received English:

> Chesnutt used a strategy in his fiction for which he is seldom given credit.
> Employing a tale within a tale technique, he framed black speech so that in his
> best stories he blends the literary and oral traditions without implying that the
> black storyteller's mode of perceiving and recreating reality is any less valid than
> the written word. Black speech in the form of Negro dialect entered American
> literature as a curiosity, a comic interlude, shorthand for perpetuating myths
> and prejudices about black people. Chesnutt's frame displays the written and
> spoken word on equal terms or at least as legitimate contenders for the read-
> er's sympathy. (Wideman, "Charles Chesnutt and the WPA Narratives" 60)

Wideman contends that Chesnutt's use of black English vernacular contains
the oral histories of his African-American characters and is a powerful vehicle for reconstructing the past so that the lies and misrepresentations of
the master class became part of the written record. He argues that Chesnutt allows the black English vernacular to come full circle: rather than being
a tool in the hand of the oppressor, it is turned against the oppressor (68).

Wideman continues to investigate black vernacular and performative tra-

ditions in "Stomping the Blues: Rituals in Black Music and Speech," which
is an extensive review of Albert Murray's *Stomping the Blues*. Murray, like
the playwright Amiri Baraka and the literary critics Houston A. Baker Jr.
and Henry Louis Gates Jr., uses the blues as the central metaphor for the
African-American oral tradition. Wideman notes how Murray employs the
complex linguistic codes of the blues, which are embedded in the black
English vernacular. He began to study how these codes could be employed
in the construction of the new voice he was seeking in his own fiction:
"Murray's central metaphor in *Stomping the Blues* (1976) is language. When
he talks repeatedly about vernacular, idiom, accent, speech, phrase, and
fluency, he is not only extending the metaphorical relationship between language and music, but he is establishing a continuity along which language
and music are two rather arbitrary signposts" (43). Subsequently, Wideman
wrote "*Of Love and Dust:* A Reconsideration," where he explores how
another southern writer, Ernest J. Gaines, and other black authors use complex linguistic codes of the black English vernacular, like the blues and signifying, to communicate complex messages. He also came to realize that
these authors select and target specific audiences, even to the point of se-
lecting audiences within audiences. Houston A. Baker Jr. helps to elucidate
the literary-vernacular function of the blues, theorizing that one way of
describing the blues is to claim its mixture of different elements as a code
radically conditioning African-American cultural signifying (Baker 5). Wideman discovered that scores of black American writers invoke the blues as a
metaphorical language, an enabling script to construct the story of a people who seemed like underdogs but were eventually able to emerge victorious. These authors employ African-American folklore and traditions like
storytelling, spirituals/gospel, myths, sermons, work songs, and the dozens/
signifying to create black characters who may exist in a racist, oppressive
world, but who summon their cultural folklore and traditions as a sustaining force (Wideman, "*Of Love and Dust*" 77).

　　This mythic archetype, the "victorious underdog" that Wideman discovered in the fiction of African-American writers, as well as the way they
employ other tropes and topoi from black literary traditions, is at the core
of his own mythic reinscription of his family's cultural ethos. As critical as
Wideman's scholarly engagement with writers like Chesnutt and Murray and
others was in expanding his understanding of black vernacular culture in
the development of a new fictive voice, they were equally important in fa-
cilitating a strenuous process of self-examination. Before the publication of
Hiding Place, Damballah, and *Sent for You Yesterday,* Wideman had not

resolved his estranged relationship with his family and his native Homewood. Such a resolution would mark a more tangible engagement with the
vernacular aspects of African-American culture that heretofore had been
limited to the realm of scholarly discourse.

His distance from his family is emblematized by his estranged relationship with his younger brother, Robert. In *Brothers and Keepers* (1984)
Wideman ponders this estrangement by reflecting on his younger brother's
cross-country flight from armed robbery and murder charges in Pittsburgh
and how "Robby's" actions would impact his own "charmed" literary life:
"Because I was living in Laramie, Wyoming, I could shake loose from the
sense of urgency, of impending disaster dogging my people in Pittsburgh.
Never a question of forgetting Robby, more of a matter of how I remembered him that distinguished my feelings from theirs. Sudden flashes of fear,
anger, and remorse could spoil a class party, cause me to retreat into silence,
lose whole days to gloominess and distance. But I had the luxury of dealing
intermittently with my pain" (5). Ignoring his brother's situation back in
Homewood presented Wideman with a dilemma he could not easily resolve:
"denying disruptive emotions were a survival mechanism I'd been forced
to learn early in life. . . . My life was relatively comfortable, pleasant, safe.
I'd come west to escape the demons Robby personified. I didn't need out-
law brothers reminding me how much had been lost, how much compromised, how terrible the world still raged beyond the charmed circle of my
life on the Laramie plains" (11). Even in Laramie, however, Wideman could
not escape the demons that haunted him. He continued to feel an overwhelming guilt about abandoning his family—guilt he determined to resolve—and
he began by interpreting the personal identity crisis he was experiencing.
Wideman embarked upon an immense personal journey, contemplating his
life as an African-American intellectual in white academic society and what
this position means in relation to his first three novels and his alienation from
his family.

John Edgar Wideman and other young "Negroes" of his generation, who
had taken the first bold steps into the exclusive institutions of the Ivy League
like the University of Pennsylvania, became what the white world expected
them to be on its terms. They had to assimilate into a world that was designed to reject them, donning the "mask" while they were doing so. For
Wideman the process of cultural assimilation also meant literally and figuratively turning his back on his family and friends in the Homewood ghetto, a common transformation for young blacks of his generation. The African-American social and cultural revolution of the late 1960s and 1970s had

not yet occurred and all things "Negro," especially music, dance, art, and literature, were considered inferior. Thus, for a young black man to excel in the larger white world he had to aspire to participate in the higher—that is, "whiter"—aspects of the culture.

Such a cultural transformation explains why Wideman's earlier novels, *A Glance Away, Hurry Home,* and *The Lynchers,* de-emphasize African-American folklore and vernacular traditions by intermingling them with tropes from European literary traditions. Eventually, however, through his assiduous studies of African-American literary and critical discourses, Wideman came to realize that in these earlier works he consciously privileges the mainstream literary traditions over African-American folk and vernacular ones. He has stated that in these works, he had tried to legitimize his interpretations of African-American folk culture with allusions to the European intellectual tradition. In one interview he comments that in his earlier works, "A quote from T. S. Eliot would authenticate a quote from my grandmother. The quote from my grandmother wasn't enough. I felt I had to legitimize it with a Joycean allusion to buttress it" (Bonetti 89). He says that after grounding himself in African-American folkloric and oral culture through his reading of black authors and authoring scholarly essays himself about the black oral-literary nexus, he came to realize that black vernacular speech could do everything any other varieties of European literary discourses and languages could do:

> There is no privileged position from which to view this fictional world, no terms into which it asks to be translated, its rawness is not incidental, not local color or exoticism from which other, more familiar voices will relieve you. *The Black English Vernacular creates the only valid terms for its world; the authority of its language is not subordinated to other codes; the literary frame is not visible.* . . . *African-American writers have created their own code of discourse from the resources of their oral tradition and the models of American literature. African-American vernacular speech like any other variety of languages defines reality for its users.* In American literature it could not perform this function until it divested itself of the frame [mainstream American literature], those elements in a literary tradition which resolve in favor of the literate, conflicting versions of reality codified into written and oral modes of expression. ("Defining the Black Voice in Fiction" 81–82; emphasis added)

His scholarly articles and experiments with the black English vernacular in his own writing establish the theoretical groundwork for the Homewood Trilogy. This trilogy is also impacted by two tragic events in his family: the incarceration of his younger brother, Robert, for life without the possibility of parole, and the death of his maternal grandmother, Freeda French.

These two events provided Wideman with opportunities to reintegrate himself into his family in meaningful and fruitful ways.

After his maternal grandmother's funeral in Homewood, while his family assembled for food and drinks, they revealed to Wideman how he could employ their collective folk memory in his fiction. At this gathering, his relatives began telling and retelling old family stories spanning their history from Africa, slavery in the American South, and eventually resettlement in the urban North:

> Aunt May was drinking a lot of Wild Turkey. She is a little old lady and she sits in a chair and her feet don't touch the floor—and she began to tell stories. Everybody was telling stories but sooner or later she just took center stage and told the story of Sybela Owens and how my family came to Pittsburgh—I listened. I'd heard these stories before but it was the first time I had heard them in a way that made them special. *I couldn't let these stories wither away. I had to write them down. It became clear to me that I need not look any further than the place I was born and the people who loved me to find what was significant and lasting in literature.* (Bonetti 86; emphasis added)

This experience enabled Wideman to reconnect with his family, eclipsing his physical, psychological, and artistic distance from them. He began to realize how he could make his family's voice his dominant fictive voice by combining their memories and stories with what he had learned about the black English vernacular in his scholarly pursuits. Through his family's storytelling experience, he began to realize that they could provide him with important mythic archetypes, tropes, and topoi for his fiction. Not only are these communal remembrances and oral traditions the basis of the literary sensibilities of the black nationalist aesthetic movement of the 1960s, they also form the foundation of the entire African-American literary tradition.

For the first time since his childhood, Wideman began to listen carefully to the remembered experiences of his family members' folk culture. This listening would bring him an insight remarkably close to the realization that Larry Neal came to while formulating the theoretical underpinnings of the Black Arts movement with Baraka in the 1960s. Neal, who did graduate work at the University of Pennsylvania while Wideman was an undergraduate there, came to believe that what he and his colleagues in the Black Arts movement would consider the black aesthetic would always exist in creative productions of African-American folk culture. During the development of the Black Arts movement, Neal would insist that an authentic black culture be rooted in African-American folklore expressed in the black English vernacular (Neal 21).

After his family's storytelling session following his grandmother's funeral, Wideman began to see his family's storytelling as a potent form of cultural resistance. He grasped that their storytelling is a literary language that is as capable of communicating the complexities of the universal human experience as any other literary language. In a practical sense this experience with his family's storytelling resembles what writers like Gaines, Gayl Jones, and August Wilson capture in their works: "Storytelling in the Black English Vernacular can do everything any other variety of literary languages can do. . . . There is no privileged position from which to view their construction of the world, no terms into which it asks to be translated, its rawness is not incidental, not local color or exoticism from which other, more familiar voices will relieve you" (Wideman, "Frame and Dialect" 36). Wideman goes on to assert that his family's storytelling *is* African-American literature, because it reinforces social, ethical, and aesthetic values to construct a world on their own terms—a world where black people have a measure of power and dignity (35).

According to Melvin Dixon, Wideman's new insight into his family's collective folk memory, which is open to the dialectic of remembering and forgetting, informs his reading about the African-American literary tradition. The act of reading history and literature is reconstructing what no longer exists, but his family's memory is life itself, vulnerable to the vicissitudes of time, containing nourished recollections (Dixon 18). Wideman is exposed as an insider to the treasure chest of his family's folklore and traditions to which an outsider, a collector, could never have had access. Zora Neale Hurston says in *Mules and Men* (1935) that "Folklore is not as easy to collect as it sounds. The best sources are where there are the least outside influences and these people, usually being underprivileged, are the shyest. They are more reluctant at times to reveal that which their soul lives by" (2). Wideman, however, was welcomed with open arms into the intoxicating circle of his family's history through their storytelling. He notes that the storytelling session that followed his grandmother's funeral was the first time he felt accepted in his family as a full-grown adult and thereby an equal member of their speech community: "I was hearing my grandmother's life. . . . As Aunt May talked about the old days I saw my grandmother as a little girl and courting and I saw John French coming to steal her away from Aunt Aida and Uncle Bill. And I saw Uncle Bill sitting there with a shotgun waiting for John French. I knew I couldn't allow these stories to wither away. I had to write them down" (Bonetti 86).

As each of Wideman's family members took turns narrating, their recollections were individual stories, but they were often told collectively as well. Their stories were told in a call-and-response fashion, rooted in Western Africa in an extended metaphorical blues language replete with complex linguistic codes like signifying and the dozens, spirituals, and sophisticated nonverbal keys. Their storytelling rituals epitomized the black English vernacular, unmediated by the frame of standard received English. Typically, a single narrator would hold the floor, but often other family members who remembered significant parts of a story—sometimes forgotten or purposely omitted by individual narrators—would contribute vital details on important family history. Wideman says the way that storytellers connected to the family and the Homewood community was through their storytelling, which enabled them to maintain their place in the grand narrative of the clan.

Wideman articulates further the process through which familial history gets told and retold, constructed and reconstructed in *Fatheralong: A Meditation on Fathers and Sons, Race and Society* (1994). Indeed, it is the telling and retelling of family (hi)stories that form the basis of his Homewood Trilogy, which restores his personal sense of belonging to his family and native Homewood community. He maintains that all of the individual narrators of his family's histories told one story, and they did not call their individual historical narratives stories. Wideman recalls that his family members gave their individual recollections highly evocative names, calling them "letters from home," "watermelons," and "onions." He reaffirms one of the colorful names of their individual narratives in his own writing:

> Stories are onions. You peel one skin and another grins up at you. Peeling onions can make grown men cry. Which raises other questions. . . . Or you might say an onion is the light and the truth, or at least as much truth and light as you're ever going to receive on this earth, source and finished product all rounded into one. . . . Each skin, each layer a different story, connected to the particular, actual onion you once held whole in your hand as the onion is connected to the stars, dinosaurs, bicycles, a loon's cry, to the seed it sprouted from, the earth where the seed rotted and died and slept until it began dreaming of being an onion again, dreamed the steps it would have to climb, the skins it would have to shed and grow to let its light shine again in the world. (*Fatheralong* 61–62)

The Wideman family's folklore and history were a sacred "memory vault" of one continuous story or "onion" through which Wideman filtered his readings about the African-American literary tradition and his research on the development of the black English vernacular in American literature. For the first time, he had been able to listen to these stories and realize that his classical education had caused him to devalue the literary potential and power of his family's collective folk imagination. This connection with his family's stories has enabled Wideman to personalize the experience of his own blackness and rediscover his identity as a unique African-American intellectual. Therefore, his family's history and vernacular culture became central in his reconstruction of his past selves in the Homewood community, the American South, and, finally, Africa. Through the melding of personal, collective, and cultural histories presented in the Homewood Trilogy, Wideman is able to fictionalize the past and write as a black intellectual who resolves, at least to some degree, his previous discomfort with the phenomenon of Du Bois's double consciousness.

The Homewood Trilogy evinces Wideman's extensive use of his family's folkloric history to create an African-American fictive, mythic community comparable to Faulkner's Yoknapatawpha. Moreover, Wideman's Homewood artistically goes beyond the myopic racial restrictions promulgated by 1960s black nationalist ideology while also superseding the mainstream modernist and existentialist discourses that dominated his earlier novels. The residents of Homewood are primarily African Americans who negotiate their reality through various historical periods while allowing their folklore and traditions to nurture, sustain, and fortify. Most importantly, they interpret their reality collectively rather than as individuals lost in black nationalist politics or modernist or Eurocentric fantasies. Their survival depends on their communal identity expressed through their storytelling. Although Wideman gives his characters in the trilogy a high degree of African-American cultural uniqueness, matters of race do not consume those characters in his mythical community.

᠁   ᠁   ᠁

The Wideman scholar James W. Coleman contends that it is in the first book of the trilogy, *Damballah*, that Wideman presents a wide range of African-American folk characters who draw upon various aspects of their cultural traditions—stories, folk beliefs and rituals, and religious songs and rituals—to triumph over racism, poverty, hardship, and pain (79). Wideman's collective vision and identity function beyond simple racial categories to glorify a struggle of the universal human spirit (79). According to the epigraph to Maya Daren's study on African cosmology, *Divine Horseman: The Voodoo Gods of Haiti* (1972), "Damballah" is an African God whose deity when literally translated means to gather the family. Thus, by titling his opening story "Damballah," Wideman is stretching his hand back, gathering his family's history into solid contemporary ground beneath his feet (Janifer 371–72).

By invoking Damballah, Wideman gives his characters a sense of extension and of the ancient origins of race. In the Fon religion, Dambada Hwedo is a personification of forgotten ancestors, those who lived so long ago that their names are forgotten (Wilson 242). Wideman is thus attempting to put those forgotten ancestors and their histories in touch with a contemporary family history. He brings the past lives of his ancestors to life, demonstrating how his family directly experiences history in their upsurge and decline, through their cycle of joys and sorrows. *Damballah* is also the linking book of the Homewood Trilogy, where we are introduced to the presiding figures of the community and encounter the sustaining legends and myths that will surface—fleshed out or told from other vantage points—in the other books of the trilogy (Birkerts 43). The story "Damballah" serves simultaneously as a framing device and overarching metaphor for the entire Homewood Trilogy. Various other stories in *Damballah* introduce and prepare us for the characters we will meet from the diverse branches of Wideman's family tree. All of these stories have to do with this clan, and Wideman provides a genealogical chart for the entire trilogy at the beginning of the book. Although this chart is not historically accurate, it does match the imaginative flow of the different stories as he traces his family's collective history from capture in Africa, slavery and escape in the American South, and resettlement and daily life in the North.

Wideman gives *Damballah* an overall sense of unity by using a well-defined setting, Homewood, by presenting central themes from different viewpoints through diverse characters from his family tree, and by depicting the development of an authorial attitude toward the setting of the subject matter (Janifer 373–74). In his article "The Psychic Duality of African-Americans in the Novels of W. E. B. Du Bois," James Stewart identifies an African-American character with ties to the African continent that functions as a counterforce against racism and wholesale cultural subordination in the New World (96). Wideman begins *Damballah* with a comparable character named Orion, an African slave brought to the New World who systematically rejects his owner's attempts to socialize him into an American bondsman. Orion is so intent on maintaining his memories of his African identity that he refuses to speak English, saying "No more would he ever speak the words of the white people who had decided to kill him" (18). Although

Orion's story begins in America, there is an implicit prehistory in Africa. The story opens with Orion standing in a river performing his ritual of communing with the African continent and summoning Damballah's spirit. Orion insists upon remembering this prehistory, and he is able to pass this sacred history on through a young slave boy who has been secretly watching him summoning the spirit of the African God, Damballah (Wilson 242). Through his memories of Africa and the God of his ancestors, Orion is in touch with the deeper kinds of prophetic knowledge that this African divinity represents. He knows that since he insists on keeping his memories of Damballah and the African continent alive in the New World, he will be killed. For some time Orion also knows of the little slave boy, and eventually he comes to see the boy as a vital link to telling future generations of their African past and the spirit of resistance embodied in the divinity called Damballah.

Aunt Lissy, the cook and surrogate mother of the slaves on the plantation, fears Orion's attempts to maintain his African identity and to pass on the spirit of the African God Damballah through the boy. She knows that the punishment for this type of resistance is death. Hence, she wants the boy to stay away from Orion, who rejects Christianity and his Americanized name, Ryan: "'That Ryan, he a crazy nigger. One of them wild African niggers acts like he fresh off the boat. Kind you stay away from less you lookin' for trouble'" (18). When the boy repeats to Aunt Lissy the word "Damballah" he has learned from Orion, she attempts to punish him but only manages to steel his resistance. By embracing the supernatural entity contained in the word, the boy has been imbued with the inward flame of the African God of his ancestors.

Because he repeatedly observes Orion's African ritual of standing in the river and invoking the ghosts of his ancestors personified in Damballah and has been passed the sacred word, the boy becomes Orion's spiritual heir. Once Orion anoints his heir to carry on the spiritual work of their African God in the New World, he launches his final revolutionary attack by publicly rejecting his master's Christianity. In the midst of one of his master's carefully orchestrated Christian services for the slaves on his plantation, Orion publicly calls on the metaphysics of his own ancient African God by screaming for Damballah. By openly rejecting the Christianity his master attempts to impose on him, Orion also defies his master, who sees Orion's act of resistance as potentially encouraging an insurrection among the other slaves. Aunt Lissy is outraged by Orion's "wild" African behavior as well, and she predicts his untimely death.

68 Raymond E. Janifer

As the master observes Orion publicly confronting the sovereignty of the Christian religion, he reaches a damning conclusion that will culminate in Orion's premature death. Orion eventually knocks an overseer off of his horse, "breaking half his bones," and, instead of running away, he confronts the mistress of the plantation and stares deeply into her eyes, "naked as the day he was born" (22). Finally, Orion is dragged away, murdered, castrated, and his remains are thrown into a large tub in the barn. The boy to whom he passed the spirit of Damballah goes into the barn and retrieves his head, believing that it contains Orion's ghost, which is still alive and must be freed to travel home to Africa. He then throws Orion's head into the river where he first saw him perform the African ritual.

The author's acknowledgment of Orion as an African relative is a direct indication that an Afrocentric worldview plays a dominant role in *Damballah* and therefore throughout the Homewood Trilogy. When Wideman introduces Orion as the first member of his family in the New World, he reclaims African history and Afrocentrism as the foundation for the folklore and traditions his family will develop and perpetuate in America. Orion's passing of the spirit of Damballah to the young boy is the first instance of the passing of the African and African-American folklore and traditions that sustain Wideman's family in Homewood to the present day. Wideman makes certain that the story "Damballah" emblematizes the entire Homewood Trilogy and concretizes the passing of the spirit of his family from Africa to the American South and finally to the urban North of Pittsburgh's Homewood. As Dorothy Mbalia observes, by naming the first story of the novel "Damballah," a story that reflects the ethereal roots of African-American people in Africa, and by using the name of that story for the entire work, Wideman reflects his increasing consciousness of himself as an African (52).

In *Damballah*, the first novel of his Homewood Trilogy, Wideman employs his family's oral histories to enact its core message. Orion's story epitomizes the central point of this message: the perpetuation and immortality of African and African-American familial and cultural rituals, customs, and lore. "Damballah" is about the ability, passed through the spirit of the ancestors, to conjure up resistance by developing a cultural countervision. Resistance is inherent in telling one's own story in one's own cultural language; for Wideman, a significant part of that language is a black English vernacular, a language that reverberates with the speech patterns, folkways, and family ethos that sustain generations of Africans, African Americans, and transplanted Homewood denizens.

Works Cited

Asante, Molefi. *Afrocentricity.* Trenton, N.J.: Africa World Press, 1988.

Baker, Houston A., Jr. *Blues, Ideology, and Afro-American Literature: A Vernacular Theory.* Chicago: University of Chicago Press, 1984.

Birkerts, Sven. "The Art of Memory: The Stories of John Edgar Wideman and the Homewood Books." *New Republic,* 13 July 1992, 42–49.

Bonetti, Kay. "Interview with John Edgar Wideman." *Missouri Review* 9.2 (1986): 75–103.

Coleman, James W. *Blackness and Modernism: The Literary Career of John Edgar Wideman.* Oxford: University Press of Mississippi, 1989.

Daren, Maya. *Divine Horsemen: The Voodoo Gods of Haiti.* New York: Dell, 1972.

Dixon, Melvin. "The Black Writer's Use of Memory." In *History and African-American Culture.* Ed. Genevieve Fabre and Robert O'Meally. New York: Oxford University Press, 1994. 18–27.

Giroux, Henry A. "Slacking Off: Border Youth and Postmodern Education." *Journal of Advanced Composition* 14.2 (1994): 347–88.

Hurston, Zora Neale. *Mules and Men.* New York: Harper and Row, 1935.

Janifer, Raymond E. "The Black Nationalistic Aesthetic and the Early Fiction of John Edgar Wideman." Ph.D. dissertation, Ohio State University, 1997.

Lustig, Jessica. "Home: An Interview with John Edgar Wideman." *African American Review* 26.3 (1992): 453–57.

Mbalia, Doreatha. *John Edgar Wideman: Reclaiming the African Personality.* Selingsgrove, Pa.: Susquehanna University Press, 1995.

Neal, Larry. "The Social Background of the Black Arts Movement." *The Black Scholar* 18 (1987): 11–22.

Samuels, Wilfred D. "Going Home: A Conversation with John Edgar Wideman." *Callaloo* 6.1 (1983): 40–59.

Stewart, James. "The Psychic Duality of African-Americans in the Novels of W. E. B. Du Bois." *Phylon* 44.2 (1983): 93–107.

Wideman, John Edgar. *Brothers and Keepers.* New York: Penguin, 1984.

———. "Charles Chesnutt: *The Marrow of Tradition.*" *American Scholar* 42 (Winter 1972–73): 128–34.

———. "Charles Chesnutt and the WPA Narratives: The Oral and Literate Roots of African-American Literature." In *The Slave's Narrative.* Ed. Charles T. Davis and Henry L. Gates. New York: Oxford University Press, 1985. 59–78.

———. *Damballah.* New York: Vintage, 1981.

———. "Defining the Black Voice in Fiction." *Black American Literature Forum* 11 (Fall 1977): 79–82.

———. *Fatheralong: A Meditation on Fathers and Sons, Race and Society.* New York: Pantheon, 1994.

———. "Frame and Dialect: The Evolution of the Black Voice in American Litera-
    ture." *American Poetry Review* 5.5 (1976): 34–37.
———. *Hiding Place.* New York: Vintage, 1981.
———. "*Of Love and Dust:* A Reconsideration." *Callaloo* 1 (May 1976): 76–84.
———. *Sent for You Yesterday.* New York: Vintage, 1983.
———. "Stomping the Blues: Rituals in Black Music and Speech." *American Poet-
    ry Review* 7 (1978): 42–45.
Wilson, Matthew. "The Circles of History in John Edgar Wideman's Homewood
    Trilogy." *College Language Association Journal* 33.3 (1990): 239–59.

4

Commodity Culture and the Conflation of Time in Ishmael Reed's *Flight to Canada*

A. T. SPAULDING

From the opening pages of *Flight to Canada* (1976), Ishmael Reed conflates time to establish a link between the historical condition of slavery and the material conditions of contemporary culture. The novel begins with a poem, entitled "Flight to Canada," in which Raven Quickskill, the poem's author and the novel's protagonist, recounts his escape from slavery in bold and ironic strokes, making anachronistic references to "jumbo jets" and his ability to move freely between the North and the South. The poem marks Reed's use of material anachronism in conjunction with the infusion of a present-day worldview characterized by Raven's assertive and signifying language:

> I flew in non-stop
> Jumbo jet this a.m. Had
> Champagne
> Compliments of the Cap'n
> Who announced that a
> Runaway Negro was on the
> Plane. . . . Last visit I slept in
> Your bed and sampled your
> Cellar. Had your prime
> Quadroon give me
> She-Bear. Yes, yes. (3–4)

Raven's poem stands as an emblem of Reed's own revision of the slave narrative. Both the novel and the poem re-form the slave narrative through a manipulation of time as a means of opening up an aesthetic space in the face of the oppressive conditions of slavery. The conflation of the antebellum South with post–civil rights America allows Reed to deploy Raven's story as a version of his own, forcing us to acknowledge the relationship between the past subjugation of African Americans under the system of slavery and the current cultural practices of appropriation, commodification, and exploitation that restrict the black artist in contemporary America. By conflating the two periods and their material, social, and cultural conditions, Reed juxtaposes his own situation as a black writer with Raven's as a slave narrator; their stories entwine in a common quest to achieve a liberating identity in the face of an oppressive economic and cultural system that seeks to contain and define them.[1] As a result, Reed constructs a postmodern slave narrative that moves beyond a historical representation of the individual slave's quest for freedom and towards a critique of the American slave system and its legacy in late-twentieth-century culture. As such, Reed's postmodern slave narrative becomes a narrative of liberation for both the escaped slave of the nineteenth century and the contemporary black artist enshackled by capitalist culture.

It is this complex orientation towards time that distinguishes Reed's postmodern revision of the slave narrative from traditional forms of historical fiction. Traditional historical novels such as *Gone with the Wind* (1936) or even Margaret Walker's *Jubilee* (1966) seek to convey the antebellum South and its social conditions with attention to verisimilitude and "realistic" detail.[2] These texts approach the antebellum South as a discrete and contained moment in time; they remain firmly grounded in the specific historical periods the creative narratives attempt to evoke. Reed's primary goal in *Flight to Canada,* however, is to collapse the present and the past by creating a text that explicitly connects slavery and its current legacy. In the present moment of writing about the past, his text foregrounds its simultaneous occupation of two distinct time periods, each informing the other in a mutual interchange, a mutual commentary. As the present moment allows him to reflect on the past in retrospection, the past informs the act of revision and provides Reed and his readers with a historical context that informs the present. Ultimately, Reed's treatment of slavery constitutes a circular orientation towards time and becomes a critique of both the present and the past through the legacy of slavery.

The conflation of time in *Flight to Canada* also distinguishes it from the European and Euro-American postmodern historical novel by emphasizing the material links between slavery and contemporary culture over the more abstract and indeterminate connections between past and present. As Brian McHale points out in *Postmodernist Fiction,* though such novels as John Fowles's *The French Lieutenant's Woman* (1969) and Stanley Elkin's *George Mills* (1982) engage the past from a present vantage point, the Euro-American postmodern historical novel occupies multiple time periods through the use of creative anachronism. McHale defines "creative anachronism" as a technique in which the contemporary sensibilities or worldview of the author or narrator offer commentary on the historical events of the text. In most cases, McHale argues, this manipulation of time "does not penetrate the fictional world but remains at the level of discourse, and the narrator, being our contemporary, is perfectly justified in making such allusions" (93). As it manifests itself in the Euro-American postmodern novel, creative anachronism produces a disjuncture between the historical elements of the narrative by filtering them through the contemporary perspective of the author or narrator. As such, in the Euro-American postmodern historical novel, the machinations of the present moment's engagement with the past lie solely with the abstract presence of an authorial figure and remain distinct from the events of the text.[3] As a result, these novels investigate the past primarily as a discursive abstraction, raising questions about the nature of historical reality itself and our ability to access that reality without the presence of narrative discourse.

In contrast to the abstract form of creative anachronism, McHale points out that one of the few examples of *material* anachronism occurs in Ishmael Reed's fiction, particularly in *Flight to Canada,* "where 20th-century technology . . . is superimposed on nineteenth century history" (93). Reed's use of material anachronism in conjunction with the creative anachronism found in Euro-American postmodernist historical fiction explicitly merges the past and the present periods beyond the level of discourse; physical objects mark contemporary culture and its relationship to the slave South. Even as Reed uses creative anachronism to infuse a twentieth-century sensibility into the period of American slavery, his use of material anachronism asserts the concrete connections between a nineteenth-century culture based on the exploitation of human beings as commodities and the commodification of the black artist. In this sense, Reed's revision of the slave narrative expands on the postmodernist dimensions of the European and Euro-American postmodern historical novel.

The elaborate juxtaposition of the slave South and our present condition in *Flight to Canada* functions ultimately as a critique of the dominant culture's commodification of the slave narrative as a popularized depiction of the quest for freedom and its ensuing result: the commodification of the escaped slaves who constructed them. Through the conflation of time and the repoliticizing of the slave narrative through a contemporary worldview, Reed raises serious questions that face both the contemporary black writer's and the slave narrator's quest for a liberating identity. How can the slave narrator/black writer create the self through a medium marketed and controlled by the dominant and oppressive culture? How can the slave narrator/black writer hope to exploit a system designed to exploit those within it? Rather than sacrificing the quest for a liberating, black identity in the face of these obstacles, Reed shifts the battlefield, transforming the slave narrative from a discourse of emergent subjectivity to a discourse of critique. Reed deromanticizes the slave narrative as the act of writing the slave's self into being and instead engages the slave narrative as the act of *reading* the cultural context of slavery.[4] This shift in focus from writing as a romantic act to reading as an act of critique allows Reed to construct the slave narrative as an interrogation not only of the slave's acquisition of selfhood but also of the culture that continuously and insidiously attempts to strip the slave and the contemporary black artist of his or her identity.

Raven's assertion in the narrative section that opens the novel, "Little did I know when I wrote the poem 'Flight to Canada' that there were so many secrets locked inside its world. It was a reading more than a writing" (5), suggests that the act of writing may embody something much more than the romantic creation of the self. Reed's use of the word "reading" proffers that, first and foremost, the act of writing produces a reading of the world. While this is perhaps true of any text, it is all the more true for the slave narrative, whether in its traditional form or in its contemporary incarnation. The slave narrative serves not only as an account of the slave's quest for freedom but also as an account of the slave system itself. Rather than a personal exploration of subjectivity, the emphasis on the written act as a reading of American slavery foregrounds an element of reflection on the world that limits and contains black subjectivity.

Reed's concept of reading as a crucial component of the slave narrative, while a revision of the traditional form, still maintains a link with those narratives written by the escaped slaves of the nineteenth century. Houston A. Baker Jr.'s reading of Frederick Douglass's 1845 *Narrative* foregrounds Douglass's skill as a reader and interpreter of texts when he writes: "He [Douglass] refuses the role of hapless victim of texts (the slave master's false moral rhetoric) and becomes, instead, an astute interpreter and creator of texts of his own. . . . Douglass' acquired skills as reader enable him to provide his own interpretations of received texts" (43). In this light, Douglass first must acquire and present a critical reading of slave culture before he can set about the task of narrating his own story. This process of developing his own critique of slavery, in turn, constitutes a fundamental aspect of his slave narrative that works in tandem with his romanticized creation of self through the written act. Rather than a complete reversal of the traditional slave narrative, Reed's postmodernist revision assumes the slave's status of selfhood and focuses primarily on the critique of the commodity culture that subjugates that self.

In Reed's shift of focus towards a discourse of critique, the slave narrative as an aesthetic form and as a commodifiable object is subject to interrogation in the novel. His revision of the slave narrative itself is both parodic and pragmatic, infused with the contemporary view of a postmodern culture wrought by consumerism and commodification. From this perspective, Reed transforms the subject of the slave narrative from the abstract quest for a previously unrealized humanity to a quest for the concrete means of obtaining capital—the economic ability to achieve freedom. The quest for freedom for the escaped slaves in *Flight to Canada* has less to do with reaching the North and more to do with successfully negotiating the market forces of capitalist culture. Reed's novel deploys capitalism as both the means to obtain freedom and as the primary obstacle by which the dominant culture can strip his characters of that freedom.

Raven Quickskill's situation as the primary black artist and slave narrator in the novel illustrates both the dangers commodity culture poses to the slave narrator and the potential ways commodity culture can be manipulated in the black artist's quest for freedom. Raven's poem "Flight to Canada" represents the potential to manipulate and the dangers of becoming exploited by a culture that views the slave narrative as not only a protest against slavery but also as a creative text for popular consumption. Though written before he fully attains his freedom, Raven anticipates the rise of his celebrity status, satirizing this ironic aspect of self-promotion when he writes of how he is received on the plane:

Passengers came up
And shook my hand
& within 10 min. I had
Signed up for 3 anti-slavery
Lectures. Remind me to get an
Agent. (3)

Raven's initial ability to exploit this system of commodification allows him to use the literary success of the poem as a means to escape slavery. It provides him with instant support from the antislavery movement and the economic means to obtain and maintain his freedom. Raven realizes that the literary representation of his escape will be commodified instantly; his freedom will not effect the formation of a new identity as a free black man but instead the creation of a consumable product. Through Raven's glib references to getting an agent and signing up for antislavery lectures, Reed acknowledges the slave narrative's status as a commodity, a literary object containing not only its own formal and aesthetic conventions but also a conventionalized relationship with its external means of production and consumption.

The slave narrative's transformation into commodity extends beyond the formal aspects of the text into the literary and political practices of conventionalizing the way the slave experience is written and consumed by the dominant culture. Raven assumes his own humanity and moves beyond the dominant culture's view of the slave narrative as an entertaining illustration and expression of his humanity and, through his mocking and confrontational tone, foregrounds his own pragmatic attempt to exploit its political and economic dimensions for his own ends. As a result, Reed transforms Raven, as slave narrator, from the image of the slave achieving freedom through struggle and self-definition to the image of the shrewd cultural player who attempts to take advantage of the system.

As a cultural player, Raven manipulates the stylistic conventions of the slave narrative and the economic/political forces that produce and define the text and its author. Initially, Raven successfully exploits his newfound fame in the North as a result of the success and popularity of his poem. After escaping from the slave-owner Arthur Swille's plantation, Raven does become a celebrity, speaking at antislavery lectures and even visiting the White House as a personal guest of Abe Lincoln. Upon his arrival in the North, Raven achieves a "star-status" equal to Walt Whitman, with whom he interacts during the formal reception at the White House. Clearly moving well beyond establishing his own humanity, Raven uses the poem to defy the Fugitive Slave Law and to enter a society guided by its consumption of artistic texts and popular personalities. Raven plays the game of cultural commodities and achieves the celebrity status that his own poem anticipates.

Reed further reinforces this ironic view of the slave narrator by introducing into the novel William Wells Brown, the author of one of the first novels published by an African American (*Clotel,* 1853) and the author of his own slave narrative in 1847. Rather than the romantic image of the former slave who creates himself and achieves freedom through the acquisition of language and the act of writing, Reed's fictionalized Brown represents the simultaneously fictional and historical model of the black writer who exploits the capitalistic system from within. Reed replaces the image of the escaped slave who struggles to survive an equally hostile northern freedom with the image of the culturally savvy ex-slave who acknowledges the complex cultural dynamics that construct his escape from slavery as a commodity, a form of consumable entertainment. The fact that Reed incorporates Brown into his novel, as opposed to other famous slave narrators such as Frederick Douglass or Henry Bibb, is significant in that Brown achieved success both as a slave narrator and as an author of fiction. Upon their chance meeting in the novel, Raven designates Brown, who appears confident and dashing in a "tall silk hat" and "black kid gloves," flashing business cards which describe him as an Anti-Slavery Lecturer and Writer, as his main inspiration for the poem: "I read your novel *Clotel* and . . . I just want to say Mr. Brown, that you're the greatest satirist of these times. [. . .] my poem 'Flight to Canada' is going to be published in *Beulahland Review*. It kind of imitates your style, though I'm sure the critics are going to give me some kind of white master. A white man. They'll say he gave me the inspiration and that I modeled it after him. But I had you in mind" (121). That Raven views *Clotel*, a novel generally regarded as one of the first fictional narratives by an African American to portray the tragedies and horrors of slavery, as a satire of the times and as a model for his own work establishes a view of nineteenth-century textual production by black writers as a means to reflect and critique the culture of slavery through irony. While the white public to which the escaped slaves or free blacks write consumes these texts merely as melodramas or exposés on the tragic lives of enslaved African Americans, Raven (and ultimately Reed himself) implies that these black writers also achieve a critical and aesthetic distance from their narratives. It is from this vantage point that black writers use irony and satire to interrogate the dominant culture that commodifies the black body and the black text. If we are to accept Raven's view of *Clotel*, and perhaps the work of other escaped slaves, these narratives critique the very discourse they reproduce. *Clotel*, with its melodramatic portrayal of tragic mulattos and the domestic upheavals caused by slavery, also stands as a critique of a culture that can only consume the horrors of slavery as melodrama. Brown's work serves as a precursor not only to Raven's poem but also to the novel that contains it: Reed's own *Flight to Canada*. Reed's novel stands as a satire of two historical moments simultaneously: the nineteenth-century culture that interpellates his characters and the current capitalist culture that impacts his own aesthetic production.

William Wells Brown's appearance in the novel is a form of creative anachronism that conflates the historical slave experience with a late-twentieth-century sensibility marked by mass consumerism. It is through the revision of this historical figure and the portrayal of Raven's own manipulation of the historical condition of slavery through twentieth-century technology and cultural sensibility that Reed presents us with a representation of the black writer who resists exploitation by manipulating the system for his or her own ends. Reed's portrayal of Brown confirms his emphasis on the pragmatic view of the slave narrator and provides Raven with his primary model for cultural, aesthetic, and economic liberation in the novel. Rather than succumbing to the pitfalls of consumer capitalism, William Wells Brown offers Raven a model of existence that turns the commodity culture back onto itself in order to achieve freedom, prosperity, and artistic success.[5] Brown has achieved a status and freedom that other escaped slaves in the novel, including Raven, have yet to reach, based primarily on his ability to tell his own story and manipulate the market that consumes it.

While Brown represents the successful manipulation of market forces, Reed also addresses the problems that prevent the black writer (past and present) from achieving a liberating identity, even in this active form of resistance. One problem created by the slave writer's own commodification of his or her experience is the potentially degrading prospect of the slave becoming the object of consumption for the pleasure of others. Simply put, as the dominant culture consumes his or her artistic text, the fugitive slave faces the prospect of "selling out." This is particularly true of the nineteenth-century slave narrator who must tell his or her story to a predominantly white consumer market. In order to appeal to that readership, the black writer, in an effort to increase consumption, must produce a representation of slavery accessible to that audience. Reed suggests that, as representations of the slave experience become commodities purchased by members of the dominant culture, the black text replaces the black body as the commodified object of slavery. The process of commodification constitutes a potential reenslavement of the black artist.

Raven realizes that by representing the black slave experience in his poem he enters a complex battlefield of economics, politics, and aesthetics, each entwined with the other. Raven's poem allows him to assume an empowered position in spite of his status as a fugitive slave when he is thrust into the cultural limelight for his literary success. And yet, in his own pursuit of freedom in the novel and in his aesthetic representation of it, the poem also allows the dominant culture to contain and objectify his identity as an escaped slave. In essence, Raven's literary representation marks a paper trail by which his former "master," Arthur Swille, and the forces of the slavocracy can not only capture him but can confine and define him as well.[6] Even after the Civil War has ended, Raven realizes that Swille will continue to pursue him and that, although the physical shackles of slavery have been broken, the hegemony of cultural slavery still threatens to reenslave him. It is this realization that leads to Raven's continued quest for his cultural and aesthetic freedom even after he achieves physical freedom when he reaches Canada.

In essence, Raven's flight to Canada represents a quest not only for a liberation from slavery but for cultural, economic, and aesthetic liberation as well. In the course of his quest, Raven encounters two characters who also attempt to subvert the threat of cultural slavery: Stray Leechfield, a friend of Raven Quickskill and formerly a fellow slave on Swille's plantation, and Quaw Quaw Tralaralara, a Native American woman and Raven's lover. It is through his relationships with these characters that Raven begins to interrogate his own position as a commodity in a commodity culture. Leechfield and Quaw Quaw represent to Raven contrasting attempts to subvert the mechanism of cultural slavery and ultimately provide him with unsuccessful models in this quest. Through the conflation of time, Reed constructs Raven, Leechfield, and Quaw Quaw as characters who respond to the threat of cultural slavery with a twentieth-century preoccupation with cultural commodities and market forces. Stray Leechfield represents the attempt to achieve freedom by manipulating the game of cultural commodities on purely economic terms. He reproduces an aesthetic version of slavery in an attempt to buy his freedom from Arthur Swille. Quaw Quaw Tralaralara represents the attempt to transcend cultural slavery by creating a marketable and universal form of aesthetic expression. Raven, in response to these two approaches, seeks to construct an ethnic and subversive aesthetic in order to critique and subvert the hegemony of capitalism.

For Stray Leechfield, the foundation of American slavery has the same roots as the American Dream: economic prosperity. It is this belief that drives him to subvert his enslavement on purely economic terms by achieving prosperity and trying to buy his freedom.[7] When he first appears in the text, Leechfield, unlike William Wells Brown and Raven Quickskill, achieves economic success by exploiting his situation as a field slave rather than selling his own aesthetic representation of slavery. In a conversation with Abe Lincoln, Arthur Swille describes with incredulity how Leechfield achieved prosperity even in slavery:

> He was stealing chickens—methodically. . . . He had taken so many over a period of time that he was over in the other county, big as you please, dressed up like a gentleman, smoking a seegar and driving a carriage which featured factory climate-control air conditioning, vinyl top, AM/FM stereo radio, full leather interior, power-lock doors, six-way power seat, power windows, white-wall wheels, door-edge guards, bumper impact strips, rear defroster and soft-ray glass. . . . He had set up his own poultry business, was underselling everybody in eggs, gizzards, gristles, livers—and had a reputation far and wide for his succulent drumsticks. Had a white slave fronting for him for ten percent. (36)

Leechfield's successful foray into the capitalist system allows him to leave briefly his position as a slave and enjoy the prosperity of entreprenurialism. But Reed suffuses Leechfield's economic resourcefulness as a slave with the flamboyance and materialism of twentieth-century consumerism. Leechfield's degeneration into consumer culture is embodied by the all-purpose status symbol: the luxury car. The intrusion of material anachronism in the text forces us to draw a connection between Leechfield's desire for freedom and contemporary consumerism. It is through the accumulation of goods that Leechfield believes he can achieve freedom, prosperity, and class status. Leechfield ultimately succumbs to the excesses of commodity culture and fails to realize that, in spite of material prosperity, he remains a slave. When Swille's hired hand discovers that he has been stealing chickens and selling them, Leechfield must kill him and flee northward. Ultimately, Leechfield's manipulation of economics allows him only a limited sense of freedom, and he must flee to escape the physical bonds of slavery.

Once Leechfield establishes himself in the North, he must find another means of securing his freedom. In an effort to make enough money to buy himself from Swille, Leechfield desecrates his own body as a means to exploit a dominant culture preoccupied with the aesthetic representation of slavery. When Raven escapes Swille's plantation and arrives in Emancipation City, he finds Leechfield in an office in an old warehouse marked "Leechfield & Leer." Upon entering the office, Raven describes, with horror and dismay, Leechfield's latest attempt to achieve prosperity in the face of cultural slavery: "O my God! My God! My God! Leechfield was lying naked, his rust-colored body must have been greased, because it was glistening, and there was . . . there was— the naked New England girl was twisted about him, she had nothing on but those glasses and the flower hat. How did they manage? . . . The Immigrant [Leer] was underneath one of those Brady boxes—it was flashing. He [. . .] he was taking daguerreotypes, or 'chemical pictures'" (71). Raven discovers that Leechfield has entered into the pornography business with Mel Leer, a Russian immigrant and former indentured servant. Leechfield, despite having escaped the physical bonds of slavery, still degrades and commodifies his body in the pornographic depiction of the slave experience. When he senses Raven's disapproval, Leechfield asserts, "'shit, everybody can't do anti-slavery lectures. I can't. I have to make it the best I can, man. I don't see no difference between what I'm doing and what you're doing'" (72). From Leechfield's perspective, the act of fetishizing the slave experience in pornographic pictures equals Raven's reconstruction of slavery in his poems and antislavery lectures: each commodifies slavery in an attempt to profit from its popular representation. To regard the act of recounting the horrors of slavery and the individual quest for freedom as a marketable resource opens the door for any version of the slave's self to be regarded as a fetishized commodity, whether it is the sexualized image of Leechfield's black body or Raven's textualized persona of the escaped slave. For Leechfield, the main purpose is to achieve the economic means to buy freedom; the particular form and content of his aesthetic representation remains a superfluous afterthought.

If Stray Leechfield represents the one-dimensional view of slavery on economic terms, Quaw Quaw Tralaralara, the popular and sensationalist Native American tightrope artist, represents the limitations of transcending cultural slavery on purely abstract and aesthetic terms. In a conversation with Raven, Quaw Quaw argues that "'slavery is a state of mind, metaphysical'" and that Raven's approach to his own art is too limited in conception. She states: "'You're just not broad enough Quickskill. You're [. . .] you're too [. . .] too ethnic. You should be more universal. . . . Politics. Race. People write and paint about politics because they have nothing else to say'" (95–96). It is from this perspective that Quaw Quaw constructs her own performance art as a means to achieve popularity and cultural success. When Raven encounters her in Canada, he sees her performing her brand of universal aesthetics to much fanfare and excitement: "She was in Indian clothes. She was coming across Niagara Falls. She was walking a tightrope across Niagara Falls. . . . Carrying the banner, she did a somersault. The crowd gaped and murmured. . . . She kept coming across the tightrope as the crowd on both sides grew hushed. It even seemed that the Falls had hushed. . . . She reached the other side and the crowd went wild, joining hands and jumping about, whistling, stomping their feet" (156–57). Quaw Quaw literally and figuratively walks a tightrope between an individual and personalized expression of her identity and the pyrotechnics that mark her artistic representation. The audience she reaches consumes her tightrope act as a flamboyant display in the tradition of sideshow and circus acts rather than as an expression of any cultural tradition. It is a universal aesthetic in so far as it projects a quality of nothingness—an absence of substance that represents only sheer entertainment value. Raven ultimately criticizes Quaw Quaw for being an "ambitious mountain climber" and for selling short her own cultural heritage.

Just as Leechfield fails to realize the hegemonic power of cultural slavery by focusing on economics, Quaw Quaw, in her attempts at achieving a universalism through sensationalism, fails to interrogate the ways in which the dominant culture consumes and misinterprets her art. And in the process of commodification, the dominant culture obscures and contains her cultural identity. In response to Quaw Quaw's suggestion that his art should be more universal and less political, Raven points out that slavery has its roots in the links between aesthetics and politics: "'what Camelot can't win on the battlefield it'll continue in poetry. . . . They're going to get your Indian and my Slave on microfilm and in sociology books; then they're going to put them in the space ship and send them to moon. And then they're going to put you on the nickel and put me on a stamp, and that'll be the end of it. They're as Feudalist and Arthurian as [Jefferson] Davis, but whereas he sees it as a political movement, they see it as a poetry movement'" (96).

Just as Leechfield never fully understands that he cannot buy himself from Swille and slavery through his pornographic pictures, Quaw Quaw's attempts to create a liberating identity through her tightrope act and pretensions towards universalism ultimately fail to free her from the hegemony of the dominant culture. Both Leechfield and Quaw Quaw acknowledge only one dimension of their oppression and fail to engage slavery through the complex links between aesthetics, economics, and politics. More than just economic and physical enslavement, Reed's construction of Quaw Quaw and Leechfield suggests that, through a system of commodification, the mainstream American culture seeks to control and reduce black subjectivity to a consumable status.

The dilemma of the black artist and seemingly untraversable mountain of cultural slavery leads Raven into pursuing a means by which he can tell his story in the face of a hegemonic commodity culture. Raven initially believes that the way he can achieve cultural freedom is through his own visionary aesthetic and creative power:

While others had their tarot cards, their ouija boards, their I-Ching, their cowrie shells, he had his "writings." They were his bows and arrows. He was so much against slavery that he had begun to include prose and poetry in the same book, so that there would be no arbitrary boundaries between them. He preferred Canada to slavery, whether Canada was exile, death, art, liberation, or a woman. . . . "Flight to Canada" was responsible for getting him to Canada. And so for him, freedom was his writing. His writing was his HooDoo. Others had their way of HooDoo, but his was his writing. It fascinated him, it possessed him; his typewriter was his drum he danced to. (88–89)

By blurring the boundaries between poetry and prose, between fiction and history, Raven attempts to create a personalized expression of his experience and a satire of the times. "Flight to Canada" marks his attempt to create a text that reinscribes and reinvests the representation of slavery with a creative and critical power. Itself a mixture of prose and poetry, of the historical with the fictional, Ishmael Reed's *Flight to Canada* also marks a significant departure from the standard conventions of the slave narrative. According to Joe Weixlmann, Reed produces "an overt representation of freedom" by constructing the novel as "diversity-in-action" (65). In this sense, Reed, like Raven, explodes the slave narrative form and achieves a kind of "aesthetic Canada" through the liberation of artistic vision. Both the poem and the novel in "theme and form combine to produce empowered and empowering objects that deny both facile categorization and promote a genuine sense of literary and sociopolitical freedom" (Weixlmann 67).

And yet, even Raven's attempts at liberation through his defamiliarizing and (re)visionary literary form could potentially succumb to the consumptive powers of commodity culture. In true postmodernist fashion, Reed turns to another historical literary figure to point out the dangers black writers face in having their stories appropriated by the white literary establishment. In the opening section of the novel (entitled "Naughty Harriet"), Reed indicts Stowe for her appropriation of Josiah Hensen's story in her famous novel, *Uncle Tom's Cabin* (1852): *"The story she 'borrowed' from Josiah Henson. Harriet only wanted enough money to buy a silk dress. The paper mills ground day and night. She'd read Josiah Henson's book. That Harriet was alert.* The Life of Josiah Hensen, Formerly a Slave. *Seventy-seven pages long. It was short, but it was his. It was all he had. His story. A man's story is his gris-gris, you know. Taking his story is like taking his gris-gris. The thing that is himself"* (8). According to Richard Walsh, this act of plagiarism, which provides the fuel for the novel's interrogation of cultural slavery, "stands for the cultural appropriation by which minority cultures are suppressed and for the subsequent oppression of their people, the essence of Reed's metaphor of slavery" (66–67). I would argue that Reed's conflation of time elevates this from pure metaphor into a level of direct critique of a culture that continues to appropriate, market, and trivialize black subjectivity through its literary texts.

Reed further complicates the political, economic, and aesthetic nexus of cultural slavery through the character Yankee Jack, a successful businessman and Quaw Quaw's husband. Known as the "Good Pirate," Yankee Jack builds Emancipation City, a refuge for escaped slaves, and fashions himself as a distributor of cultural objects and artifacts. But behind Yankee Jack's marriage to Quaw Quaw and his seemingly benevolent interest in the affairs of escaped slaves in Emancipation City lie his sinister role in the subjugation of oppressed peoples. In his poem "The Saga of Third World Belle," Raven exposes Yankee Jack's murder of Quaw Quaw's father and the pillaging of her culture:

> Your favorite pirate uses
> Your Dad's great chief's skull
> As an ashtray
> And sold your Mom's hand-knitted
> Robes to Buffalo Bill's
> Wild West Show
> He buried your brother alive
> In a sealed-off section of the
> Metropolitan Museum. (123)

If Stowe stands as a symbol for cultural appropriation in the text, as Richard Walsh suggests, Yankee Jack represents the *agent* of cultural commodification, exploitation, and appropriation, nullifying black identity by packaging, marketing, and debasing it. For Reed, Yankee Jack embodies the oppressive vehicle of cultural commodification hidden beneath the surface benefits of exploiting this system. Beyond exploiting the economics of commodification, Yankee Jack exerts control over minority culture from a dominant position. Raven confronts Yankee Jack about his role in the cultural enslavement of minorities, stating: "'You call yourself a "distributor," attempting to make yourself respectable. You decide which books, films, even what kind of cheese, no less, will reach the market. At least we fuges know we're slaves, constantly hunted, but you enslave everybody. Making saps of them all. You, the man behind a distribution network, remaining invisible while your underlings become the fall guys'" (146). Reed portrays Yankee Jack as the embodiment of capitalism itself, guided solely by the prospect of profit. But, as Yankee Jack himself points out, he is just a middleman protecting the dictates of the dominant culture from a position of power. It is the dominant position that allows him to capitalize on minority cultures and determine which cultural expressions are civilized and which are savage.

With all the obstacles and potential pitfalls of cultural commodification, the process of creating a liberating black identity by writing the self into being or by exploiting the effects of commodification on purely economic or aesthetic terms becomes a seemingly impossible enterprise. Clearly the production of the slave narrative specifically and the black artistic text in general needs to involve more than a romanticized notion of identity, a false and oversimplified conception of universality, or a preoccupation with the accumulation of wealth.

At this point I must assert that my emphasis on Reed's inclusion of the concept of reading as a cultural critique of commodification in the slave narrative works on two fundamental levels. First, it highlights the fact that as the creator of the slave narrative, the author (Douglass, Reed, or even Raven as a fictional author and an extension of Reed himself) produces his or her own critical reading of the cultural context of slavery. Second, the written text as reading must, in turn, produce additional readings as it is consumed and interpreted as a cultural text. What Reed makes clear through his explicit inclusion of the consumptive act of reading and the productive act of interpretation into his novel is the fact that these functions operate under the same potentially oppressive system of capitalism as the act of writing. Just as Reed faces the dilemma of being exploited by commodity culture like Raven, his fictional counterpart, so too does the reader face the prospect of complicity in that exploitation. Like the symbol of appropriation, Harriet Beecher Stowe, and the agent of capitalism, Yankee Jack, the reader's consumption of the text creates the possibility of tracking down the black artist by commodifying blackness and, therefore, undermining the potentially liberating function of the text.

As Robert Elliot Fox points out in his reading of *Flight to Canada,* the poem "Flight to Canada" "symbolizes, for Reed, the way misinformed criticism 'catches' or categorizes black artists" (71). By shifting the focus from a romanticized creation of the self as the primary liberating function of the slave narrative to a politicized critique of commodity culture, Reed presents the reader with a means of interpreting the text that avoids a commodification of blackness. Reed politicizes the aesthetics of writing and reading and creates a text that appropriates and objectifies the oppressive aspects of our capitalist culture with an eye towards critique. In terms of the readings his text produces, the object of consumption and critique shifts from blackness itself to the culture that seeks to commodify the black text and the black body.

Ultimately, Reed's postmodern revision of the slave narrative reinvests the genre with its inherently political and historical dimensions. By politicizing the act of writing and the act of reading in his novel, Reed merges aesthetics and politics to produce a discourse on our commodity culture. By reinventing the narrative form of the slave narrative and by shifting the focus of the reader's gaze from the narrating slave to the oppressive culture that produces that slave, Reed presents us with the means to critique from within. The issue of the escaped slave's humanity is no longer contestable, no longer an issue of representation. For Reed and Raven, the narrative act serves not as a means of illustrating their humanity but as a means of speaking out in a critical and creative voice. Our task when reading their texts (as well as other slave narratives, both traditional and postmodern) is to assume the slave's dignity and humanity and to interrogate the capital culture that dehumanizes and commodifies him or her. From this critical perspective, every act of reading these narratives can produce an oppositional and potentially liberating space of critique.

Notes

1. In "'A Man's Story Is His Gris-Gris': Cultural Slavery, Literary Emancipation, and Ishmael Reed's *Flight to Canada*," Richard Walsh asserts that Reed uses anachronism to "negate the sense of history as a linear evolution" and to draw parallels between the Civil War South and the civil rights movement of the 1960s (59). As a writer who emerged during that era, this conflation of time equates Reed's own struggle with that of his character Raven.

2. Though Margaret Mitchell's depiction of slavery in *Gone with the Wind* can hardly be characterized as accurate—marked as it is by its melodramatic plot and its portrayal of slaves as content with their condition—the novel does seek to evoke the historical moment to its readers without any overt intrusion of twentieth-century culture or sensibility.

3. McHale cites the moments when John Fowles's narrator in *The French Lieutenant's Woman* comments on the events of the text from a contemporary perspective in spite of the fact that the narrative takes place in the nineteenth century. The narrator also infuses the title character with a modern sensibility that belies her time and circumstance.

4. This marks a movement away from the dominant (and dominating) culture's view of black writing as an illustration of the slaves' humanity. The slave's ability to write, Henry Louis Gates Jr. asserts in *Figures in Black*, served as a primary argument by abolitionists against slavery (11). In *To Tell a Free Story,* William Andrews also points out that one of the aspects of the slave narrative that made it so popular in the nineteenth century was its connection to the "revolutionary romanticism" of the era. Many liberal readers of the day "celebrated the fugitive slave as a kind of culture-hero who exemplified the American romance of the unconquerable 'individual mind' steadily advancing towards freedom and independence" (98). In both of these views, the act of writing serves as a means of projecting either a basic humanity or a romanticized self to its white readership.

5. While Reed has stated that the slave narratives by Henry Bibb, Frederick Douglass, Solomon Northrup, and others are "the best examples of what it means to live free," he specifically discusses William Wells Brown's successful manipulation of the economic and commercial aspects of his life through his money-lending business (Domini 110). In this sense, Brown seems to represent, for Reed, the combination of artistic and economic acumen.

6. The narrator of the text attributes Raven's success and his perpetual fear of reenslavement directly to his poem: "'Flight to Canada' was the problem. It made him famous but had also tracked him down . . . It had dogged him" (13). The connection between the artistic representation of slavery and the dogs used to track and capture escaped slaves suggests that the dangers associated with Raven's depiction of slavery and the success it brings him pose more than just an abstract threat to his freedom: it represents a violent reenslavement of his identity.

7. Leechfield states his view of slavery when Raven questions his motives in selling pornographic pictures depicting the sexual depravities of slavery: "'I sent Swille a check. Look, Quickskill, money is what makes them go. Economics. He's got the money he paid for me, and so that will satisfy him. Economics'" (74).

Works Cited

Andrews, William L. *To Tell a Free Story: The First Century of Afro-American Autobiography, 1760–1865.* Urbana: University of Illinois Press, 1986.

Baker, Houston A., Jr. *Blues, Ideology, and Afro-American Literature: A Vernacular Theory.* Chicago: University of Chicago Press, 1984.

Domini, John. "Ishmael Reed: A Conversation with John Domini." In *Conversations with Ishmael Reed.* Ed. Bruce Dick and Amritjit Singh. Jackson: University Press of Mississippi, 1995. 128–43.

Fox, Robert Elliot. *Conscientious Sorcerers: The Black Postmodernist Fiction of LeRoi Jones/Amiri Baraka, Ishmael Reed, and Samuel R. Delany.* New York: Greenwood, 1987.

Gates, Henry Louis, Jr. *Figures in Black: Words, Signs, and the "Racial" Self.* New York: Oxford University Press, 1988.

McHale, Brian. *Postmodernist Fiction*. New York: Metheun, 1987.

Reed, Ishmael. *Flight to Canada*. New York: Atheneum, 1976.

Walsh, Richard. "'A Man's Story Is His Gris-Gris': Cultural Slavery, Literary Emancipation, and Ishmael Reed's *Flight to Canada*." *Journal of American Studies* 27.1 (1993): 57–71.

Weixlmann, Joe. "African American Deconstruction of the Novel in the Work of Ishmael Reed and Clarence Major." *MELUS* 17.4 (1991–92): 57–79.

5

Clarence Major's *All-Night Visitors:* Calibanic Discourse and Black Male Expression

James W. Coleman

Readers who have followed Clarence Major's career realize that as his career has developed his work has become more experimental and increasingly foregrounds the great limitations of fictive portrayals and expression that are the concerns of such white radical metafictional writers of the Fiction Collective as Ronald Sukenick, Raymond Federman, and Harold Jaffe. Major also experiments in his first novel, *All-Night Visitors* (1969), but the experimentation presents itself in the form of a pursuit of the potentialities of black male expression. Postmodern, metafictional, and poststructuralist interpretive strategies are relevant for an analysis of *All-Night Visitors,* but in this essay I want to utilize various critical paradigms, especially Anglo-American anthropological and African-American poststructural constructs, that highlight Major's experimental project in terms of black male writing. My purpose is to show that *All-Night Visitors* is a black male text that reflects the problems of black male freedom, empowerment, and voice in ways that are characteristic of other contemporary black male texts.

Black poststructuralists like Karla F. C. Holloway develop their theoretical paradigms through a method of "shift":

> Shift happens when the textual language "bends" in acknowledgement of [black] "experience and value" that are not West-

ern. A critical language that does not acknowledge the bend or is itself inflexi-
ble and monolithic artificially submerges [the significance of this black "experience and value"]. In consequence, critical strategies that address the issues
within these texts must be mediative strategies between the traditional [white]
ideologies of the theoretical discourse and the [black] ancestry of the text itself. Such mediation demands a shift in the scope (if not the tone) of critical terminology—a redirection that calls attention to different (and often contradictory) [black] ideologies [and paradigms]. (62)

So "shift" means taking critical paradigms developed by white theorists for
non-African-American cultures and "bending" them so that they become
relevant for the reading of African-American texts. Because Holloway is
talking specifically about the texts of contemporary African and African-
American women writers, I "bend" the quotation to make it more generally black. I adapt her concept of shift to explain the kind of critical paradigms
that are relevant to Major's experiment with creating a humanistic black
male text. For example, I utilize the paradigm of the black phallic trickster,
which the black vernacular and postructuralist theorist Houston A. Baker
Jr. develops by giving an African-American male shift to paradigms of the
white anthropologists Victor Turner and Cliffort Geertz (Baker 180–85).
And I later shift the paradigm of the black phallic trickster further, to make
it the variant paradigm of black phallic duplicity, a construct especially relevant to black men and black male texts because of their particular locus
in the nexus of Western culture, politics, ideology, and racism. I also shift
Turner's concept of liminality for my analysis of African-American texts.

All-Night Visitors is basically a discursive experiment with a deeply traditional Western grounding. The central discourse focuses on erotic encounters between the black main character, Eli Bolton, and several different
women. On the surface, the discourse amalgamates a central vulgar, pornographic description and theme, the stereotyping of the black male as sexual beast and the sexist objectification of women through the first-person
point of view that privileges the sexual feeling and gratification of Eli. Eli's
primary mode of expression is through crude, vulgar language and sex, and
he constantly shows his insatiability.

What I have just described shows the text's deep traditional Western
grounding in the pervasive cultural and literary discourse of Caliban and
Calibanic phallicism. Roberto Fernandez Retamar traces the history of this
discourse in his essay "Caliban: Notes toward a Discussion of Culture in
Our America." Retamar locates one of Shakespeare's main sources for Caliban in a Montaigne essay ("De los Canibales," or "On Cannibals"), but

finds the most influential Western inscription of Caliban in *The Tempest* (14–
16). In the play, Prospero takes Caliban's island and gives the "gift" of language to Caliban, who can only "gabble," to make him an effective slave
in doing Prospero's bidding. Caliban hates Prospero and reviles him and the
"profit" Caliban himself has gotten from language, the ability to curse his
persecutor. Caliban shows his resentment when he tries to rape Prospero's
daughter Miranda and perpetuate his progeny on the island. In spite of Prospero's imperialism, the play's point of view makes Caliban an "Abhorred
slave, / Which any print of goodness wilt not take." Caliban is a member
of a "vile race, / . . . Who hadst deserved more than prison" (39). Shakespeare plays on the anagram Caliban/cannibal (Retamar 11, 14–15) and
situates Caliban in terms of the European perception of savage dark and
black non-Europeans.

As Retamar points out, we see the Caliban/cannibal in the "African black
who appeared in those shameful Tarzan movies" (14), and according to the
black feminist theorist Hortense Spillers, this character has a portrayal,
"feared and despised, from Caliban, to Bigger Thomas" (8).[1] The point is
that this figure and image of Caliban, which is male and highly black, pervades Western discourse. This figure is the inarticulate sexual predator who
has somehow missed or misappropriated Western education and civilization. He expresses himself in crude vulgarity and raw, physical sex. The fear
of miscegenation associated with him is great. This black male needs to be
controlled and locked away, and this discourse of Caliban effectively circum-
scribes and imprisons the black male.[2]

Major's portrayal of Eli on its surface clearly situates him within the
Western discourse of Caliban. Eli is the crude, vulgar rapist and beast who
threatens to pollute with his phallus, just as Caliban would pollute Miranda and pollute the island with his issue. And, very importantly, this characterization of Eli takes on greater resonance today because of stereotypes of
black men similar to the Calibanic expressed at certain times in feminist
critiques of black male sexism.[3]

Part of the discursive experiment, however, is the attempt to appropriate and subvert what Major intends to be the surface level of Calibanic discourse. Major does this by subverting the paradigm of Calibanic phallicism
with black phallic tricksterism; in the process, he changes the black phallus from a symbol of pollution to one of productivity and proliferating
meanings.

In his adaptation of the work of Victor Turner and Clifford Geertz, Houston A. Baker Jr. develops a black theoretical shift to create the paradigm of

the black phallic trickster (180–85). Baker shifts Turner's and Geertz's analyses of phallic rituals in other cultures to fit the phallic symbolism and ritual of Ralph Ellison's Trueblood scene in chapter 2 of *Invisible Man*. Baker says that the "black phallus is a dominant symbol in the novel's formal patterns of behavior. . . . [It] offers an instance of ritual in which the black phallus gathers an extraordinary burden of disparate connotations, both sensuous and ideological. . . . Ellison recognizes the black phallus as a dominant symbol of the sometimes bizarre social rituals of America and incorporates it into the text of the novel" (181). Baker concludes that "Trueblood's sexual energies, antinomian acts, productive issue, and resonant expressivity make him—in his incestuous, liminal moments and their immediate aftermath—the quintessential trickster" (184).

Trueblood's successful black phallic tricksterism consists of sexual vitality, rebellious sexual acts opposed to society and morality, the production of progeny, and an economically rewarding and richly resonant linguistic expression. Trueblood's liminal status—outside the conventions and laws of society in a wide-open place of process and discovery—is important to his tricksterism.

Eli fits a pattern of black phallic tricksterism similar to Trueblood's. On the subversive level of the discourse of *All-Night Visitors*, Eli's sexual vitality is rebellious and oppositional in a society that proscribes certain behavior by black males. Eli produces no progeny, but much more importantly, the resonance of his language practice creates a figurative and symbolic haven of humanity for him and others. Eli's language practice projects him to a liminal place far away from the horror, brutality, and inhumanity of everyday life and maintains his liminal place, "'betwixt and between,'" in terms Baker takes from Turner (183), ever in productive process. Most importantly, Eli tries to open linguistic space in the imprisoning discourse of Calibanic phallicism with his methods of black phallic tricksterism.

In my use of the concept of liminality, I have shifted Turner's meaning in some specific ways that I need to explain briefly. I have taken the anthropologist's analysis of cultural rites and applied it to a literary text. But even more importantly, I shift Turner's idea of societal "rites of transition"—that is, "separation, margin (or limen), and aggregation"—to focus on its second-term liminality, as opposed to the entire process. For Turner, the process ends in aggregation and, concomitantly, completion, closure, or consummation (94). Making liminality primary is relevant and necessary for a significant number of contemporary black male texts, including *All-Night Visitors*, because these texts foreground liminality.[4]

In *All-Night Visitors* Eli's most significant place is symbolically "betwixt and between," in the margins of liminality. Oppressive racial/cultural conditions keep Eli, along with the characters in other contemporary black male texts, in a position of liminality and preclude aggregate consummation. Eli liminally and symbolically shows his humanity over and over, but the society will not grant him the "culturally recognized degree of maturation" (Turner 93) requisite for societal acceptance and transition into the state of manhood and humanity, his aggregate state. Nor do Eli and other black male characters have the male cultural resources and the physiological/racial qualities to help them achieve aggregation.

For Eli, aggregation becomes secondary; it manifests itself in terms of a wild and, in the final analysis, contrived act of selfless humanity, after which Eli states his own manhood (199–203). Eli's claim of manhood in aggregate societal terms brings the text to an "ending," but it pales in comparison to the text's primary emphasis on Eli's liminality.

Because Major's project in *All-Night Visitors* is an experiment, I want at this point to look more closely at some of its specifics in the text to see how the experiment works and to talk about its possible success or failure.

Major attempts to focus and create the black male self, Eli's self, in *All-Night Visitors*. The various discourses in the novel present two different sets of linguistic signs of this black male self. One set of signs engenders Calibanic phallicism and negative contemporary feminist stereotypes of black male sexists/rapists. The other set of signs brings forth images of a much more cerebral, spiritual, humane, and ultimately loving black male. At this level, the black phallic trickster speaks with proliferating, subversive meanings. These two different sets of signs come together in the novel's central discourse, in which Major experiments with a creation of a black male self. Major tries to give the positive conceptions of black maleness ascendance over the negative by giving the discourse a superficial, shallow level of meaning as well as another level, on which one can see positive, humane qualities of black maleness—the levels of Calibanism and black tricksterism, respectively. Major wants to show that the Calibanic level of discourse does not bear the primary meaning and that the main character, who is the black phallic trickster, takes control of the discourse of the text and appropriates and subverts it against its will to make it do what he wants.

The appropriation and subversion take several forms. First, the narrator subverts and appropriates the linguistic signs of the discourse. Superficially, the linguistic signs are Calibanic and suggestive of male sexism in the context of contemporary thinking. The narrator subverts this stage of the discourse with signs that invite us to analyze and participate in the process of self-definition that he undertakes. In this process, the exploration of the higher humanity of the black male self and the self of the female other becomes a dominant topos. This takes the emphasis away from Calibanism and male sexism. Second, Eli Bolton, the artful phallic trickster, creates an urgent tension in the language and sometimes accelerates its rhythm to suggest an almost supernatural level of black human being, a positive black maleness. This is another part of the process of human exploration and definition. Further, Eli subverts the privileging of male feeling, gratification, and well-being at important places with language that focuses on the definition of nonstereotypical female humanity. We cannot separate this strategy from the first two strategies described above. Finally and more generally, Eli sets up a contrasting context between the text's erotic discourse and the dehumanization and horror of the alternative experiences available to him. When we see how hypocritical, brutal, and callous the rest of the world is, we understand that Eli's definition so completely in terms of intense and ultimately honest, sensitive, and humane feeling subverts the discourse of Calibanism and sexism. The discourse thus becomes a parody of all its surface meanings. I will later demonstrate these points with specific examples from and discussions of the text.

There is something especially exciting about *All-Night Visitors:* The characteristic resistance of the novel's discourse to the kind of appropriation that Eli attempts gives it a vital tension and anxiety. It constitutes a discourse that is highly charged and that generates negative, inflammatory, emotional reactions in a culture that stubbornly refuses expropriation from the meanings and contexts of that culture. For many, nothing beyond the negative will be a possibility.

The following quotation from Mikhail Bakhtin's "Discourse in the Novel" describes the struggle that takes place among the word, the speaker of private, subversive intention, and a generally agreed-upon, embedded discursive intention:

> As a living, socio-ideological concrete thing, as heteroglot opinion, language, for the individual consciousness, lies on the borderline between oneself and the other. The word in language is half someone else's. It becomes "one's own" only when the speaker populates it with his own intention, his own accent, when he appropriates the word, adapting it to his own semantic and expressive intention. Prior to this moment of appropriation, the word does not exist in a neutral and impersonal language (it is not, after all, out of a dictionary that the speaker gets his words!), but rather it exists in other people's mouths, in other

people's contexts, serving other people's intentions: it is from there that one must take the word, and make it one's own. And not all words for just anyone submit equally easily to this appropriation, to this seizure and transformation into private property: many words stubbornly resist, others remain alien, sound foreign in the mouth of the one who appropriated them and who now speaks them; they cannot be assimilated into his context and fall out of it; it is as if they put themselves in quotation marks against the will of the speaker. Language is not a neutral medium that passes freely and easily into the private property of the speaker's intentions; it is populated—overpopulated—with the intentions of others. Expropriating it, forcing it to submit to one's own intentions and accents, is a difficult and complicated process. (293–94)

The Calibanic, male sexist discourse in *All-Night Visitors* is clearly the kind that does not "submit . . . easily . . . to [this] seizure and transformation into private property." Eli's subversive trickster's voice risks becoming the voice of the discourse that it attempts to undermine. Examples from the novel will allow me to analyze further its discursive practices and then to talk about the success or failure of Major's experiment.

The first section of *All-Night Visitors,* entitled "Tammy," is about Eli's relationship with a very young white woman whom he does not love, but the pure pleasure of their sex takes Eli into his spiritual depths. At the end of the "Tammy" section, Eli gives the following description of the climax of oral sex:

I can't *hold* on much longer, the emission is pushing against the many bevels of the dammed-up walls of myself. *Oh shit,* I think, *oh shit,* this is too much! I really begin to submerge, sink down into levels of self as I feel it lift—I am dying, flowing down as the *splash!* enters the first stages of its real career issuing out of the gun, it is coming—now—out—of—the—fire arm *valve,* its ordeal beats me back into ancient depths of myself, back down to some lost meaning of the male, or deep struggling germ, the cell of the meaning of Man. I almost pass into unconsciousness the rapture is so overpowering, its huge, springing, washing infiltration into Her, an eternal-like act, a Rain, I am helpless, completely at her mercy, wet in her hands, empty, aching, my ass throbbing with the drained quality of my responsive death. (14)

The Calibanism and sexism in this passage largely reside in the black male voice cursing, expressing his insatiability as he coerces a white woman to perform oral sex, and showing concomitantly what a sexual beast he is. But the preponderance of the language and its tone and rhythm here focus toward the intellectual analysis and figuration of the humanity of the male self and the sacrifice of that self to the female. There is a "pushing against the many bevels of the dammed up walls of myself," a submersion "into levels of self," a search for the "lost meaning of the male," a giving up of the self to "Her" in a "responsive death" that goes on to a surrendering sleep at the end. When read aloud, the accelerated rhythm of the language suggests the heightened human feeling that Eli attains.

If this is true, then it would seem that Eli's tricksterism works, and he expropriates the discourse from its Calibanic, sexist context. But we should not underestimate the power of the discourse to elicit negative emotional responses that would prevent other perceptions and experiences of the text. This is particularly true today, given the highly justifiable outrage in our society about sexism and female degradation through pornography.

In another section entitled "Anita," which is about a black woman, Eli curses and expresses some of the same bestial characteristics that he expresses in the quotation above. But near the end, he calls Anita the "knowledge-able Black Mother of a deep wisdom, intrinsic in every fuse, every chromosome, every crevice of her epidermis, enormous in the internal cavities of her mouth, anus, the atoms of her urethra, the tissues of her every thought, liquid of her nerves, the intelligence of her tracts, digestive system, the energy of her bladder, every foetal tissue of her, every psycho-biological process of her protoplasm!" (104). A large part of this passage subverts male privileging with language that suggests an intellectual creation and description of female humanity; in this context, the male also implies his empathy. This de-emphasizes the passage's Calibanism and sexism.

But this passage has a particular significance in terms of feelings about sexism in the contemporary black community. The segment of the language that reduces the woman to a sexual object ("the internal cavities of her mouth, anus, the atoms of her urethra") will likely evoke a negative response from many readers and cause them not to look further. The sexual exploitation and abuse of black women by black men has been an issue in the public mind for some time now, and many readers (women, in particular) do not tolerate this kind of sexism at any level in discourse. These readers will not see any value in separating the levels of discourse and analyzing what Eli does: The main point is that a black man subjects a black woman to his will. The text's full narrative will likely further valorize this reaction. In the narrative, Anita is never a woman whom Eli likes or appreciates. His true love is a white woman, Cathy, and he portrays Anita in direct, unfavorable comparison to her. Probably no issue in the black community has been more a source of controversy and anger than the contention that black men prefer white women over black women. Some black readers will hate Eli for his preference of a white woman. Other white readers will hate him for his phallic pollution of a white woman.

Eli describes a time with Cathy after lovemaking as follows:

> I lay down, in the still coolness of the morning, upon the dark bed beside Cathy, who is sleeping very soundly. It is almost daybreak; the worst hour in the world has gone by, and I survived it: I am still breathing. I am *not* lonely. I feel the comfort of her closeness. There are only the sounds of the night, muffled. The city out there, being milked by the mystic revolutionaries, despite God's coming, for collateral.
>
> Our lovemaking was like a rite in a hungry hour of ritual. A cycle we needed. Grateful, now: we are transformed. The entrance behind us, yet before us.
>
> Gently, I take her into my arms, and she, like a comfortable babe not even waking up while she's handled, comes in her sleep snug against me. Her hot sleeping lips part, the kiss. The taste of night. Of Cathy, her warm sturdy flesh. Our legs lock, our sex coming together, hot.
>
> I know I will be mad when she leaves me. (132–33)

Eli objectifies Cathy less than he does the other women, tries to portray her in positive terms, and tries to show his love for her. But readers will read his words about Cathy in the general context of the novel and experience them in terms of all the discursive weight that has accrued. The larger narrative context has helped to establish firmly an idea that prevents a positive perception of Eli.

At one level, Eli is the Calibanic sexual predator and rapist of Cathy. Early in the novel we have seen that Eli, in his despair and frustration over Cathy's termination of their relationship, raped her on the street (while two people watched from a room above) as he temporarily slipped into insanity and paradoxically tried to keep her through his act. Many will not sympathize with Eli because of his mental state and will read his act as a manifestation of his black male oversexuality and bestiality. Major himself has said that he knows he risks confirming myths and stereotypes through Eli's portrayal (*Dark and Feeling* 135). And Keith Byerman states that Eli is "very much the stereotype of the sexually prodigious black man, whose oversized penis corresponds to his insatiable sexual appetite" (258).

Eli hopes to make the point that he raises himself above this, though. Besides his attempted subversion and appropriation of discourse that I have been discussing, Eli also establishes a clear contrast between the world inside himself and the outside world. This outside world is horrible. Eli experiences virulent racism; lives in an orphanage and experiences its callous, brutal life; sees the cruelty of a fatal stabbing on Chicago's streets; and witnesses unspeakably cruel racist atrocities as a soldier in Vietnam. Eli's internal world, where he defines himself in terms of heightened feeling that sometimes attains an altered state of intense humanity, is undeniably preferable to the world outside. In this context, Eli's Calibanic and sexist discourse obviously becomes a parody of itself; its surface meaning yields to the figuration of his internal world and its humanity. Through his appropriation and subversion of discourse, Eli practices a form of black phallic tricksterism. But this is only true if readers will see the need to go or want to go beneath the surface. This brings me back to a consideration of the success or failure of the novel's discursive experiment, which I will make brief concluding remarks about shortly.

Eli also wants to show that his humanity makes him a true lover. Near the end, he thinks about the "eminence of each second [he and Cathy] had spent together. Only one who has known the profoundest most unselfish love, an overwhelming voluptuousness of love—only this person knows the luxury of such selfless outpouring of so much that is beautiful in the loving of someone" (182–83). Eli concretizes his love and humanity in the last paragraphs of the novel through the symbolic act of giving up his apartment to a destitute woman and her children (202).

Not all readers will accept or appreciate what Major has done. But it is a fact that the words and linguistic structure of *All-Night Visitors* can force the careful, sympathetic reader below the surface. Here Major deals with an experimental redefinition of the black self and experiments by giving Eli the role of a black phallic trickster.

Major turns the discursive redefinition of self in the direction of the positive, but he reemphasizes the positive in the context of indeterminacy and open-endedness. The black phallic trickster expresses his liminality through language. The positive self evolves and re-evolves continually in the tension of the language evoking it in the ever-changing situations that Eli encounters. The linguistic signifiers continually produce and reproduce the meaning of the self and text, particularly in the instances of heightened expression. There is always ambiguity. The process is ongoing; the true, full meaning of the self remains ambiguous and open-ended.[5]

By the end of *All-Night Visitors*, Eli has "become firmly a man," but this does not represent closure in the trickster's process of productive liminality. He remains keenly attuned to this development that defines him. He is "vibrantly alive," feeling the "private crevices of this *moment*" open in him (emphasis added). The last sentence in the book says, "I stood there until daybreak" (203). He looks at the dawning of a new day, which will be part of the ongoing experience of self-definition in which he involves himself. This ongoing quest for the human self projects Eli above the horrible alternative experiences available to him and keeps him meaningfully alive.

My ultimate goal in this essay is to show how *All-Night Visitors* reflects the problems of black male texts and black male characterization, and I now want to look at the text as a unique male mode of expression.[6] I would start by saying that the text depicts an individual, liminal black male self defined by language in terms of the moment. The individual male self, the self of Eli, struggles for a symbolic kind of discursive freedom in an evil present that would destroy him; the open-endedness of language as a symbol of liminal status is crucial in the struggle for freedom. The primary confinement of the black male is discursive; a linguistically symbolic liminality mediates this confinement and also isolates the male from the horrors of the everyday, physical world. And the struggle is decidedly an individual one.

Karla F. C. Holloway's *Moorings and Metaphors* provides a useful approach to identifying the terms by which *All-Night Visitors* reflects black male texts generally and how these texts relate to the alternative possibility of black women's texts. Several key terms provide a basis for Holloway's analysis and definition of black women's texts: motherhood, orality, community, spirituality, ancestry, (re)memory, mythology, and, most important structurally, recursion. Holloway says that in the texts of black women, motherhood, "embraced or denied," "physiological or visceral," is central to a black woman's sense of self (26, 28). Black women's texts define themselves through recursion, "a certain depth of memory that black women's textual strategies are designed to acknowledge" (13–14). The creative potential of black motherhood is central to a sense of a black female self capable of (re)membering and recovering the past and achieving wholeness through a process of recursion. Recursiveness involves layers and circles of text constantly enfolding themselves (102, fig. 1). Mythologies, the (re)membered and revised histories and self-definitions that black women generate from their collective oral, communal voices (34), layer the recursive process in the present and past. The orally, communally generated mythologies enfold the physical world and the spiritual world. Mythologies generate (re)membered and revised black female histories that foreground black female ancestry (101–2). They draw together (re)memory and metaphor as sources of deep, powerful spirituality (33–35). The text does not directly reflect the culture of black women, but it does suggest black women's ways of doing and saying things (4–5).

Holloway finds that black male texts lack the orally, communally gener-

ated mythologies that revise history and redefine self, and they also lack the
fortifying spirituality so important in black female texts (6–11). It seems to
me that Holloway says that black male writers fail to find ways, potential
or realized,[7] to make the black male self whole in a deeply grounded, recursive context.

I agree with Holloway, but I do not find this to be a shortcoming in *All-
Night Visitors* and other contemporary black male texts. Like other contemporary black male texts,[8] *All-Night Visitors* concerns itself with the
potentials and problems of discourse that have a strong foundation in the
written Western tradition. Major manipulates language to open up liminal
places in discursive traditions that confine and oppress black men. Eli's predicament is liminal and open-ended. He finds no way to restore, or potentially restore, a self mutilated by the indelible inscriptions of Western discourse and concomitantly buffeted and fractured in an oppressive everyday,
physical world. But Major, like other contemporary black male writers,
follows the compulsions of his physiology/race, oppressive Western culture,
and black male culture.

The point about physiology/race in contemporary black male texts, especially in *All-Night Visitors,* is that the black phallus is such a physical
presence and carries so much ideological weight and symbolic creative potential. Symbolically and realistically, the black phallus is different from the
black womb, which is so implicitly important in Holloway's argument about
black women's sense of self centered in the potential for motherhood (26–
31). In realistic terms, I find myself reminded of the old black saying "Mama's baby, Papa's maybe." In other words, the black phallus can never be
sure of its specific generative power.

In *All-Night Visitors,* the black phallus is a great physical presence, but
Major gives it no physical generative power. Its physical presence symbolizes the power to figure liminal places in an oppressive Western discursive
tradition, but it does not carry the symbolic and actual generative potential
of the womb. Its externality and uncertain specific generative potential will
not allow it to become a symbol or reality that places Eli in a deep recursive process that recovers and restores the self.[9]

Another point about black phallic tricksterism in *All-Night Visitors,* which
is true for other black male texts as well, is that the phallic trickster is always aware, on some level and to some extent, of his phallic duplicity.[10] Eli
is, after all, a trickster, and in spite of genuine, sincere motives in the overall context of the novel, he realizes at some point that "all I want her for is
to fuck her" (3). Phallic duplicity is tantamount to duality and fracture, and

it does not have the moral weight, depth, and surety to provide a basis for full renewal. The phallus as reality and symbol offers possibility but not potential or actual fullness and certainty. For Eli, it symbolizes the possibility of making open-ended linguistic places in an oppressive discursive tradition.

The Western discursive tradition has, of course, misrepresented black women also, which is one reason that contemporary black women writers have had to revise their representations in their own work. But the case is altogether different when one compares the possibilities that black male and female writers have for revision and reconstruction. Because of their gendered access to black female characters with a potentially sure and full, orally, communally, and recursively generated sense of self, black women writers have revised and reconstructed their portrayals on their own terms and in their own unique ways. This is, I believe, a significant part of the point of Holloway's book. But in the context of what I have said about the real and symbolic potential of black male physiology/race and the precarious moral position of black phallic tricksterism, black male writers cannot so fully escape the confines of the Western discursive tradition. Eli, the black phallic trickster, uses language to create open-ended, liminal places in the Calibanic Western discursive tradition. However, he does not supplant this tradition with a new history and mythology, as do black women writers who write recursively because of their cultural grounding and gendering in black womanhood. Major has no access to a safe, sure place outside the Western discursive tradition, so he can only try to distance himself from it liminally.

Holloway and other critics make much of the supportive communities in the texts of black women writers and implicitly or explicitly criticize the strong individuality of black male texts.[11] I believe that this is unfair and unrealistic. Black male texts, like black female texts, do not mirror culture but do indirectly reflect the culture's rituals and modes of interaction. And I would assert that the cultures of black men and women are markedly different. The culture of black women is indeed largely communal and supportive, as Holloway says throughout her book. But the culture of black men, at least in its secular aspects, focuses itself much more toward individual assertiveness and competition. And consequently it does not surprise me to find this individuality, particularly in the form of black tricksterism, reflected in black male texts such as *All-Night Visitors*.

I would say that signifying and playing the dozens are the dominant tropes of black male discourse and culture. Prominent black scholars have not called these tropes uniquely male, but the phallic competition and tricksterism embedded deeply in much of the discourse of the dozens and signifying do testify to their black maleness. Both Stephen Henderson and Henry Louis Gates Jr. use "Rap's Poem" by H. Rap Brown as a signature statement of signifying and black language practice.[12]

> A session would start maybe by a brother saying, "Man, before you mess with me you'd rather run rabbits, eat shit and bark at the moon." Then, if he was talking to me, I'd tell him:
>
>> Man, you must don't know who I am.
>> I'm sweet peeter jeeter the womb beater
>> The baby maker the cradle shaker
>> The deerslayer the buckbinder the women finder
>> Known from the Gold Coast to the rocky shores of Maine
>> Rap is my name and love is my game.
>> I'm the bed tucker the cock plucker the motherfucker
>> The milkshaker the record breaker the population maker
>> The gun-slinger the baby bringer
>> The hum-dinger the pussy ringer
>> The man with the terrible middle finger.
>> The hard hitter the bullshitter the poly-pussy getter
>> The beast from the East the Judge the sludge
>> The women's pet the men's fret and the punks' pin-up boy,
>> They call me Rap the dicker the ass kicker
>> The cherry picker the city slicker the titty licker. (qtd. in Henderson 187–88;
>> Gates 72–73)

The poem ends on an individual competitive note: "'And ain't nothing bad 'bout you but your breath'" (qtd. in Henderson 188; Gates 73).

The signifying language play of much of the quotation suggests a phallic trickster who is duplicitous, but duplicitous phallic virtuosity is a concomitant of subversive linguistic virtuosity. Brown implies a subversion of white discourse in a quotation that Gates uses from Brown's *Die Nigger Die!* "'I learned to talk in the street . . . not from reading Dick and Jane going to the zoo and all that simple shit'" (72). I find "Rap's Poem" to be very male, very competitive, and linguistically subversive. And in spite of the group interaction and call-and-response implied here, the intention of this competition is to achieve individual ends, to see who can prove himself the baddest and set himself apart from the group, as one to be revered and perhaps even feared. This is individual expression that constantly addresses the ongoing moments of black male cultural interaction and implicitly the confining places of white discourse and culture.[13]

Black male texts such as *All-Night Visitors* reflect this black male trick-sterism and linguistic virtuosity that is ultimately subversive, and they also reflect an individuality that is basic to black male culture, that is deeply embedded in its cultural tropes. Eli sets himself apart and does not compet-itively signify in a black male cultural context. But he very much makes himself the individual phallic trickster whose phallic virtuosity coincides with his subversive linguistic virtuosity. In the overall setting of *All-Night Visitors,* Eli's way is a black male way of creating liminal space for himself. This black male way can only reflect the imperatives of physiology/race, oppres-sive white culture, and black male culture.

Clarence Major has always gone in directions that other "serious" black writers have not taken and done things that other "serious" black writers have not done. The risqué portrayal of Eli in *All-Night Visitors* is part of this experiment. I am saying that *All-Night Visitors* is clearly a black male writer's kind of experiment, dictated in significant ways by the ineluctable forces of black and white culture and physiology/race. Major has become more radically experimental as his career has developed. His stylistic and structural interests, similar to those in *All-Night Visitors,* almost always concern the limitations of the text and of discursive expressiveness. This, too, is very much a proclivity of several contemporary black male writers,[14] and it stands in contrast to the texts of contemporary black women writers, in which the authors successfully break the limitations of Western discourse by (re)membering, redefining, empowering, and mak-ing whole (actually or potentially) black female characters. Major's exper-imentation does increasingly follow the direction of radical white postmod-ernists and metafictionists; however, it also follows a line that is distinctly contemporary black male.

Notes

1. I am indebted to Spillers for her insights about the Retamar essay and for her very fine analysis of the various manifestations of Calibanism in narrative discourse.

2. See Wideman 115–16, 120–22, and 125–51. Wideman does a lot to reinforce my point about the pervasive effect of Shakespeare's Calibanism on Western discourse and consequently on black people. The writer/character in Wideman's text tries, unsuc-cessfully, to rewrite *The Tempest* to give it a different outcome and change Caliban's fortunes. (The text says that "Caliban . . . gets . . . exiled, dispossessed, [and made a] stranger in his own land . . . gets named just about every beast in the ark, the bestiary, called out his name so often it's a wonder anybody remembers it and maybe nobody does" [140].) Because in Wideman's text fictive discourse, or Western fictive discourse

at least, shapes reality, rewriting *The Tempest* would change an important root source of much Western discourse and change the oppressive circumstances of black Americans, particularly those of black males such as the writer/character and his son, who is locked away in a prison solitary-confinement cell (115–16).

3. See hooks (57–64) regarding this point. In analyzing the famous Central Park rape case and the white feminist response to it, hooks asks, "why is black male sexism evoked [by white feminists] as though it is a special brand of this social disorder, more dangerous, more abhorrent and life-threatening than the sexism that pervades the culture as a whole, or the sexism that informs white male domination of women?" (62). hooks comes down hard on black male sexism but suggests that contemporary white feminism attributes a special virulence to black men, thus stereotyping them and reinforcing old racist patterns.

4. Obviously, my general theory of black male texts will not apply to every writer and every text; however, no theory is ever all-inclusive. And this short essay, focusing especially on *All-Night Visitors,* is not the place to draw out the full dimensions of my theory. Here, I simply lay out its dimensions broadly enough to cover the text I am discussing. I want to say, however, that black male writers have similar concerns with discursivity and textuality and tend to problematize the portrayal of the black male self, or at least to make it tentative and open-ended (see notes 7 and 10). It is the foregrounding of tentativeness and open-endedness that significantly accounts for liminality in the texts of contemporary black male writers. My theory of black male writing covers writers as divergent as Ishmael Reed, John Edgar Wideman, Reginald McKnight, Randall Kenan, Charles Johnson, Clarence Major, and Trey Ellis.

5. Signifiers producing open-ended meaning and indeterminacy bring to mind Henry Louis Gates Jr.'s analysis of his central trope of Signifyin(g) in *The Signifying Monkey.* See my discussion later in this essay of the male tropes of signifying and playing the dozens.

6. See note 4.

7. I am implying here a much fuller restorative process in the texts of contemporary black women writers. However, the process in black women's texts is by no means an easy, simple one, and in texts such as Toni Morrison's *Beloved,* for example, it is not necessarily a successful one. But my point is that the potential for restoration does exist in the black female character, the black female self, because of the physiological and cultural resources that Holloway talks about in her book. I mean, more specifically, a sense of self grounded in motherhood (Holloway 26–31) and the mythologies, generated from black women's collective oral, communal voices, that give them the potential to revise their histories and define themselves anew (34). Holloway uses the critical term "recursion" in her analysis of this process (13–14, 102).

8. Charles Johnson's *Oxherding Tale* and *Middle Passage,* and John Edgar Wideman's *Philadelphia Fire* are clear examples of such black male texts.

9. See note 7.

10. It seems to me that the awareness of phallic duplicity is pretty widespread in the texts of black male writers. It has various forms of manifestation, and black male characters view it with different degrees of seriousness. In chapter 2 of Ellison's *Invisible Man,* Trueblood weaves an elaborate story, set around a Freudian-type dream, to explain his having had sex with his daughter. There certainly could be phallic duplicity that Trueblood is aware of, but the text leaves unclear its moral significance. The invisible narrator in the Sybil scene of chapter 24 of *Invisible Man* tries to practice phallic tricksterism and ends up with ambiguous results. The scene is comic in some ways, and the narrator seems to become aware of his phallic duplicity and its ineffectiveness. In Wideman's *Philadelphia Fire,* phallic duplicity takes a different form and presents a possibly more serious moral problem. See the section in the novel (63–65) in which the older, ostensibly more responsible writer/character watches, sexually aroused, as the young daughter of his friend and father figure takes a shower. There is symbolic violation here, and the writer/character reveals a duplicitous self that he would not want revealed.

11. It has become fashionable to criticize black male writers for a number of reasons; their emphasis on individuality instead of community is one of them. I hear critics and commentators making this criticism in my classes, at literary conferences, and in private conversations. A critical text that states this more explicitly is *Invented Lives: Narratives of Black Women, 1860–1960,* edited by Mary Helen Washington. See Washington's introduction, "The Darkened Eye Restored: Notes toward a Literary History of Black Women" (esp. xxi).

12. In *Understanding the New Black Poetry,* Stephen Henderson uses the poem as the first piece in section 3 of his critical anthology, entitled "The New Black Consciousness, the Same Difference." Henderson wants, I think, to indicate that Rap's language practice shows the new black assertiveness and confidence in the 1960s and 1970s and embodies attitudes, rituals, and modes of behavior that are central in black culture. The maleness of Rap's rap makes it clear to me that it is strongly indicative of black male culture.

13. Of course, black women and white people can also signify, especially since, as Gates quotes from Roger D. Abrahams, signifying can "'denote speaking with the hands and eyes'" (75). But first and foremost, signifying is the "black person's use of figurative modes of language use" (74). And I argue that these "figurative modes of language use" are predominantly masculine. Black women may signify, especially through innuendo and indirection, but the primary modes of rhetorical figuration are practiced, with great intention, in black male culture. And perhaps it is true that these modes sift into black female culture. Based on what Holloway says in her chapter "Mythologies" (85–109), I would, at the risk of too heavily extrapolating black women's culture from a textual analysis, say that the oral creation of female mythologies, a mode of language practice and storytelling different from signifying, defines black women's culture. What most clearly distinguishes mytholo-

gizing from signifying is that it is not language play, competitive or uncompetitive, in the way that signifying is. Similarly, indirection is not its purpose.

Signifying for black males takes other overt forms than the signifying phallic trick-sterism of "Rap's Poem." Gates quotes another example of signifying from Brown:

Man, I can't win for losing.
If it wasn't for bad luck, I wouldn't have no luck at all.
I been having buzzard luck
Can't kill nothing and won't nothing die
I'm living on the welfare and things is stormy
They borrowing their shit from the Salvation Army
But things bound to get better 'cause they can't get no worse
I'm just like the blind man, standing by a broken window
I don't feel no pain.
But it's your world
You the man I pay rent to
If I had you [sic] hands I'd give 'way both my arms.
Cause I could do without them
I'm the man but you the main man
I read the books you write
You set the pace in the race I run
Why, you always in good form
You got more foam than Alka Seltzer. (74)

The repeated references to "man" emphasize the masculinity of this discourse.

14. Some of these writers are Trey Ellis, Randall Kenan, John Edgar Wideman, Ishmael Reed, and Charles Johnson. They do not all foreground the limitations of the text and discursive expressiveness in the same way and to the same extent. Reed and Johnson, for example, celebrate discursivity more than they agonize about its limitations. Nevertheless, they do thematize textuality and discursivity. And they may extend and revise Western discursive constructs (this seems particularly true for Reed), but their process of extension and revision still acknowledges the powerful influence of Western discourse on black characterization. They never recursively break free as much as black women writers do.

Works Cited

Baker, Houston A., Jr. *Blues, Ideology, and Afro-American Literature: A Vernacular Theory.* Chicago: University of Chicago Press, 1984.

Bakhtin, M. M. "Discourse in the Novel." In *The Dialogic Imagination: Four Essays.* Ed. Michael Holquist. Trans. Caryl Emerson and Michael Holquist. Austin: University of Texas Press, 1981. 259–422.

Byerman, Keith. *Fingering the Jagged Grain: Tradition and Form in Recent Black Fiction.* Athens: University of Georgia Press, 1985.

Ellison, Ralph. *Invisible Man*. New York: Random House, 1952.

Gates, Henry Louis, Jr. *The Signifying Monkey: A Theory of African-American Literary Criticism*. New York: Oxford University Press, 1988.

Henderson, Stephen. *Understanding the New Black Poetry: Black Speech and Black Music as Poetic References*. New York: Morrow, 1973.

Holloway, Karla F. C. *Moorings and Metaphors: Figures of Culture and Gender in Black Women's Literature*. New Brunswick, N.J.: Rutgers University Press, 1992.

hooks, bell. *Yearning: Race, Gender, and Cultural Politics*. Boston: South End, 1990.

Johnson, Charles. *Middle Passage*. New York: Macmillan, 1990.

———. *Oxherding Tale*. New York: Grove, 1982.

Major, Clarence. *All-Night Visitors*. New York: Olympia, 1969.

———. *The Dark and Feeling: Black American Writers and Their Work*. New York: Third Press, 1974.

Morrison, Toni. *Beloved*. New York: Knopf, 1987.

Retamar, Roberto Fernandez. "Caliban: Notes toward a Discussion of Culture in Our America." *Massachusetts Review* 15.1–2 (1974): 7–72.

Shakespeare, William. *The Tempest*. 1611. Rpt., New York: Washington Square Press, 1994.

Spillers, Hortense. "Introduction: Who Cuts the Border? Some Readings on 'America.'" In *Comparative American Identities: Race, Sex, and Nationality in the Modern Text*. Ed. Hortense Spillers. New York: Routledge, 1991. 1–25.

Turner, Victor. *The Forest of Symbols: Aspects of Ndembu Ritual*. Ithaca, N.Y.: Cornell University Press, 1967.

Washington, Mary Helen, ed. *Invented Lives: Narratives of Black Women, 1860–1960*. New York: Doubleday, 1987.

Wideman, John Edgar. *Philadelphia Fire*. New York: Holt, 1990.

6

"I Was My Father's Father, and He My Child": The Process of Black Fatherhood and Literary Evolution in Charles Johnson's Fiction

WILLIAM R. NASH

Throughout his fiction, Charles Johnson uses African-American fatherhood to explore various individual and group male identity formation processes. In his most recent novel, *Dreamer* (1998), the two main black male characters never knew their fathers and suffer profound identity crises as a result. This treatment of fatherless men deviates from a pattern in his previous works, where he concentrates on the presence rather than the absence of father figures. From his first published novel, *Faith and the Good Thing* (1974), to his National Book Award–winning *Middle Passage* (1990), Johnson creates black fathers unable to parent because of a crippling sense of racial victimization and psychological emasculation that leads them to deny their responsibilities to children and spouses. In essence, these black males cannot be *fathers* because they do not believe American society will let them be *men*. This position reflects much common mythology about African-American fatherhood and resonates with many scholars' takes on the ultimate relationship between race and parenting.[1] For Johnson, however, this position is not an end but a beginning, not a fact to live with but a state of being to revise. The failed fathers in his work never win; instead, they become the standard against which to evaluate all other textual models of African-American manhood.

Johnson complicates his ideas of black manhood and fatherhood in *Oxherding Tale* (1982) and *Middle Passage,* as well as in the title story from *The Sorcerer's Apprentice* (1986), by showing the failed fathers confronting male children who choose different definitions for their own manhood. Andrew Hawkins (*Oxherding Tale*), Allan Jackson ("The Sorcerer's Apprentice"), and Rutherford Calhoun (*Middle Passage*) escape the traps that envelop and destroy their respective fathers, all of whom bear physical and emotional scars from slavery, by embracing a more flexible understanding of racial identity. Recognizing the connections between black and white cultures, Andrew, Allan, and Rutherford learn multiple understandings of what it means to be a black man. As they reconcile their racial heritage with their more fluid sense of their individual identities, the sons also come to terms with their fathers. In each work, the newly enlightened son can help his father dismantle emotional and psychological barriers associated with the father's narrow, racialized worldview. This gift of nurturance contributes to Johnson's larger project of breaking down all limiting definitions by reversing the father and son roles; as Andrew Hawkins reflects in this moment in *Oxherding Tale,* "'I was my father's father, and he my child'" (176).

In addition to deepening our understanding of the possibilities inherent in black manhood, the father/son theme in Johnson's work also illuminates the difficulties facing the black artist who confines himself to previously established, rigid definitions of what *black* literature can be. The failed fathers in these texts all adhere to a worldview similar in some ways to the fundamental principles of the Black Arts movement of the 1960s, "the aesthetic and spiritual sister of the Black Power concept [that] proposes a radical reordering of the western cultural aesthetic" and that favors an essentialist notion of racial identity (Neal 797). Although Johnson was initially interested in the ideas behind the Black Arts movement, referring to himself as "once a convert," he ultimately rejected its ideology, labeling it "a serious roadblock for genuine black fiction and philosophy" (Johnson, "Where Fiction" 48). He shows the son figures evolving through the same pattern in each of these works. In response to their fathers' rigidity, the sons develop creative models, illustrating the variations within the body of black literature by drawing on numerous literary traditions as a part of their creative process. Acknowledging the legacy of the literary tradition he belongs to and simultaneously illustrating the flexibility of definitions attached to it, Johnson replicates the actions of his son characters. Like them, the author engages with his community's legacy—in this case literary—and adds elements from other traditions he finds personally compelling.[2]

This challenge to established perceptions about black identity is the fruit of a philosophical system synthesizing phenomenology and Buddhism that undergirds all of Johnson's published fiction.[3] This system rests on two fundamental convictions: that individual identity is an illusion that causes more pain than it gives pleasure, and that one can bracket all preconceptions one brings to every encounter to achieve the fullest possible experience of the event. That purified perception amplifies the possible meanings each encounter bears.

Freedom from the illusion of identity and preconceptions that shape experience are essential to Johnson's vision of a new way to understand black manhood. With regard to preconceptions, collectively defined ideas about racial identity perpetuate oppression and injustice; if one were able to set aside such burdens, Johnson contends, then the possible definitions of black being multiply. Also, in terms of the rigid preconceptions that confine us most, conventional interpretation of the American historical record preserves and extends the power of preconceptions such as those the sons in his books try to escape. Being unbound from history, as Johnson's son narrators often are in their moments of enlightenment, allows for the development of new ways of understanding being in the world. In thinking about identity as illusion, Johnson denies the efficacy of the divisive markers we establish: gender, class, and especially race. As one learns that the separation individuals experience is often self-inflicted, then one can transcend, and thereby either deny or redefine, the false categories that drive the divisions, a process that also radically alters one's understandings of black being by opening it to endless variations.

As he struggles to broaden understandings of black being and to open new possibilities of being in the world that breech established boundaries, Johnson simultaneously seeks to challenge and revise accepted perceptions of what black literature can be. Throughout his novels, Johnson works to achieve the fundamental goal of his aesthetic program: the creation of a philosophical African-American fiction transcending the "splinter[ing of] 'perspective'" and achieving what he calls "whole sight," an array of visions unified in the attempt to articulate experiences of blackness, rather than "*the* black experience" ("Whole Sight" 2; emphasis added). A literary version of his statements about black manhood, his aesthetic offers new possibilities for African-American literature that subvert or transcend the limitations of systems such as the Black Aesthetic, which interprets African-American identity through a single model for black perception reliant on a dualistic interpretation of race.

Creating a program for achieving this whole sight, he suggests that black writers experiment with the "galaxy of . . . forms that are our inheritance as writers" (4), an idea we can see him working out in his own novels as he takes forms that have characteristically been the province of black artists and expands them to illustrate all the different things they can be. *Oxherding Tale,* for example, is an amalgamation of slave narrative, historical novel, philosophical treatise, Buddhist parable, and bildungsroman. *Middle Passage* is "basically three novels in one. You've got a love story. . . . a story of the slave trade . . . then finally, you have the story of a mad ship captain, this kind of ultimate Ahab" (Johnson, "Philosopher," 17). In these blends, Johnson claims a space for himself as an artist, directly challenging the established understanding of what black literature is and suggesting a much broader possibility for it. His artistic evolution in many ways reflects the sons' struggles with their fathers; just as they are breaking away from parental expectations about what their racial and personal identity will be, Johnson is breaking away from established authorship models that limit the range of black literature.

Like Allan Jackson, the title character of "The Sorcerer's Apprentice" who can only heal his father when he stops imitating the left-handed sorcerer and doing things his own right-handed way (168), Johnson must find his own voice to tell the stories that he has to tell in the way that best suits his purposes. His struggle to find that voice dates to the period of his own apprenticeship, when he wrote six novels, all still unpublished, all adopting the voices and models of writers he admired. After working through these "strictly naturalistic novels inspired by. . . . Richard Wright, James Baldwin, and John A. Williams," Johnson realized that these authors "were not . . . anywhere close to [his] emerging version of how the world worked" and set them aside to take up the philosophical model he develops throughout his published body of work (Introduction to *Oxherding Tale,* xiii). In the process of expanding the work of his predecessors, Johnson reconnects with his literary ancestors, a development he mirrors in the works through the evolution of the son/father relationships.

Johnson's consideration of fatherhood links him to a recent trend in African-American literature: writers remembering their fathers and/or speculating about the necessary components of successful parenting for African-American males facing the pressures of life in American society. Collections such as Gloria Wade-Gayles's *Father Songs* (1997), Andre C. Willis's *Faith*

of Our Fathers (1996), and *Black Men Speaking* (1997), which Johnson co-
edited with John McCluskey Jr., feature the perspectives of numerous scholars, critics, and activists and emphasize the differences between the mediated perceptions and the realities of black manhood and fatherhood. A more
sustained single meditation on parenting for African-American males appears in John Edgar Wideman's account of his own family, *Fatheralong: A
Meditation on Fathers and Sons, Race and Society* (1994). A poignant,
philosophical account of episodes from his childhood and his recent interactions with his father, Wideman's book explores the author's personal history and also discusses the difficulties black fathers face. He says, in explaining why African-American fathers often fail their families,

> Ideas of manhood, true and transforming, grow out of private, personal ex-
> changes between fathers and sons. Yet for generations of black men in Ameri-
> ca this privacy, this privilege has been systematically breached in a most shameful
> and public way. . . . Arrayed against the possibility of conversation between
> fathers and sons is the country they inhabit, everywhere proclaiming the inad-
> equacy of black fathers, their lack of manhood in almost every sense the term's
> understood here in America. (64–65)

For Wideman, the process of connecting generations, of allowing sons to
accept their fathers and vice versa, necessarily involves their accepting "the
stigma of race" (70). Though Wideman and Johnson share fundamental
concerns about black manhood and fatherhood, for much of Johnson's
career he has resisted the conclusions that Wideman draws in *Fatheralong*.
From *Faith and the Good Thing* to *Middle Passage*, the fathers who fail their
sons are all marked by the stigma of race; the sons who manage to free themselves and become better fathers are the ones who manage either to sidestep or reclaim that stigma and create a more flexible definition of their racial
being. Though Johnson does not deny the reality of the barrier, he refuses
to grant it the power Wideman does.

What Wideman does directly, Johnson does more obliquely. As he says in
a recent interview, "As I look at my fiction, I see a recurrent pattern—the
exploration of father/son relations, and perhaps this is because my dad is
the only man on earth I've ever felt I had to please or answer to uncondi-
tionally" (Nash 50). One event from his childhood seems to dominate his
consideration of fathers and sons. In "The Second Front," Johnson recounts
the story of his expressing a desire to be a professional cartoonist and quotes
his father's reply: "'They don't let black people do that'" (179). This belief
in the professional restrictions placed on black Americans resonates pro-

foundly with the attitudes of Johnson's father characters: blackness for them operates within a set of preconceived boundaries they dare not violate. In that equation, Johnson resembles the son figures who resist the imposition of boundaries and achieve the goals their fathers deem unattainable by transcending the narrowly racialized view of self that causes their elders so much pain. Inadequately equipped to meet the demands of their sons' growth, the fathers fall behind and remain bound by their limited and limiting identities. Their failure leads the reader to momentary despair; Johnson, however, consistently relieves that frustration by demonstrating how the sons free themselves from what binds their fathers and then use what they have learned to teach the fathers their new way of seeing race. As each son becomes his "father's father," he reinforces the message: despite the racial oppression that the African-American community has suffered, one can learn new ways of understanding race that allow for self-love and human connection and that stop the cycle of oppression for future generations.

The fathers' failure stems primarily from a socially constructed self image and a negative interpretation of their individual and collective heritage. George Hawkins (*Oxherding Tale*), Richard Jackson ("The Sorcerer's Apprentice"), and Riley Calhoun (*Middle Passage*) are men broken by their experiences in bondage; their fragmentation takes various forms, but each deeply feels the impact of slavery. For Richard Jackson, the scar is clearest in his smashed thumb, a wound he received when a wagon wheel rolled over his hand on "Freedom Day" (152). Rubin Bailey, the sorcerer who will take Richard's son as an apprentice, heals the former slave's physical injury. He cannot, however, help Richard with the emotional damage that slavery inflicted upon him. Only Richard's son, Allan, can use the lessons Rubin teaches him during his apprenticeship to work the final spell that will liberate and heal his father.

In contrast to Richard's crushed thumb, which is a survivable injury, Riley Calhoun is literally destroyed by his situation: vaguely aware of his free heritage and unwilling to submit to the soul-crushing force of bondage, he flees, leaving home and family behind. And, "since he had never ventured more than ten miles from home, wherefore he lost his way, was quickly captured by padderolls and quietly put to death, the bullet entering through his left eye, exiting through his right ear, leaving him . . . rotting in a fetid stretch of Missouri swamp" (170). His desertion leaves his sons, Rutherford and Jackson, unable to correct the flawed lessons he has taught them. Before his death, Riley understands himself to be a racial victim, one who turns suffering to nefarious purposes as he drinks, womanizes, and generally victimizes his community under the umbrella excuse that "it wasn't really *his* fault he acted thataway" so much as it was the fault of the system (169). His legacy, such as it is, comprises his sense of suffering and this concomitant idea of entitlement to exploit others; as the novel begins, this burden marks the narrator Rutherford Calhoun, whose life of thievery and self-indulgence demonstrates how completely he is his father's son.

While Riley and Richard bear physical marks of their suffering, George Hawkins carries primarily psychological scars that he passes on to his son Andrew. Formerly the most privileged house slave on Cripplegate plantation, George falls to the position of oxherd after he disgraces himself on the night his son is conceived. Drinking on the front porch with his master, Jonathan Polkinghorne, George agrees to his owner's suggestion that the men change beds and partners for one night. Though Mattie, George's wife, turns Polkinghorne away, George slips into bed with Anna Polkinghorne, who grabs him eagerly before she realizes who he is. The results of their union are a demotion for the slave, permanent estrangement of the plantation master and mistress, and Andrew, the racially mixed protagonist who suffers the consequences of his father's indiscretion.

In addition to feeling unwelcome in his master's house and somewhat disconnected from his father's, Andrew must also bear the brunt of George's ideological reaction to these events. Once content with his situation and reluctant to criticize the Polkinghornes, after his banishment George becomes increasingly militant and vocal on the subject of race. As he develops and argues his views, he burdens his son with an enormous responsibility: "'Whatever you do, Hawk—it pushes the Race forward, or pulls us back. You know what I've always told you: If you fail, everything we been fightin' for fails with you. Be y'self'" (21). As George well knows, Andrew is both black and white, as well as being educated in a classical tradition that takes him far beyond the limits of his father's racialized logic; therefore, "being himself" means something different from what George has in mind. Similarly, George points out to Andrew that his mixed heritage will enable him to pass; however, he then tells him that choosing to act white to gain freedom would "'be like turnin' your back on me and everythin' I believes in'" (21). Blinded by his devotion to his limited idea of race, George can see that Andrew might make other choices but cannot validate them because they threaten his way of being in the world, a way he maintains in order to understand and perpetuate the victim consciousness that defines and drives him.

George's quest for and preservation of a racialized masculine identity close him to numerous other personal possibilities; they also create profound crises for his son, who seeks a different understanding of himself as a man and as an African American. Pressured to resist a more flexible sense of self by a father who demands loyalty and whom he loves desperately, Andrew cannot access any elements of his identity that exist beyond the parameters George establishes without betraying his father. In a sense, then, George demands that his son divide himself, placing primary importance on the facets of his identity that perpetuate George's idea of black manhood. For Andrew, as for Rutherford Calhoun in *Middle Passage,* the fallout from his father's active conviction that black men must know who they *are* means that he cannot meaningfully express or connect to any sense of who he can *be* by looking at himself, his race, and the world differently from his father. When Andrew finally learns to accept and rely upon his different understanding of the world and himself, he can reconnect with his father, transcending George's memory and healing the psychological rift that both have experienced but that he can save his children from.

The fragmentation the narrators feel parallels a physical and emotional split that each experiences in his relationship with his father. One of the scars of slavery each father bears and bequeaths to his son is an unwillingness to care too much about anyone or anything that he might lose. For George, the betrayal he feels in the wake of his fall from house to field slave makes him suspicious, resentful, and untrusting; therefore, he can hardly express his emotions. He tries to reach out to his son but can only do so by impressing the importance of his racial identity on him. When Andrew compromises that racial identity by passing for white, he suffers the guilt of having betrayed his father. Because they cannot connect either physically or emotionally, he has no way of escaping that burden. Andrew's sense of self-separation therefore intensifies as it blends with his isolation from his failed father, isolation that comes largely because race shapes even love in George Hawkins's world.

Like George Hawkins, Riley Calhoun (*Middle Passage*) and Richard Jackson ("The Sorcerer's Apprentice") are so emotionally debilitated by slavery that they are ill equipped to nurture their sons properly. Riley Calhoun's greatest failure literally takes his life; Richard Jackson's is less extreme, but his emotional limitations nevertheless keep him from connecting with his son, Allan. Although quite proud of the sorcerer's apprentice, "however pleased Richard might have been, he gave no sign. . . . He was the sort of man who held his feelings in, and people took this for strength" (152). As Allan rightly surmises, this is not strength but the result of his father's experiences with slavery, which include a real fear of loving anything symbol-

ized in his physical injury. His "thick, ruined fingers," crushed under the
wagon on the day he was physically freed, cannot hold anything. They reflect
his emotional slavery and his inability to make contact with his son, the
burden bondage has placed on him as it has made him unwilling or unable
to express his emotions freely (168). Though Richard is the one of these three
fathers who will love and the one who will actually benefit from reestab-
lishing a connection with his son, until Allan turns elsewhere for insight and
finds ways to transcend those limitations they cannot connect because his
father remains emotionally enslaved. Only when the son establishes an alternative can the father be completely free.

Richard's successful escape from the bonds that hold him and his recognition of the value in Allan's artistry suggest that "The Sorcerer's Apprentice" has particular significance for Johnson. He invests the characters in
this story, which he wrote while preparing *Oxherding Tale* for publication,
with literary and personal power as he works out his relationship between
race and artistry and strives to articulate an aesthetic identity that counters
his father's ideas about what black artists cannot do.[4] Allan learns to be a
sorcerer and uses his magic to help Richard love, thereby creating a new way
of being in the world that liberates him and his father. Similarly, Johnson
uses the magic of his literary artistry to expand ideas about racial identity,
a refutation of his father's statements about the racialized parameters of his
creative opportunities even as he pays tribute to his elder.

Andrew, Rutherford, and Allan transcend their fathers' limited views by
turning away from the men who fail them to explore the identity models that
other black males offer them. In each of Johnson's novels, the son's escape
from the oppression of a constricting racialized identity comes through contact with surrogate father figures. However, the father role never falls to one
man; all of the protagonists must balance numerous substitute fathers' teachings and determine what ways of being in the world benefit them most. This
selection process within the text mirrors the scenario Johnson establishes for
the reader as he encourages him or her to evaluate the various role models
available to black men. Many of the potential substitute fathers are as deeply flawed and wounded as the actual ones, which complicates the choices the
protagonists must make as they try to avoid duplicating their original difficulties; however, the situation is never hopeless in Johnson's work. Consistently through the novels up until *Dreamer* (1998), Johnson offers the same
answer: the most effective alternative approaches belong to "fathers" who
exist outside established boundaries of racial definition.

In *Oxherding Tale, Middle Passage,* and "The Sorcerer's Apprentice," the substitute fathers are all descendants of the Allmuseri, the mythical tribe of African wizards Johnson creates and uses as a primary vehicle for his unlimited vision of race.[5] The Allmuseri arrive in America as part of the forced removal of West Africans through the transatlantic slave trade. We see that journey in *Middle Passage;* in *Oxherding Tale* and "The Sorcerer's Apprentice" the Allmuseri figures are lineal descendants of the tribe who are already established in America. Their experiences in bondage are what they have in common with the actual father figures in the texts; the difference between the fathers and the wizards appears in their reactions to the experience.

The Allmuseri, whose name comes from "al-museri" and means "a mosque or spiritual gathering place," are able to resist the damaging effects of slavery because their unique worldview saves them from the sense of dividedness and victimization that marks each of the failed father figures in the texts. They are a profoundly spiritual people dedicated to maintaining their belief in the interconnectedness of all things and thereby to resisting the temptation of desire, a state of mind that emphasizes separation and causes much human suffering. In *Oxherding Tale,* for instance, the Coffinmaker, Reb, lives a life unmarked by any cravings. Andrew observes that the Allmuseri craftsman is "the man, at country market, who looked at the stands and rejoiced at what he *didn't* need; the man who, when most vigorously at work, seemed resting" (46). As Johnson explains, in the novel "Reb is the resident Taoist," interested in "transcending dualism" and able through his enlightenment to escape the victim's consciousness and to work instead to nurture others (Nash 56). As Andrew seeks to free himself from his father's influence and the curse of seeing the world in bifurcated terms, Reb offers him another way of being in the world that substitutes a celebration of human connection for the abiding sense of separation that prevents George from loving his son.

In addition to teaching the sons about the possibilities for human connection that counter the common perception of divided racial identity, the Allmuseri also offer them a new way of seeing that transcends the limitations and definitions of identity that cause the failed fathers so much trouble. Riley, George, and Richard all struggle with a racialized sense of self that springs from collective and individual identities shaped by the national discussion of race that fixes their status. Conversely, the Allmuseri offer the sons a language free of definitions and fixedness, as well as a model of life that negates the limiting power of history as a definer. Experiencing the Allmuseri ethos, the sons can reassess and modify their senses of what they have learned from their fathers.

The presentation of the Allmuseri language and worldview is an issue in every work where they appear; the clearest, most detailed version of their beliefs and characteristics comes in *Middle Passage*. Rutherford describes their hands, noting that "their palms were blank, bearing no lines" (61); he then explains their language:

> When Ngonyama's tribe spoke it was not so much like talking as the tones the savannah made at night, siffilating through the plains of coarse grass, soughing as dry wind from tree to tree. Not really a language at all, by my guess, as a melic way of breathing deep from the diaphragm that dovetailed articles into nouns, nouns into verbs. I'm not sure I know what I'm saying now, but Ngonyama told me the predication "is," which granted existence to anything, had over the ages eroded into merely an article of faith for them. Nouns or static substances hardly existed in their vocabulary at all. A "bed" was called a "resting," a "robe" a "warming." (77)

Taken together, these details illustrate the Allmuseri's complete liberation from conventional limits. As Ashraf Rushdy notes, their language "is transcendent and embodies in every instance the pre-conditions of 'intersubjectivity and cross-cultural experience'" (378). In addition to addressing lexical issues at the heart of Johnson's aesthetic, the description of the Allmuseri's anti-essentialist speech has important implications with regard to race. With a language that does not accommodate for fixedness, the Allmuseri cannot be plagued by the sorts of definitions that mark words like "black" and "manhood" for George, Riley, and Richard. Furthermore, their language only addresses current experience, an indication of their escape from history. This idea of their freedom from history resonates also in the detail that there are no lines on their palms. The lines on our hands, one of which is the lifeline, mark us indelibly and fix us chronologically. As history and the Western sense of time are two of the most basic ways that we understand ourselves as individuals, the Allmuseri's lack of these attributes emphasizes their freedom from this sense of separation. Protected by this language and worldview, they usually avoid the trap of individual identity and the related concept of race, since race implies the separation that they reject. In every way they provide the sons and the reader with a powerful counterexample to the failed fathers' racialized sense of suffering.

The only time the Allmuseri fail to maintain their unity comes when they rebel aboard the slave ship *Republic* in *Middle Passage*. In a sequence of events that clearly evokes the historical record of the *Amistad* mutiny, the tribe rises up and seizes control of the ship.[6] In their violent effort to save themselves, the tribe necessarily becomes "part of the world of multiplicity, of *me* versus *thee*" (140). The situation and the Allmuseri's reaction to it remind the reader of slavery's effects on even the most enlightened consciousness. Like the failed fathers in the text, the Allmuseri can be pushed to act out the hostilities that slavery instills in all affected by it. Fortunately for the sons and the tribesmen, however, the Africans have one transcendent quality that helps them recover and reestablish the order of things most consistent and harmonious with their worldview.

Significantly, every member of the tribe is a wizard. By definition, wizardry or magic involves the transformation of perceptions. In other words, the tribe's life eschews established points of view and belief systems; they live outside "the world of multiplicity, of *me* versus *thee*" because they can see differently, and they use their magic to affirm what the rebellion threatens. Furthermore, the Allmuseri teach the protagonists to cultivate new ways of seeing that enable them to avoid the suffering their fathers experience. Freed from that pain, the sons can reconnect with their fathers and disrupt the cycle of oppression.

The sons' encounters with these Allmuseri substitute fathers propel each towards an enlightenment that emancipates them from their cycle of suffering. Transcending that pattern, the sons then can begin to heal the breech their fathers' limited, racialized worldviews have caused. For Allan Jackson, the lessons he learns from the sorcerer Rubin Bailey give him the courage to love his father and to literally reach out to him. As he finally accepts the limitations of his new training and the shift in perception of himself and the world that comes with it, Allan works his best spell by freeing his father from his inability to love. Rutherford Calhoun has no chance to reconnect with his father physically, but he fuses with him spiritually as he finally understands what motivated Riley. Furthermore, he modifies that awareness into something even more useful as he adopts Baleka, one of the Allmuseri children who survives the wreck of the *Republic,* and parents her with a wholeness and sensitivity he has never shown before. As the son rears a daughter rather than another son, Johnson further breaks down limits by breaking the pattern of gender relationships as well. Absolutely contrary to his alienation from his father, Riley, Rutherford experiences with Baleka a union that echoes Reb's connection to all things in *Oxherding Tale.*

In that novel, Horace Bannon, the Soulcatcher who pursues runaway slaves, emphasizes Reb's lack of desire and his sense of connectedness in a final conversation with Andrew: "'Did you know if yo friend passed a butcher shop, and if somebody was sledgehammering a shorthorn, the back of

Reb's neck bruised?'" (171). Johnson evokes the same image in *Middle Passage*. Explaining his devotion to Baleka to Isadora Bailey, whom he fled New Orleans to escape marrying and whom he now wants to marry at journey's end, Rutherford says "'Whenever Baleka is out of my sight I am worried. If she bruises herself, *I* feel bruised'" (195). The former thief, who thought of himself entirely in individual terms, has experienced a fusion with his father that enables him to be a better parent to his adopted daughter. Significantly, she is a tangible reminder of the experience of slavery; however, unlike his father before him, Rutherford manages to transform that experience into something empowering rather than a license for profligate behavior. In knowing the Allmuseri, Rutherford breaks the cycle of victimization, comes to see the world differently, and thereby frees himself from the racialized limitations that drove Riley to his death.

The transformations Rutherford and Allan undergo show different elements of a total process Johnson expresses most fully in *Oxherding Tale*. Andrew Hawkins, the narrator, stands prepared to die at the end of the novel, defeated by Bannon, the bounty hunter also known as the Soulcatcher, and the desire he has failed to master. His ultimate despair manifests itself in his conviction that his father, George, whom the slave hunter slew in the aftermath of the Cripplegate slave revolt, must have died hating him for betraying the race by choosing to pass for white. Bannon spares Andrew, however, because he has vowed to quit slave catching if he ever met a man he could not capture; his method of pursuit involves learning what the fugitive slave wants and replicating and internalizing that wish so that he can think like, and therefore catch, his prey. Because Reb—Andrew's Allmuseri surrogate father—was immune to desire and therefore impossible to entrap, Soulcatcher offers Andrew a life lesson rather than a bullet in the brain. He tells Andrew how Reb got free and in the process explains what he has learned about George.

Bannon's knowledge of George's life and death, and especially the way he shows it, makes him an invaluable resource for Andrew; not only does he know what the elder Hawkins thought and felt, but that awareness literally manifests itself on his body. What appears to be an intricate pattern of tattoos on the slave catcher's chest is actually a record of all his experiences.[7] In gazing into the expanse of images, Andrew comes to a new understanding of himself and his relationship to his father, an awareness that his encounter with Reb has prepared him for:

> Not tattooes at all, I saw, but forms sardined in his contour, creatures Bannon
> had killed since childhood . . . all were conserved in this process of doubling,

nothing was lost in the masquerade, the cosmic costume ball, where behind every different mask at the party . . . the selfsame face was uncovered at midnight, and this was my father . . . the profound mystery of the One and the Many gave me back my father again and again, his love, in every being from grubworms to giant sumacs . . . and, in the final face I saw in the Soulcatcher, which shook tears from me—my own face, for he had duplicated portions of me during the early days of the hunt—I was my father's father, and he my child. (175–76)

The "process of doubling" emphasizes that son and father are no longer separate. Indeed, in the detail of Andrew's seeing himself as his "father's father," we note that they are indistinguishable, a state of being that expands their roles as well as our awareness of the falseness of such labels. With his recognition of this interconnectedness he shares with George, Andrew can reconcile his way of being in the world with his father's and thereby can embrace and propagate the multiplicities of black manhood he and his father represent. The link between his worldview, which rejects distinctions of any sort, and George's validates him and his decision to resist his father's limited, divisive understanding of himself. He further affirms that broader position by naming his racially mixed daughter Anna, after the white biological mother who could not embrace or even acknowledge him in his own childhood. That he can give her name to one he loves suggests he can overcome the divisions that neither of his biological parents could reconcile, a position that affirms a more flexible understanding of racial identity and, as in the case of Rutherford and Baleka, a challenge to the limitation of gender roles as well. Like the other sons, Andrew takes the lesson of his unbound, Allmuseri surrogate father and uses it to expand his understanding of himself as a black male, a process that enables him to forgive his biological father even as he realizes the flaws in his father's position.

The repeated pattern in each of these earlier works is thought-provoking for the reader; however, there are difficulties associated with it that critics have recognized and that Johnson has recently addressed in his new work. Although the Allmuseri present an attractive option for developing different understandings of racial identity and particularly of black manhood, their appeal is essentially intellectual. Unmarked by time and therefore freed from history, the tribesmen do not offer an immediately applicable approach to being in the world; one living in America cannot easily ignore the legacy of racial oppression and systematic emasculation that the Allmuseri sidestep. As a result, the affirming construct of black manhood Johnson inscribes in his earlier works is attractive but somewhat abstract. In *Dreamer*, however, Johnson modifies his approach and offers readers a more concrete method of transcending racial limitations and understanding the possibilities inherent in black male being.

The novel celebrates the life and legacy of Dr. Martin Luther King Jr. and demonstrates how his philosophy of nonviolence and his hope for the preservation of "the beloved community," a recognition of the fundamental human connections that transcend race, class, and gender, offers the novel's protagonist, and by extension the reader, a new model of black manhood. Once again, the young black male narrator must choose between competing visions of the world that older black men offer him. In *Dreamer*, King is one possible substitute father. Significantly, the other surrogate father in the novel, Chaym Smith, is King's physical double and a lineal descendant of the Allmuseri, able to trace his origins to Baleka Calhoun, the Allmuseri daughter Rutherford adopts at the end of *Middle Passage*. Like the Allmuseri of the earlier novels, he practices methods of emphasizing his connectedness to all things: in an amalgamation of Reb, Rubin, and Ngonyama, Smith is a painter, musician, carpenter, martial artist, Zen Buddhist monk, and philosopher. He has, in the course of his travels, embraced the various *Ways* (in the Buddhist sense) to enlightenment that have saved his predecessors. However, none of them can save him. Smith's experiences with racial oppression and human venality, compounded by the failure of all his efforts at transcending race, have corrupted his vision, making him an unfit role model for the narrator, Matthew Bishop. Embittered in the course of his quest for acceptance, Smith tells Bishop, "'There's two kinds of people in this world. Predators and prey. Lions and *lunch*'" (65). His hostility and fracturedness evoke the state of the Allmuseri crew in the wake of the rebellion aboard the *Republic*, as he has fallen deeply into the separation that they feel at that moment. Unlike them, though, he does not fear for his soul and try to reconnect but rather embraces that isolation as his way of being in the world. Initially, Smith rejects everything that the 1960s civil rights movement stands for, going so far as to wipe himself on a statement of nonviolent principles after defecating (93). Although compelling, he sets a dangerous example for young Bishop; only after he begins to understand King can Smith break out of his destructive patterns and learn a new way of being in the world himself, one that more closely matches the experiences of his fellow tribesmen.

In a sense, King must parent both the young narrator and this mysterious Allmuseri who is his physical double and bring them to enlightenment. By removing power from the tribe that has traditionally provided the best model for black manhood in his work and vesting it in an actual historical figure whose vision for himself and his community effected significant social change in America, Johnson extends and strengthens his suggestions about the multiplicity of meanings black male identity can comprise. He also takes an even stronger position on the importance of black fatherhood as a means of accessing that open vision. Neither Smith nor Bishop knows his father's identity; this ignorance symbolizes a powerful psychological gap that both men must overcome. It also functions as a pointed commentary on contemporary African-American life, as the absence of fathers represents a lack of leadership for African Americans and a threat to the process of community building. The reconnection process Johnson shows in *Oxherding Tale,* "The Sorcerer's Apprentice," and *Middle Passage* cannot occur if there are no elders with whom to reconnect. As Smith says to his young friend when Bishop confirms his fatherlessness, "'That's what I figured. You like most of the rest of us. Brothers, I mean. You're illegitimate. No father prepared the way for you. You want to be among the anointed, the blessed— to *belong.* . . . But you don't fit. You got to remember that nobody on earth likes Negroes. Not even Negroes. We're outcasts. And outcasts can't never create a community'" (65). This statement resonates profoundly with the racialized victim consciousness that plagues Johnson's failed fathers in his earlier novels; it also intensifies the danger that lurks around the edges of George's, Richard's, and Riley's lives. Like them, Smith is a failed father of sorts. When he meets the three young sons of a prostitute living in his tenement building, Smith informally adopts them. He makes a good faith effort at nurturance, taking the boys places, feeding them, and trying to be a positive presence in their lives. He even goes so far as to marry their mother, whom he does not love, in an effort to save the youngsters. Ultimately, however, economic and social pressures destroy him; he and his wife descend into a vortex of substance abuse and domestic violence that ends only with the murders of the woman and her sons. Chaym has no knowledge of who committed the crimes, as he was wandering the city in an alcoholic daze the night they occurred; nevertheless, he becomes the prime suspect and ends up confined to a mental institution.

Whether or not he committed the murders, Chaym believes that he did commit a crime before the boys and their mother died by surrendering to the external pressures he had hoped to spare the youngsters. He cannot parent effectively, at least partially because he has neither a role model to draw on nor a belief in the possibility that he can make emotional connections with others because of his double illegitimacy, which is both personal and racial. Chaym and Bishop share this emotional paralysis, though the younger man lacks Chaym's bitterness, a fact reflected largely in Bishop's ability to follow King's teachings. Bishop also hopes to make an enduring emotional connection with Amy Griffith, his co-worker in training Smith for his role as King's double. Amy represents the stable life that Bishop values; furthermore, her family is a living manifestation of the attitudes King champions in his campaign for social justice.

Behind the value of King's teachings, Johnson evokes the image of his family and emphasizes the importance of King's relationship with his father, Martin Luther King Sr., commonly referred to as "Daddy King." Raised in a unified, two-parent household with a father who was simultaneously demanding and supportive, King Jr. has a stable emotional foundation on which to build his dream of the beloved community. As Johnson notes in a chapter devoted to King's thoughts about his own children, he also has learned to be a good father, one who can set aside his work occasionally for his children and who knows that good parenting is part of the challenge his commitment to building community demands of him.[8] The parenting he practices at home becomes something of a model for his actions in the movement, as he nurtures Smith out of a sense of responsibility and provides Bishop with the surrogate father model he needs to deal successfully with the pressures of the turbulent civil rights struggle.

By placing these characters in the context of the civil rights movement, Johnson also shifts the perspective somewhat on the issue of racial identity as it connects to the ideas of manhood and parenting that he presents. Though he still rejects the limiting victimized consciousness of black identity that Smith voices in this novel, the author sees a value in racial awareness that has not been present in his work to date. The accounts of Amy's self-reliant family, as well as the story of the congregation of Calvary African Methodist Episcopal Church in Evanston, demonstrate Johnson's reverence for the model of African Americans who see their racial identity as a point of pride rather than a stigma. Significantly, the members of this congregation were, as Bishop notes, "in their own way, initially outcasts" (125). However, they build community with one another in the face of systematic oppression rather than turning on one another, as Smith asserts in his "lions and lunch" analogy. Their blackness becomes not a license to harm one another but an indication of their collective experience and their commitment to improving their individual and communal lots.

Their attitude reflects a positive racial consciousness one does not find elsewhere in Johnson's work. His modification of his position marks the literary manifestation of his own personal explorations. For instance, the account of Calvary A.M.E. Church and particularly the story of Robert Jackson, the contractor who rejects the idea of racial limitations and establishes himself in business in Evanston, mirrors Johnson's story of his great-uncle, William Johnson, who lived the life attributed in the novel to Bob Jackson. Even more important than his financial success, though, is Will Johnson's example for his great-nephew and his peers: "despite the lack of opportunities in the first half of this century, our elders in the pre–civil rights era raised strong, resourceful sons and daughters; their intention—their personal sacrifices and life-long labor—was to prepare their offspring for the chances they themselves were denied. Black men today can do no less" ("Second Front," 183). With this call, Johnson articulates an enlightened understanding of black identity that emphasizes change while still affirming racial heritage.

Although this might appear at first glance to be a radical shift in Johnson's beliefs, I contend that it is consistent with his aesthetic principles. In his earlier works, he shows characters who transcend a dualistic mindset by rejecting negative, limiting perceptions of their racial identities. Often these characters speak of their racial identity with fierce pride; in *Oxherding Tale,* George Hawkins loudly proclaims the superiority of African and African-American culture to Andrew. His conviction arises, however, in response to his fall from grace at Cripplegate. Prior to his demotion, the text tells us, he was a firm adherent to his master's views. At bottom, his militant, pro-black views are more defense mechanism than true belief. What Andrew must learn in response to his father's lessons, to borrow a phrase from bell hooks, is "to see darkness differently" (113). This action places him in the minority of black characters in the text rather than in the majority. In *Dreamer,* Johnson offers another perspective on this issue by providing the image of a generation of African Americans in Evanston with an indomitable group image. The presence of this core community with this established view of blackness in the text allows Johnson to pursue another path towards his ultimate goal of "whole sight." He illustrates the rich and varied interpretations of racial identity to support his claim that discussing experiences of blackness is more fruitful than holding fast to a unified conception of a single "black experience."

One sees the shift in Johnson's approach to these issues clearly as he recasts the cartoonist anecdote from his own childhood, which he presents in what he calls the "most complete" version in "The Second Front." Initially an indicator of his father's rigidity and adherence to the racialized worldview that characterizes most of Johnson's narrators, the story in its most recent form reinforces the modified vision of race and fatherhood appearing in *Dreamer*. As Johnson's understanding of the relationship between race and fatherhood has changed and as he has prepared for the new vision he presents in *Dreamer*, the story of that discussion has also evolved. Recounting the familiar events, the author extends his description of his father's reaction, "They don't let black people do that," and shifts the emphasis of his commentary somewhat. Following the account of his father's first comment, Johnson says, "he rethought his position and admitted his error when I brought him examples to the contrary, and he then paid for my lessons (via mail) with New York comic artist Lawrence Lariar, financially backing me up on something he barely understood—this, I came to see, is the very definition of love: helping others because you believe in them, regardless of whether their dreams outstrip your own understanding" ("Second Front" 179). With this recognition of his father's ability to change and his willingness to accept a broader definition of racial possibility than he held previously, Johnson reinforces his more grounded resolution to the conflicts plaguing his characters and the extratextual African-American community in present-day America. He further emphasizes that hope by linking the example of love his father represents to Dr. King's teachings, showing how each man provides strength and resources to face the dilemmas presented by the racialized worldview of contemporary American society.

In many ways, King's model of the beloved community resonates with the sense of interconnectedness Andrew experiences as he gazes at Bannon's tattoos. However, Johnson's choice of King and his struggle as an alternative means of exploring his ideas does make the issues more pressing and less abstract. King's language of the beloved community is a human ideal, certainly; however, it resonates with more possibility than a tattooed slave catcher might for some readers. With his presentation of the plight of many African-American males in the picture of the fatherless seekers and his suggestion of a concrete, historically tested solution to their difficulties, Johnson seems in some ways to have moved from the philosophical speculation of his earlier novels to a more direct suggestion of a pertinent response to present circumstance. Significantly, many of King's ideas are present in the earlier works. This is perhaps not surprising, as King read widely in texts of the Eastern philosophies that Johnson draws on in his fiction. What is quite striking, however, are the variations in approach to these ideas.

As Johnson notes in a discussion of his early work, one of the key features of the Allmuseri is that they "live lives of perfect peace, nonviolence, creativity, and *ahimsa* ('harmlessness to all sentient beings')" (Nash 57). The concept of *ahimsa* in particular is central to King's philosophy; like the wizards before him, he seeks to ameliorate and to transform people's perceptions. The difference, which is in my opinion very important, is that his program is applied, whereas the wizards' is much more amorphous. With this shift in his presentation of key concepts, Johnson makes his message more concrete and casts it in terms that affirm the idea of blackness even as they call for a revision of understandings of what that term signifies.

Johnson also continues his effort at revising conceptions of African-American literary identity in *Dreamer*. One important example appears in the detail of Smith's home in Chicago and his reaction to being locked out of it. Smith lives in a small room at 3721 Indiana Avenue, the same address of the squalid flat Bigger Thomas and his family occupy in Richard Wright's classic work of black naturalism, *Native Son* (1940). Wright's novel is an important book for Johnson, because in his opinion it presented the reading public for the first time with a fully articulated black life-world; forced to see all events from Bigger's perspective, the reader must understand the world in a new way. This, in Johnson's view, is the change in perceptions that all great fiction should create.

He also argues that *Native Son* teaches in a sense, as it clearly and powerfully illustrates the ways in which the mind manages and creates experience. Bigger's worldview, his fear and hatred of whites, and his sense of alienation and victimization drive everything he does, from fighting with his southside Chicago cronies to reacting to the white communist, Jan, who tries to treat him as an equal, with preconditioned responses of fear and shame. His confusion and resentment push him to the brink of hysteria and lead him to commit murder. In many ways his preconceptions are what drive him, just as preconceptions about him drive the mobs that attack him and call for his death. In making this point about how received opinions circumscribe and even determine experience, Johnson says, Wright creates "a phenomenological description of black urban life" (*Being and Race* 13) and moves a step closer towards the new philosophical fiction he envisions.

Though he recognizes that step, Johnson ultimately concludes that Wright failed to imagine the ultimate vision that the black life-world might possibly present. Bigger's experiences, while affording the reader some phenomenological access to black urban life, are also propelled by an extremely rigid and strictly limited view of black being. As in any naturalistic novel, the protagonist is at the mercy of deterministic forces. In Wright's case, those forces are the established understandings of racial identity that shape and confine Bigger's world and that lead him ultimately to his actions and his end.

For Johnson, this end is neither desirable nor inescapable. Grounded as he is in a philosophy of experience and a belief in the multiplicity of possibilities for identity formation, he cannot accept a naturalistic model of blackness. Wright's portrayal of Bigger's being may be accurate, but it unfortunately clashes with Johsnon's view of identity. He takes this issue up in *Dreamer,* housing the character who initially seems most bound to a deterministic model of blackness in the Thomases' tenement apartment. On the eve of his departure to begin transforming himself into King and outraged over being locked out, Smith sets a fire in the building that eventually destroys the entire structure. The significance of this image is unmistakable; as the double moves toward his encounter with a flexible model of perception that denies fixedness and rejects the idea of racial victimization, he destroys the symbol of that oppression. Similarly, on a literary level, Johnson denies Wright's influence with this action, casting off a model of racialized identity historically prominent in African-American fiction that will not suit his aesthetic needs and purposes. He evokes his literary heritage but then uses it to make a transformative point about his craft and the tradition to which it belongs.

Johnson extends the challenge to established models of African-American creativity as the narrator Matthew Bishop confronts separatists and black militants who advocate Black Power and Black Artistry and who reject his synthetic philosophical vision as suspect. This particular challenge resonates with Johnson's own experience.[9] Initially compelled by and ultimately resistant to the ideology of black cultural nationalism, the rejection of white influences on African-American cultural production that arose in the late 1960s and early 1970s as the aesthetic arm of the Black Power movement, Johnson developed a form of black literature that took him far from the established territory of many of his peers who gained fame during this era. By evaluating previous models of African-American expression and choosing his own way of incorporating them into his writing, Johnson followed the example of one of his most important influences, Ralph Ellison, rather than falling prey to the trap of essentialism that befell so many of his peers. He does not merely mimic Ellison, however; like the son figures in his fiction, Johnson takes what his forebears have accomplished and makes it new by doing it his own way. Of the author of *Invisible Man* Johnson says, "Ellison gets the point wrong, or backward: it is not reality or the world that is formless and fluid but human perception" (*Being and Race* 16).

Through his contact with King Bishop has a similar experience, as he sees the value of integrating multiple traditions and sources, something the minister himself did, as Johnson pointedly illustrates in his discussion of King's sermon sources: "In his sermons he was, in essence, not one man but an integrated Crowd, containing here a smidgen of Walter Rauschenbusch, there a bit of Gerald Kennedy, and everywhere the imposing influence of his father" (104). Bishop also learns that there must be moral ends attached to the creative means, a lesson that resonates with ideas Johnson learned from his mentor, John Gardner. Integrating traditions is not an end unto itself, after all. A living illustration of this idea, Smith himself is a combination of a variety of sources and influences, a range of experiences that have shaped him throughout his quest and that offer him multiple resources for expressing his bitterness. What he lacks, however, and what Johnson implicitly identifies as the great need of all creators, is an ability to take what has come before him and break it out of established uses. King blends others' thoughts into something new that serves his larger purpose, as Johnson blends an array of sources in service of his larger aesthetic project of "whole sight." When Chaym Smith can learn to see the larger framework that can hold these experiences, as he does after long exposure to King's ideas, he can become truly creative in a new and meaningful way.

When Smith achieves that creative enlightenment, he stands in a similar position to Andrew as he gazes on his father's face at the end of *Oxherding Tale*. Having been parented by one who understands the danger of limitations and who offers his surrogate sons the means of freeing themselves from their mental bonds, Smith can surpass the parameters of racial identity as he has understood them to date. The same is true for Andrew, Rutherford, and Matthew as they chronicle their transformations in the narratives they create; their process of writing takes them far beyond the boundaries that their fathers have known to a creative world where their being is effectively limitless. What Johnson shows for them is also what he sees for himself and other writers engaged in the process of expanding conceptions of what African-American literature, and specifically literature by black males, is and can be. Just as Andrew becomes his father's father as he understands the interconnectedness of all things, Johnson sees himself in relation to the African-American literary tradition he simultaneously belongs to and re-imagines. The process of seeking fathers and challenging the models that appear to fill that need mirrors the author's quest to make a space for himself. As he shows his characters articulating their new identities against the background of their heritage and simultaneously honoring and transcending that heritage, he evokes the image of his personal and professional development and reminds his reader what possibilities exist for black manhood and black literary expression.

Notes

1. Johnson's use of the father/son model as a means of exploring black male identity places him in the middle of an ongoing, conflicted, interdisciplinary discussion. In the past two decades, black manhood and black fatherhood have been the subjects of numerous essays and books that span a range of perspectives from sociological to theological, from literary to historical. In that range one finds a deluge of answers to the central question: what does it mean to be a black man and a black father in America? The sociologist Robert Staples examines the living conditions for slaves that combined to break down the patriarchal nature of many of the West African cultures from which the slaves came; the sociologist John McAdoo demonstrates that black fathers respond to their children in ways that parallel white fathers' interactions with their offspring; and the sociologist Clyde W. Franklin expounds on the various constructions of black masculinity that black studies programs need to address as they lay the foundation for further meaningful exploration of the identity formation process. The richness and difference in the understandings these studies offer emphasize the multiplicity that is so central to Johnson's work and affirm his sense of black manhood and fatherhood as multifaceted.

2. James W. Coleman addresses a similar point in "Charles Johnson's Quest for Black Freedom in *Oxherding Tale.*"

3. Johnson's interest in phenomenology dates to his graduate training in philosophy at Southern Illinois University and the State University of New York at Stony Brook; his practice of Buddhism dates to his involvement with the martial arts, which began in 1967. As numerous authors have treated his dedication to phenomenological method, I will not repeat that discussion here. For a detailed explanation of Johnson's version of phenomenology, see Johnson, *Being and Race: Black Writing since 1970,* and Little, *Charles Johnson's Spiritual Imagination.* For a thorough assessment of the Allmuseri as a vehicle for his phenomenological ideas, see Rushdy, "The Phenomenology of the Allmuseri: Charles Johnson and the Subject of the Narrative of Slavery."

4. The story also resonates with Johnson's experiences as an artist in another important way: it reflects something of his process of development as he grew through his relationship with John Gardner, his "first (and only) writing mentor" (Johnson, "John Gardner" 619). An aesthetic father of sorts for Johnson, Gardner resisted his young protégé's interests in Buddhism and encouraged him to write another book like *Faith and the Good Thing,* one that fused his philosophical interests with the diction and structure of the African-American folktale. Seeing that advice as limiting and consumed with the desire to write "a neo–slave narrative that explored fun-

damental questions about the (black) self, and deployed Eastern philosophy in the process," Johnson took a new direction for his fiction (623). The story of the apprentice's slow recognition that he need not copy his master's every move and his ultimate understanding of how his version of the craft can rectify the wounds of racialized being that limit black literature as their fictional counterparts limit Richard Jackson's experiences casts light on the author's motivations and his accomplishments as he creates.

5. For a discussion of the Allmuseri, see Rushdy. The article also discusses some healing elements of Richard and Allan Jackson's relationship.

In *Faith and the Good Thing*, Faith Cross's surrogate parent is the Swamp Woman, the local "werewitch" who teaches the heroine to conjure and thereby affirms an empowered version of the folkloric worldview of her father, Big Todd Cross. With the ability to conjure, Faith can turn what was Big Todd's escape fantasy into an effective, useful mode of being that frees her from "the history of the race" that destroys all the African-American men in the novel (195). This first exploration of parenting takes a more conventional approach to the questions of race and community and individual identity formation. The werewitch and the protagonist share a relationship much more similar to a typical mother-daughter bond, which is often the more common venue for the sorts of lessons Johnson's protagonists learn about race, identity, and community. Furthermore, as the works of Charles Chesnutt suggest, the conjure woman is a much more traditional figure in African-American literature than the African wizards.

Although Johnson does not create the Allmuseri until after completing *Faith and the Good Thing*, he is clearly experimenting with the idea for the tribe even in his first novel. The Swamp Woman belongs to a tribe from Nubia, according to the biography local residents have created for her. However, with her magic abilities, her apparent immortality (which symbolizes an early version of the Allmuseri's transcendence of time), and, most importantly, her recognition of the unity of all things that grounds the Buddhist-influenced way of being in the world that she shares with the tribe, the Swamp Woman could reasonably be described as a sort of proto-Allmuseri.

6. Johnson's use of the *Amistad* case as a specific reference point for events in the novel demonstrates the aesthetic applications of the Allmuseri's worldview for the reader. By taking up the actual historical record and revising it in his fictional presentation of similar events, Johnson challenges our preconceptions about reality and in a sense unbinds the history so that we can experience it in terms free from the limitations that the "facts" impose on our sensibilities.

7. The image of Bannon's tattoos recording his experiences evokes the image of Queequeg from Melville's *Moby-Dick*. Melville is an important literary predecessor for Johnson; the two share an interest in issues of perception and an awareness of Eastern religious thought, and Johnson evokes Melville in virtually every one of his works. In this instance, where he takes Melville's idea and reworks it, turning the idea of Ishmael's savior around and incorporating the Soulcatcher's destructive

impulses, Johnson demonstrates his technique of both invoking his literary fathers and finding his own way, the creative equivalent of the process the son characters engage in throughout each work.

8. Johnson does not treat King's relationship with his father in detail; however, the facts of their connection are pertinent to this discussion. David J. Garrow emphasizes the bond between the two ministers, explaining how the father pushed his son to serve with him at Ebenezer Baptist Church in Atlanta but then accepted his decisions to emphasize his civil rights work over his ministerial duties. Apparently, King was better equipped to resist his father's pressures than his brother, A. D., whose relationship with Daddy King was quite conflicted. One has the sense, however, that what Johnson shows of the two M. L. Kings' relationship is somewhat idealized.

9. In 1968, Johnson had an experience at Southern Illinois University that would shape his career as an artist and define much of his visual arts output. Going to a campus lecture by the dramatist and poet Amiri Baraka, Johnson was fully exposed to the ideas of the Black Arts movement and "the ideology of 'blackness'" that characterized it. Flanked by imposing security guards, refusing to take questions from white audience members, and motivated by a passion for the aesthetic revolutionary doctrine he sought to convey, Baraka urged those with creative talent to "take [their] talent back to the black community" (Boccia 614).

Johnson raises the specter of this experience in *Dreamer* when Matthew and Amy attend a lecture by the activist Yahya Zubena at the Black People's Liberation Library. A black-only event, the lecture quickly descends into the kind of nationalist diatribe that Johnson typically associates with the Black Power movement and the ideas of the Black Aesthetic. When Yahya learns that Amy and Matthew have worked with King, he refers to them as "'Uncle Tom nigguhs'" and shouts them down so that he can address the "'real black people in the room'" (173). In this encounter, Johnson redraws the boundaries of a powerful personal experience and demonstrates the danger behind this flawed message. The encounter with Baraka was important to his artistic development and led him to complete *Black Humor* (1970), the first of his two books of comic art that he published in the 1970s. At that point in his growth, the mentor figure was important to him; as he writes *Dreamer*, he revises the significance of the experience and celebrates Matthew's and Amy's recognition of the need to evaluate this possible role model more carefully and to make their own decisions about what to do with what they learn.

Works Cited

Boccia, Michael. "An Interview with Charles Johnson." *African American Review* 30.4 (1996): 611–19.

Coleman, James W. "Charles Johnson's Quest for Black Freedom in *Oxherding Tale*." *African American Review* 29.4 (1995): 631–44.

Franklin, Clyde W., II. "'Ain't I a Man?': The Efficacy of Black Masculinities for Men's Studies in the 1990s." In *The American Black Male: His Present Status and*

His Future. Ed. Richard G. Majors and Jacob U. Gordon. Chicago: Nelson-Hall, 1994. 271–84.

Garrow, David J. *Bearing the Cross: Martin Luther King, Jr., and the Southern Christian Leadership Conference.* New York: William Morrow and Co., 1986.

hooks, bell. "An Aesthetic of Blackness: Strange and Oppositional." In *Yearning: Race, Gender, and Cultural Politics.* Boston: South End Press, 1990. 103–13.

Johnson, Charles. *Being and Race: Black Writing since 1970.* Bloomington: Indiana University Press, 1988.

———. *Dreamer.* New York: Scribner's, 1998.

———. *Faith and the Good Thing.* New York: Viking, 1974.

———. "John Gardner as Mentor." *African American Review* 30.4 (1996): 619–24.

———. *Middle Passage.* New York: Atheneum, 1990.

———. *Oxherding Tale.* New York: Grove Press, 1982.

———. "The Philosopher and the American Novel." In *In Search of a Voice.* Ed. Charles Johnson and Ron Chernow. Washington, D.C.: Library of Congress, 1991. 1–8.

———. "The Second Front: A Reflection on Milk Bottles, Male Elders, the Enemy Within, Bar Mitzvahs, and Martin Luther King, Jr." In *Black Men Speaking.* Ed. Charles Johnson and John McCluskey Jr. Bloomington: Indiana University Press, 1997. 177–88.

———. "The Sorcerer's Apprentice." In *The Sorcerer's Apprentice: Tales and Conjurations.* New York: Atheneum, 1986. 149–69.

———. "Where Fiction and Philosophy Meet." *American Visions* 3 (June 1988): 36, 47–48.

———. "Whole Sight: Notes on New Black Fiction." *Callaloo* 7.22 (1984): 1–6.

Johnson, Charles, and John McCluskey Jr., eds. *Black Men Speaking.* Bloomington: Indiana University Press, 1997.

Little, Jonathan. *Charles Johnson's Spiritual Imagination.* Columbia: University of Missouri Press, 1997.

McAdoo, John L. "Black Father and Child Interactions." In *Black Men.* Ed. Lawrence E. Gary. Beverly Hills, Calif.: Sage, 1981. 115–30.

Nash, William R. "A Conversation with Charles Johnson." *New England Review* 19.2 (1998): 49–61.

Neal, Larry. "The Black Arts Movement." In *Cavalcade: Negro American Writing from 1760 to the Present.* Ed. Arthur P. Davis and J. Saunders Redding. Boston: Houghton Mifflin, 1971. 797–810.

Rushdy, Ashraf H. A. "The Phenomenology of the Allmuseri: Charles Johnson and the Subject of the Narrative of Slavery." *African American Review* 26.3 (1992): 373–94.

Staples, Robert. "The Myth of the Black Matriarchy." In *The Black Male in America.* Ed. Doris Y. Wilkinson and Ronald L. Taylor. Chicago: Nelson-Hall, 1977. 174–87.

———. "The Myth of the Impotent Black Male." In *The Black Male in America*. Ed. Doris Y. Wilkinson and Ronald L. Taylor. Chicago: Nelson-Hall, 1977. 133–44.

Wade-Gayles, Gloria, ed. *Father Songs: Testimonies by African-American Sons and Daughters*. Boston: Beacon Press, 1997.

Wideman, John Edgar. *Fatheralong: A Meditation on Fathers and Sons, Race and Society*. New York: Pantheon Books, 1994.

Willis, Andre C., ed. *Faith of Our Fathers: African-American Men Reflect on Fatherhood*. New York: Penguin, 1997.

7

Prodigal Agency:
Allegory and Voice in Ernest J. Gaines's
A Lesson before Dying

HERMAN BEAVERS

It's because she wants it told.
—Quentin Compson, *Absalom, Absalom!*

The son was separated from the father on the auction block
and they have been looking for each other ever since.
—Ernest J. Gaines

For you were the Father who gave him riches. You loved him
when he set out and you loved him still more when he came
home without a penny.
—Augustine, *Confessions*, book 1

Ernest J. Gaines's sixth novel, *A Lesson before Dying*, is rightly described as a coming-of-age novel chronicling the journey
of its narrator, Grant Wiggins, from disillusionment to purpose. But such an assessment is of limited utility if we are to
discern fully the task Gaines has set for himself, which is nothing short of ruminating upon the black community's political shortcomings. Gaines postulates that only a politicized
community can successfully resist hostile acts of misrepresen-
tation. Thus, even as Grant's main task is to usher Jefferson,
a young black man sentenced to die for a murder he did not
commit, into manhood by teaching him how to die with dignity, we discover that "manhood" involves a politics of self-
definition that the community either fails to reinforce or en-

acts by the adoption of public idols who undermine the process. Ultimately, Gaines asserts, the quest in this novel is not personal but communal in nature. While individual acts of resistance are important in Gaines's fictions, such initiatives take on broader meaning in the context of the collective because they acquire symbolic importance in future struggles. In organizing *A Lesson before Dying*, Gaines utilizes Christ's parable of the prodigal son to press home this main point and thus reveals that his purpose is to create a fiction whose energies are more allegorical than realist.

Certainly, it takes some conceptual wrangling to reach such a conclusion. When we think of the parable of the prodigal son, what most often comes to mind is a story concerning the fall from grace into sin, prompting a fall from affluence into poverty, the prodigal son's reluctant return, the father's joyous restoration of his son to affluence, the proverbial slate wiped clean. But at the heart of this best known of parables lie issues of memory and conflict. The prodigal son forgets his upbringing to embrace a life of debauchery and sin. What rescues him from a life among the hogs is his recollection of his father's abundance. In the case of the father, he forgets the son's sins to welcome him home. And in the case of the elder brother, he remembers all the things he has done to demonstrate his piety, even as he forgets that obedience to the Father is a matter of faith, not works.

The parable of the prodigal son serves an important function in *Lesson* because Gaines's intent is to disrupt neat categories and thus trouble narrative closure. However, since we associate the parable with the journey or quest narrative and thus privilege the point of view of the prodigal, a number of features are in need of discussion. First, the substance of the parable regarding the prodigal's wanderings has been transformed into a spiritual pilgrimage. For what gives persuasive weight to the prodigal's tale is that he has lived to tell his story and has overcome great obstacles to do so. In spite of the parable's ending, where the prodigal son is clothed, fed, and celebrated, at a subtextual level the prodigal son continues to be marked, bearing traces of his past affliction.

Though the parable seems to insist through the prodigal son's restoration that all is as it should be, his transgression is remembered by the elder brother, which means the parable does not fail to register the discontinuity intrinsic to the prodigal's return. This is an essential element of the parable, because the lessons of redemption are not always self-evident. Hence, the parable demonstrates a tension that lends itself to literary discourse. As Geoffrey S. Proehl points out, the parable begins to appear in literary texts as early as Augustine's *Confessions,* where he employs it "as a metaphor for his own spiritual journey." Moreover, the parable of the prodigal son "emerges in an autobiographical context within a reflective, confessional mode" (46). Proehl observes further:

> As a whole, the parable provides a simple structure with which to organize the narrative of a specific life, especially from the perspective of a certain end point: after having passed through a period of crisis, after coming home. At the same time, connecting the narrative structure of the parable with a specific life story ... naturalizes and validates that pattern, makes it seem less like the prefabricated structure that it is and more like a living organism.... Of note here is the ability of the story to inspire and absorb imaginative additions, especially in the scenes of riotous living. (48)

Gaines's use of this parable situates our reading of the text in familiar territory even as it posits a new way to think about how *communitas* and manhood bear an integral relation. To accomplish this, Gaines opts to tell the story from a different point of view, not from that of the prodigal but from that of the elder, "good" son.

As I will argue, Gaines's novel harnesses memory and voicelessness in order to insist upon the community's role in developing political agency in a troubled body politic. This would begin to explain why Gaines chooses not to organize *Lesson's* plot around proving Jefferson's innocence. Rather, he organizes the story around Grant's efforts, the college-educated young black man teaching in the plantation school of his childhood. Like the elder son, a model of obedience and steadfast service to his father, Grant is the necessary choice to narrate events in *Lesson* because he is situated to consider life in the Quarters within the context of change and stasis. As a schoolteacher, he can see where the past, present, and future converge because the school represents temporality; those who enter are either impervious to change, indifferent to it, or, in Grant's case, desirous of it. Grant's dissatisfaction with life in the Quarters means he is not prone to romanticize the plantation. Having experienced life in the world beyond the Pichot plantation, he is both insider and outsider. Grant represents, literally and conceptually, the proverbial crossroads: a product of the plantation, his education has rendered him politically inert. Though his role as teacher is, in part, to initiate his students' journey to literacy, he has few tools to accomplish this, save his own realization that voicelessness means someone else can be appointed to tell your story.[1] What he does not know at the beginning of the novel, however, is that the success or failure of an act of narration relies on the self-awareness of the narrator; telling someone else's story is likewise an instance of recognizing your own story.

◻ ◻ ◻

The parable of the prodigal son, as a story "of the death and resurrection of the self," is, as Jill Robbins asserts, "the story of a conversion" (317). In this regard, *Lesson* can be located alongside two of Gaines's previous novels, *In My Father's House* (1978) and *A Gathering of Old Men* (1983), in a trilogy of works that have the issue of conversion at their heart. In the case of Jefferson, Gaines is less interested in redeeming him spiritually than he is in depicting his redemption from the social death visited upon Jefferson by white supremacy's ability to denigrate black bodies, consigning them to a category beneath humanity. This is a compelling story, to be sure, but by rendering it through Grant's perspective, Gaines suggests that redemption is a process that is neither solitary nor closed. Even as we see Grant slowly beginning to accept his role as Jefferson's mentor and role model, we need to understand that what gives their relation its poignancy is its irreconcilability; he can do nothing to save Jefferson's life. If Jefferson achieves manhood, there will be no tangible evidence.

Gaines does not wish the reader to understand Grant through the aegis of myth; hence *Lesson* cannot be read as a novel of reconciliation (May 54). His use of the parable of the prodigal is meant to articulate the difficulty that arises out of incompatibility. Hence, Gaines ruptures the illusory nature of Grant and Jefferson's "reconciliation" to create a novel that partakes of what John May describes as the twofold function of parable: "The surface function of parable is to create contradiction within a given situation of complacent security but, even more unnervingly, to challenge the fundamental principle of reconciliation" (54). The real enemy, though it is never articulated as such, is white supremacy. Jefferson's transformation occurs even as it leaves the basic workings of white supremacy untouched, in spite of it. The parable of the prodigal son gives us the elder brother because it needs to register disruption in the conventions that underwrite notions of the elect.

Grant's narration, unlike that of *In My Father's House* and *A Gathering of Old Men* (which are told in the third-person and through shifting points of view, respectively), suggests that even as he discovers that Jefferson has died with dignity, he also realizes that his real work—confronting white supremacy—is yet to begin. Gaines underscores this by setting the novel in 1948 rather than in the present. While this temporal discontinuity might suggest that a sufficient amount of time has elapsed to allow the reader to look back with satisfaction at the civil rights movement's successful transformation of the South from a region where black men could not get a fair trial or participate in electoral politics to a place where blacks exercise power within the body politic, I want to argue that Gaines's novel takes into account the community's fall into a circumscribed politics whereby icons and images cease to fuel resistance and come to be interpreted as acts of resistance in and of themselves.

Thus we need to understand *Lesson* as an allegorical novel, not because it follows the parable of the prodigal son "to the letter" but rather because it insists that we leave its pages with a sense that what appeared to be the resolution of a simple binary is, in fact, a mystery of immense proportions. The tears that Grant sheds at the novel's conclusion simultaneously mark the magnitude of communal failure and the fact that he remains unreconciled to his real task: confronting white supremacy unabashedly. Because a parable "discloses a society's fears, its abject humility in the face of failure and mystery" (May 54), *Lesson* critiques communal behavior, juxtaposing it with what we know is the contemporary black community's failure: in spite of its urbanity and sophistication, it fails to alter the paths of young black men.

Lesson's complexity can be linked to allegory's function in the body politic and its investment in regenerative acts of interpretation, the recycling of antiquated texts, finding new uses for them. The parable of the prodigal son allows us to understand the forces acting upon both fathers and sons, but the novel's opening scene points to an issue often associated with powerlessness: shame. As both the parable and Jefferson's trial portray it, shame is a powerful inducement, if only because it centers itself on the relation between existence and self-worth. Gaines's decision to set the novel in 1940s Louisiana means that he has chosen a time period when Jim Crow laws are in full swing and there is little in the way of political resistance. The trial calls into question the community's ability to project itself into the future, to see itself as a political entity beyond its present existence. Using the parable of the prodigal son allows Gaines to fashion a novel whose characters are trying to repudiate the poetics (and thus the politics) of bewilderment and disenfranchisement. However, because they have grown so accustomed to scarcity and lack, they do not possess the means to sustain resistance in the face of white hostility. Likewise, they fail to recognize that their negative response to the verdict, while foreclosed in the legal and political realms, can be manifest through strategies that fuse the symbolic and physical worlds.

Because the parable posits shame and depleted resources as the starting points of redemption, Jefferson's trial represents the site from which the community's transformation will commence. To rejuvenate their community, however, they require a means of reconstituting the "heroic." The problem is that they are bewildered as to the proper way to proceed. In keeping with his other works of fiction, Gaines's novel once again depicts "black men who face the problem of being denied the dignity and self-worth found in the status of 'manhood'" (Augur 75). Though Grant's plight is radically different in origin, we would do well nonetheless to think of Faulkner's Quentin Compson as a figure of companionable weight. When we compare Grant Wiggins and Quentin Compson, we find that both come to us as struggling prodigals. Like Quentin, Grant is recruited for a difficult task that involves an act of narration. Unlike Quentin, however, who slowly comes to understand why Miss Rosa calls him to her hot, windowless office, Grant does not discern the larger design inherent in Miss Emma's request; he sees it as an imposition, not as a circumstance of conversion. But Quentin's realization that Miss Rosa's main reason for recruiting him is "because she wants it [patriarch Thomas Sutpen's story] told" (5) is useful for our purposes here because their interplay points to Faulkner's desire to problematize that which stands as the historical by positing not one story of the Fall but three, all of which work to complicate narrative truth. Gaines's use of the parable is, in the way of parables, a disruptive act because it is neither neat nor certain; it asserts that the path to redemption is mysterious, unknowable. Because the parable of the prodigal son disrupts the link between obedience and redemption, we are forced to reimagine the routes leading to such a state.

But thinking about Miss Rosa brings us to the question of what Miss Emma wants. What does she expect from Grant Wiggins when she insists, "I don't want them to kill no hog . . . I want a man to go to that chair, on his own two feet" (13)? Does she merely wish for Jefferson's story to be told, and will such an act provide the Quarters' residents on the Pichot plantation with what they need to sustain themselves in the face of Jim Crow laws? These questions lie at the heart of *A Lesson before Dying* and suggest that there are issues of reading and audience that warrant attention. Though she is present for the trial, Miss Emma is aware that, save for the defense attorney's cursory mention of her importance to Jefferson, she is invisible. But rather than contesting the fact that the trial has been a travesty or that Jefferson is sentenced to die for a crime he did not commit, the most devastating issue for Miss Emma is the implication that Jefferson is not fit to be

considered a man. In Miss Emma's view Jefferson's situation reflects negatively on both her and the Quarters. Unlike *Absalom, Absalom!* which is
concerned with breaking a silence of long standing and then contending with
the din that results, *A Lesson before Dying* is a novel concerned with the
community's search for an adequate witness, with the importance of insti-
tuting a poetics that can shape collective acts of testimony to counter the
narratives produced by white supremacy. And where Faulkner's novel has
at its core the notion that such a search is fraught with danger (hence, Quentin's demise), Gaines's novel explores the redemptive power of testimony.
Thus, *Lesson* is deeply concerned with acts of witnessing, but it argues that
Jefferson's plight represents a moment when the community must redefine
what constitutes proper forms of testimony.

   This begins to explain why, given her close relationship with Reverend
Ambrose, Miss Emma chooses Grant and not the preacher as the intermediary. Her conclusion needs to be understood in light of Gaines's definition
of manhood as "taking responsibility for the whole, all humanity," something the preacher does as a matter of course but something Grant, in his
self-absorption, cannot manage as the novel begins. Miss Emma (along with
Grant's aunt, Tante Lou) is a vehicle through which Gaines can highlight
and articulate a number of political moves. Though in Gaines's fictional
world she certainly would not characterize her request as the emblem of a
political position whose aim is to disrupt the cultural discourse of white
supremacy, neither can Miss Emma be dismissed as politically inert. For Miss
Emma knows that a politics of expediency exists in the Quarters that places
the safety of the collective over individual needs. However, she also recognizes the fact that Grant's resistance to helping Jefferson issues from the idea
that "manhood" is often synonymous with self-reliance and self-determination. Miss Emma knows she needs to find a way to recast what it means
to be a man, so she fixes her efforts on Grant, using self-deprecation and
an indirection that ultimately rests on her confidence that Grant's respect
for his elders will not allow him to refuse her. "'He don't have to do it'"
(13), claims Miss Emma, even though she means to communicate the urgency of the situation to Grant. Later she says, "'He don't have to go'" (78),
but she does so only because she recognizes that the enterprise will fail if
Grant is indifferent to the task. But this intimates that she knows Grant better
than he knows himself. Moreover, she knows that the community's idea of
manhood is predicated on the idea that individual transgression reflects badly
on the group. Thus, black male failure, often unavoidable and perhaps inevitable, is, for pragmatic reasons, best left to the realm of the unspoken.

As a black man whose job it is to "keep the others from ending up like [Jefferson]" (14), Grant embodies this racial pragmatism, whose normal procedure dispatches Jefferson from collective memory as soon as he runs afoul of the law. This way of thinking means Jefferson is "already dead," and, as such, he becomes a negative aspect of the communal narrative, a fixed point that the narrative will either avoid or diminish in importance.

Grant's claim that Jefferson is "already dead" foregrounds "the heroic" as a narrowly circumscribed set of public deeds. The parable of the prodigal son ends with an instance where the son's return prompts a celebration of a scale meant to communicate the magnitude of the fall from grace. Grant's role is to assume the same posture as the father in the parable—to accept Jefferson as heroic, essential to the community, worthy of celebration, even though he lacks visual evidence. But this is not the case as Grant begins visiting Jefferson in prison. As the "good son" who has followed the instructions of his elders (and to a lesser degree of whites) to the letter, Grant does not understand why it falls to him to usher Jefferson into manhood. He chafes in his election to the status of "role model," and for good reason. He knows that he is as susceptible as any other black man on the plantation to the kinds of mistreatment that Jefferson has suffered. But his education and his wider knowledge of the world provide him options that most men in the Quarters do not have. Hence, he must contend with his desire to be shut of the entire affair, to go about the act of moving ahead without the burden of Jefferson's situation, even as he fulfills his duty to Jefferson. But here Gaines demonstrates the manner in which the black community is a site of conceptual blindness and conspiracy.

This is evinced by the propensity of the Quarters' residents to sublimate their worldview to that of the whites at the apex of the body politic. Thus, even as they might fret about segregation and racism, the impulse to erase Jefferson from speech and memory is nonetheless a gesture that affirms the black community's inferiority. And as Gaines's other fictions have demonstrated (notably "Just Like a Tree" from the short story collection *Bloodline* [1968] and *Of Love and Dust* [1967]), the Quarters' denizens would silence dissent because it potentially endangers the collective. Equally problematical are the strategies the community comes to rely upon as alternative forms of heroic portraiture. The alternative, Gaines suggests, is for the black community to find its heroes in the public sphere, to capitulate to the notion that black masculinity is best exemplified by public spectacle. While there are reasons to view this as positive, Gaines's novel complicates this circumstance.

The best evidence of this comes during the discussion about the baseball legend Jackie Robinson in Claiborne's bar. Listening at the bar, Grant comes to understand that Robinson's success in professional baseball is essential in the same way that Joe Louis's two fights with the German Max Schmeling have bolstered the black community's sense of well-being. In what stands as some of the novel's most beautifully nuanced writing, Gaines depicts the old men literally acting out one of Robinson's athletic performances: "Now the old man became Jackie—not running, but showing the motion of someone running at full speed. His arms were doing what the legs could not do. He showed you the motion of Jackie sliding into the plate, the motion of the umpire calling Jackie safe, and the motion of Jackie brushing off his clothes and going into the dugout. The old man nodded his head emphatically, with great pride, and went back to the bar. Claiborne and the other old man told him that he was exactly right" (87–88). The late 1940s is a historical moment characterized by the shift from folk heroes to heroes drawn from the worlds of sport and cinema. Grant remembers "how depressed everyone was after Joe [Louis] lost the first fight with Schmeling. For weeks it was like that. To be caught laughing for any reason seemed like a sin. This was a period of mourning" (88). Thus, even the preacher in the Quarters says, "'Let us wait. Let us wait, children, David will meet Goliath again'" (88).

The preacher's revision of the biblical text suggests that the community has fallen prey to an idolatry that fixes its gaze on popular culture, as if affirmation awaits them in the pages of magazines or on the screen of a movie house. For while the scene in Claiborne's bar indicates the necessity of having successful role models, its inverse is also operative here: social and emotional investment in athletes like Joe Louis and Jackie Robinson deflects attention away from heroic acts that are not broadcast on the radio, that never become instances of spectacle—acts that fall outside of the form "history" assumes in postwar culture. Though the old man can "become" Jackie Robinson to act out his exploits, to do this implicitly denigrates his own achievements, constructs an inherent difference between acts performed in the public sphere and those that take place outside it. Moreover, it undercuts the necessity of manifesting higher levels of political consciousness or engaging in political action because athletic feats become ends in themselves. Though they assume the form of ritualistic combat, sports ultimately stifle dissent before it can become political resistance; victory becomes the most tangible evidence of the collective's self-worth. Thus, Grant remembers, "For days after that [Louis/Schmeling] fight, for weeks, we held our heads higher than any people on earth had ever done for any reason" (89).

But this memory leads him to remember a lecture at his university, where an Irish scholar lecturing on Irish literature mentions Joyce's "Ivy Day in the Committee Room." What spurs the recollection is the Irishman's claim that the story, though the product of an Irish writer, is an important piece of literature: "Regardless of race, regardless of class, that story was universal, he [the professor] said" (89). When Grant finally gets an opportunity to read the story, he fails to see what the Irishman calls "universal." It is only when he has spent enough time listening to the people with whom he lives that he comes to understand that Joyce's story is about the lasting impact of the Irish political hero, Charles Stewart Parnell. Though Joyce's story takes place long after Parnell has passed, the men in the story wear ivy leaves on their lapels as a show of respect, as a symbolic gesture meant to articulate his continued influence. But it also suggests the manner in which political forms of voice and memory can exist in such a rarefied state that they cease to be useful resources in the political arena. Gaines makes reference to this story, first, because he insinuates the idea of collective memory as a phenomenon that crosses racial and class lines. Second, he suggests that political action's relationship to the past either utilizes martyrdom to cohere into political struggle or it degenerates into nostalgia.

As Grant ruminates, he remembers a dream he had after reading about an execution in Florida. The writer relates the story of how the boy about to be executed screams, "'Please, Joe Louis, help me. Please help me. Help me'" (91). This is an important detail because it demonstrates that sports heroes, no matter how accomplished, most often cannot prevent social injustice—theirs is a limited influence indeed. Gaines forces us to draw the distinction between a martyr and a hero—how does the former become the latter? What is the efficacy of a hero? Who stands as the best representative for the community? And what sorts of criteria ought to be used to reach a conclusion? After Grant and Jefferson become comfortable enough to talk, Grant tells Jefferson:

> Do you know what a hero is, Jefferson? A hero is someone who does something for other people. He does something other men don't and can't do. He is different from other men. He is above other men. No matter who those other men are, the hero, no matter who he is, is above them. . . . I could never be a hero. I teach, but I don't like teaching. I teach because it is the only thing that an educated black man can do in the South today. I don't like it; I hate it. I don't even like living here. I want to run away. I want to live for myself and for my woman and for nobody else. (191)

Grant articulates the hero as a figure of complete selflessness. Moreover, he proposes a model in which teaching is a futile act. Imagining the "elder brother" talking to the prodigal, Gaines takes the opportunity to challenge the idea that upward mobility alone is the signifier of heroic action. While this would seem to be self-evident, the heroic ideal is often visually fixed in public discourse as middle-class, financially comfortable.[2] In creating the conversation between Jefferson and Grant, Gaines suggests that the key to redeeming young men is to intervene upon the politics embedded in notions of conversion. Rather than insisting that he is the means to Jefferson's salvation, Grant reverses this paradigm, transforming Jefferson into the symbol of his and the community's worth and possibility. His argument rests on what Jill Robbins describes as the "economy of salvation," where "[the] negative moment anticipates another moment of grace, rebirth, and conversion" (318). Like Augustine's *Confessions, A Lesson before Dying* is structured by the "economic relationship between a negative and a recuperative moment in the parable of the prodigal son . . . figured by the metaphors of death and rebirth, departure and return, sin and grace, blindness and sight, and aversion and conversion" (318).

Here, it is fitting to discuss the novel's use of two set pieces: the superintendent's visit and the Christmas program. In the former, Grant describes the visit of Dr. Joseph Morgan, a man who insists upon calling him "Higgins" rather than Wiggins. After an inspection of the students, where he calls on students to test their command of grammar, mathematics, and geography, the superintendent gives a ten-minute lecture on hygiene and diet and concludes that Grant's biggest task is to educate his students in the use of the toothbrush. Though Grant points to the paucity of textbooks and supplies as more pressing needs, the superintendent insists that what is needed is "more drill on the flag" and "more emphasis on hygiene" (57). The superintendent's preoccupation with the idea that the education of black children must center on managing their physical appearance and reciting the Pledge of Allegiance recalls Booker T. Washington's *Up From Slavery*, which returns on numerous occasions to the issue of personal hygiene, particularly the use of the toothbrush. But comic though it is, the scene represents the intertextuality between *Lesson* and Bernard Shaw's play *Pygmalion*, intimated by the superintendent's use of "Higgins" throughout his encounter with Grant. Using Shaw's pedantic linguist as a model, Gaines's superintendent is a man who sees the education of black children as a matter of superficial transformation. That he emphasizes hygiene and patriotism indicates that Grant's task is not to help students acquire literacy that could lead them to question their place in the body politic but rather to render them politically compliant. "'You have an excellent crop of students'" (56), the superintendent declares, but his words betray his feeling that Grant's job is to cultivate men and women whose lives are in the cotton and cane fields, not in books, making them mere extensions of the crops they raise. Just as Henry Higgins sought to erase all traces of Eliza Doolittle's working-class origins and to pass her off as a "countess," Grant's job is to expunge all those things that offend white sensibilities and potentially threaten white supremacy. Foremost, he must not inspire his students to challenge or disrupt the long-standing racial hierarchy.

However, the Christmas pageant represents exactly this kind of moment— a way to subvert the superintendent's racist mandate. When the pageant concludes, Grant wonders whether it signifies change in the lives of black people in the Quarters, but there are subtle details suggesting that the seeds of resistance have indeed been sown. When the traditional Christmas songs like "Silent Night" and "Little Town of Bethlehem" are sung, the audience's attention falls on the one gift under the tree, which has been purchased for Jefferson. Though this would seem to be a harmless gesture, what makes it poignant in my view is the manner in which it demonstrates the coalescence of public concerns and performative energies. Though Jefferson's name is never mentioned, the Christmas pageant is a moment when the entire community turns its concern to him. Symbolically, this moment anticipates the manner in which Jefferson's death will serve as the catalyst for political resistance. As the figure to whom all the community's resources are directed, Jefferson, like the Christ-child, becomes the means of communal salvation. Despite the fact that the reigning paradigm is that Jefferson is "already dead" as far as the Quarters is concerned, the Christmas program represents a turning point, not only in the residents' sense of possibility but also in the way that Grant utilizes his role as schoolteacher. Without any overt recognition on his part, he has politicized what heretofore has been markedly apolitical. Though the event does little to alter Grant's outsider status—he sullenly watches and laments, "But I was not with them. I stood alone" (151)—it does provide a way for the community to begin to carve out an identity that emphasizes resistance over acquiescence, for it suggests that even if they cannot stop the inevitable, they can make use of it in new, more productive ways.

It is here that we might turn to the conflict that emerges between Grant and Reverend Ambrose. Reverend Ambrose, as the community's spiritual leader, has not been chosen to prepare Jefferson spiritually for his death.

Hence, he enlists Grant to perform this role, to talk to Jefferson about the afterlife. But both Grant and Jefferson have fallen away from the church. Ambrose hopes that Grant will encourage Jefferson to give voice to his salvation before his execution, but Grant repeatedly refuses to accept this responsibility. When Grant and Ambrose have their final confrontation, it is less than three weeks prior to the execution date. Though Grant voices his doubt about the afterlife, Ambrose asserts that nothing is more important and that without this, Grant cannot know his people.

Herein lies another reason why Gaines's use of the parable of the prodigal son as an organizing strategy is so effective, for the conflict between Grant and Reverend Ambrose has to do with issues of leadership, not spiritual salvation. In Ambrose's view, Grant's role as schoolteacher makes him the community's potential leader. Hence, it should not be lost on the reader that the church in the Quarters doubles as the schoolhouse. Clearly, Gaines is implying that the struggle between minister and schoolteacher evinces itself not only spiritually but spatially as well. As such, the issue is whether black liberation will emphasize the political realities of life in the South or whether it will continue the tradition begun during slavery of relinquishing claim on the physical world of the living to gain control of life in the hereafter. The minister is prepared to cede his claim to leadership if Grant will continue to assume the spiritual tasks of traditional approaches to leadership. But Grant represents nascent political energies that will become, by the 1960s, secular calls for black freedom. Though Grant is happy to leave spirituality to men like Reverend Ambrose, his own doubt about the afterlife makes him unfit to lead in Ambrose's estimation. Moreover, as a "backslider" Grant can only appeal to Jefferson by transforming himself, by shedding his own spiritual apathy. In Ambrose's view, it is men like Grant that produce men like Jefferson; neither literacy nor status can serve as adequate sources of redemption.

For Grant, the problem is that the minister sees the role of spiritual leader as having more to do with applying analgesic solutions to the affliction of white supremacy than attacking the root causes of the malady. Here, Grant becomes the prodigal son and Ambrose the elder brother, which suggests that their dispute centers on issues of transformation. What constitutes a successful redemption? How can the community partake of the benefits? What will be the long-term effects of Jefferson's death? For Ambrose, Jefferson must move to a place where he can embrace what it means to be a martyr, because the minister sees events through the eyes of the elderly members of the congregation whose days are limited. Hence, it is Miss Emma with whom Reverend Ambrose is most concerned. Though the only way Ambrose can access redemption is via the Christ narrative, Gaines's use of the parable suggests that the question of what Jefferson's death means to him need not conform to the community's interpretation. But by having the schoolchildren visit Jefferson in prison, Grant begins to fashion a new form of pedagogy, one that is socially engaged, designed to empower his students as it makes full use of those members of the community who, by conventional standards, are ineligible to contribute.

It is here that we come to understand the value of Jefferson's diary. By including it as part of the novel's narrative structure, Gaines suggests that representation has been at issue throughout the entire text. Though the reader may find Jefferson's writing difficult to navigate because it does not conform to conventions of narrative—that it be chronological, have a formal structure, regulate its mode of address while accounting for its audience, and adhere to standards of grammar and syntax—the novel needs Jefferson's writing in order to move towards closure.

Chapter 29 consists entirely of Jefferson's diary. It begins with Jefferson writing to Grant: "i cant think of too much to say but maybe nex time" (226). What makes the writing in Jefferson's diary so compelling is Gaines's decision to render it in all its imperfection, thereby communicating that all writing represents a tension between convention and content. As a record of Jefferson's last days before his execution, the diary serves as a chronicle of his emotions, thoughts, and memories. But it also provides that moment when, like Augustine in his *Confessions,* Jefferson can step back from his life and view it from the vantage point of an author. This position allows him to reassess his life in the Quarters. When he writes about visits from the schoolchildren in Grant's class or the other adults, he represents the Quarters as a community of people whose histories intertwine with his own.[3]

Jefferson's diary also poses the question of whether acts of representation ought to be directed towards accuracy and precision or flights of imagination. In a novel so devoted to following an allegorical impulse, Jefferson's diary insists, in keeping with the parable of the prodigal son, that we find ways to value Jefferson's writing in spite of its copious grammatical errors. In many ways, the diary is a moment when Jefferson can assess the "riches" at his disposal. Although he feels himself undeserving of them—he does not understand why people come to visit him or why Grant continues to push him to look deeper into himself as he writes—Jefferson's diary, as an act of recording his life and times, serves as a way for the community to preserve for posterity's sake the words of a hero. By including it, Gaines reinforces the importance of those often deemed unworthy of representation: rather than creating an intermediary who will give voice to their concerns, he posits that a more viable course is to engage in acts of call and response that bring their voices to the fore. It also recalls Augustine's *Confessions* when he declares, "O Lord my God, be patient, as you always are, with the men of this world as you watch them and see how strictly they obey the rules of grammar which have been handed down to them, and yet ignore the eternal rules of everlasting salvation which they have received from you" (38–39). Both Augustine's and Jefferson's writings iterate that the systems used to create conventions of literary value ignore the deeper question of spiritual content. Hence, the most important words in Jefferson's diary come when he asserts, "i ain had no bisnes goin ther wit brother an bear cause they aint no good an im gon be meetin them soon" (233). In a sentence that violates the convention of separating disparate ideas, Jefferson asserts the connection between a definition of responsibility and the manner in which human actions do not function in a moral vacuum; he concludes that association can be the evidence of moral failure, but his willingness to own his actions creates the possibility of an afterlife.

▣ ▣ ▣

Though Gaines has consistently denied having an interest in writing protest fiction, *A Lesson before Dying* utilizes allegory to posit political dissent on what is clearly an analogous circumstance in the black community: how will we deal with the increasing numbers of young black men who are either dead or incarcerated and slated to die? This question cannot be contained in a piece of realist fiction because it would mean that Gaines presumes to manifest a reductive sensibility. As a southern novelist, Gaines works from the fact that "the story of the South is the story of a region that discovered that sin has nothing to do with serpents, and self-doubt has little to do with losing Gettysburg. . . . Through allegory, the South ceases to be a place in Macon, Mobile, or Baton Rouge. Being Southern becomes a way of seeing oneself . . . the South is a necessary reminder of the human longing for restitution and the desire for salvation" (Whitt 5–6). As Jan Whitt persuasively argues, "the Southern writer acknowledges the dark side of the human soul and [is] determine[d] to turn and confront the past" (5). In talking about the "heresy of self-reliance" found in the work of O'Connor, McCullers, and Faulkner, Whitt likewise articulates the narrative tension of Gaines's novel. Writing from his regional sensibility, Gaines nonetheless engages in the act of ruminating upon "the most effective metaphor for America" (Whitt 4), the South. Grant's struggle to lead Jefferson to manhood can thus be understood as Gaines's attempt to engage an issue animating the contemporary American body politic. Further, Gaines's aesthetic concerns link him to southern writing from the thirties through the fifties, when "white southern fiction was within the national literature—a powerful, folk-based, past-conscious, often mythic expression of a storytelling culture within a larger literature" (Hobson 93). The only way to manage such a duality is through the aegis of allegory.

But how do we come to recognize allegory—and to what purpose does it work? If allegory is that instance in literary practice where the word "says one thing and means another" (Levin 23), then we need to understand *A Lesson before Dying* as a way for Gaines to explore an important aspect of the conversion narrative: the ramifications of voicelessness, not only in individual terms but in collective ones as well. What the novel posits are a number of sites where symbolism is manifest: the courts, sports, politics, the church, the school, and the village. Because the South is a place where the political nature of speech is always evident, it calls for the reader to reimagine the relationship between the body and southern speech. Gordon Teskey underscores the importance of such thinking when he observes,

> the concept of the body is the ground from which any fundamental thinking about human aggregation (thinking, for example, about human rights) must be derived. To say this is to invert the classical standard, according to which political order derives from abstract principles, to which bodies are supposed to conform. . . . But such abstractions had their beginning, if not in the body, then in more radical principles that do. Two such principles are especially important . . . the *agora*, or political space, where bodies are gathered together, and the *voice*, which issues from the interior of the body into the political space. (124; emphasis added)

As that place where we have so often looked in American history to note the nation's contradictions, the agora, as the South represents it, serves as proof that ours is an afflicted body politic (124). Allegorical writing makes us aware of the politically contested body and the inherent power of that body when it comes to voice (123). "Without voice," Teskey writes, "the body is meat" (123). Teskey's comment takes us to where Gaines's novel begins, with Jefferson being referred to as a hog. What this means, of course, is that Jefferson is completely lacking in the resources necessary to participate in social discourse. But this also points to the reasons why Gaines's novel eschews mythic strategies in favor of allegorical ones. With the advent of romanticism, allegory was denigrated as an instance where the artificial, the arbitrary, and the abstract predominate, making it "uncongenial to modern culture" (Levin 37). But, as Deborah Madsen has noted, allegory flourishes in moments of cultural disorder; hence, the political commentary in which *Lesson* is engaged would be diminished if the novel were to give itself over to realism. The novel's signifying apparatus is reliant upon the parable's irreconcilability; the reader must understand, along with Grant, that the novel's conclusion signals the work left to be done, not that which has already been accomplished.

This calls for us to ponder the significance of the novel's ending. Romanticizing Paul Bonin's (the white deputy sheriff at the prison) and Grant's agreement to be friends is, in my view, a mistake of grand proportions, first, because it denies the danger of such an alliance and second, because it denigrates the African-American drive for self-determination that would blossom in the 1950s. Paul's declaration that he will "witness" for Jefferson in Grant's classroom has to be measured against the scene with the school superintendent Dr. Morgan, which underscores the fact that the black children's "education" is still inferior to that of white children (the remedy for which will be nothing short of Supreme Court intervention). And yet, realism is misplaced because it forecloses upon the possibility embodied in the parable, which says that even the unworthy are capable of voice. Allegory's discursive mode is well suited to serve as a channel for a political discourse because its basic function is to allow "one thing [to be] said [while] another thing is indicated" (Levin 23). In the 1940s, such discursive practices were a matter of expediency; they are now important because they extend the parameters of cultural discourse, protecting language from the pitfalls of entropy. Because the body politic often attempts to mute those voices that threaten its ability to generate myth, Grant's ambivalence at novel's end signifies the space created by the undoing of one form of communal consensus—that black men are incapable of speaking for themselves, are little more than beasts—and the institution of another: that imprisoned black men should catalyze political action. As I have stated elsewhere, Gaines's use of the prison not only highlights a potential space of transformation and redemption, it likewise prefigures the manner in which the jail will become, in the next two decades, a site from which to articulate political resistance.[4] But such a realization on Grant's part, even as Paul asserts his willingness to testify to Jefferson's manliness, brings with it the knowledge that the Quarters must institute a new poetics—and politics—

of selfhood, one that speaks to the inherent value of each of its members, irrespective of station.

But this inevitably leads us back to Faulkner. For what makes the exchange between Grant and Paul so dramatic is that we see the tension between Faulkner's notion of black endurance and Gaines's revision of that ideal. Moving forward from Craig Werner's persuasive arguments regarding Faulkner in "Endurance and Excavation: Afro-American Responses to Faulkner" (in *Playing the Changes*), it could be argued that for Paul, the act of witnessing is meant to suggest that, as the "strongest man in [the] room," Jefferson has endured (*Lesson* 253). The situation takes on a different significance for Grant. Jefferson's value is to the future; thus, Paul's purpose has to be one of challenging white supremacist views of black inadequacy. But this exposes a difficult conundrum: can Paul, as deputy sheriff, perform this task without compromising his relationship to the body politic?

It must be remembered, though, that the Jefferson-Grant-Paul relationship unfolds in a novel written in the 1990s, and it is here that we begin to see the efficacy of Gaines's allegorical posture. Jefferson is surely a signifying gesture on the writings of Gaines's predecessor in southern literature, William Faulkner. Thus, he is ultimately *not* a person; rather, he represents a space in the cultural imagination, a figuration located in the realm of the abstract. In Faulkner's Jefferson County, black men like Joe Christmas, Lucas Beauchamp, or Rider in "Pantaloon in Black" all suggest that *enduring* life in the South is a greater priority than political agitation, even when they fail to survive. Gaines's use of the parable of the prodigal son shifts the terms of the discourse and thereby insists that it matters little how we have arrived at this state of affairs. Redemption is not a matter of the past but rather a new turn on the future. By naming the "hero" of his novel "Jefferson" and placing him in an allegorical tale, Gaines imbues Faulkner's locale of Jefferson with new meaning. Therefore, when Jefferson writes, "i aint done this much thinkin and this much writin in all my life befor" (229), not only does Gaines riff on the quality of silence indicative of Faulkner's black male characters' lives, but we come, like Grant, to understand that this condition is political, not the product of black idiosyncrasy.

Conceptually, Jefferson provides the Quarters with a way to rethink its relationship to the whites who cohabit Gaines's Bayonne. If they are to be redeemed, it will have to happen through the political agency they can manifest in their bodies, a fact that was demonstrated again and again during the sit-ins and marches of the 1950s and 1960s. As a novel that looks back to a nascent civil rights movement as a way to reflect upon the political impotence of the present, Gaines's *A Lesson before Dying* insists that the province between deed and word is a place that requires constant attention. By utilizing the figure of the prodigal son, Gaines suggests that the dilemma facing the body politic is not a lack of heroes but rather the narrow criteria used to define heroic action. The challenge is one of looking beyond the mythic to find heroes in the realm of the everyday, among those who have no choice but to be who they are.

Notes

1. I want to note here that Gaines's fiction has dealt with this theme. In *The Autobiography of Miss Jane Pittman* (1971), the Quarters comes to see Jimmy as "The One" in part because, in writing letters for members of the community, he has the ability to capture their voices on paper—to be more than a mere amanuensis—and thereby serve as an avenue of communication between distant spaces.

2. We might think here of popular publications like *Ebony* and *Essence,* which conjure images of black upward mobility via material success but have failed to serve as catalysts for political resistance. They represent a paradox in that they insist to black readers that self-esteem is borne of tangible or material forms of evidence. Thus, even as both publications ostensibly attempt to "uplift the race" (and in *Essence's* case, black women), they wind up having to buy into consumption as manifestations of black identity. When political dissent does appear in these publications, it is often romanticized, as if to suggest that public visibility and material success are the signifiers of political struggle.

3. The visits, like the moment at the end of *A Gathering of Old Men,* when man, woman, and child each touch the body of Charlie in a ritual meant to preserve his inner qualities, serve not only to affirm Jefferson's value in the lives of the inhabitants of the Pichot plantation but also to initiate a new process, a new way to enact communitas.

4. See my argument regarding "Three Men" in *Wrestling Angels into Song: The Fictions of Ernest J. Gaines and James Alan McPherson,* 27–31.

Works Cited

Auger, Philip. "A Lesson about Manhood: Appropriating 'The Word' in Ernest Gaines's *A Lesson before Dying.*" *Southern Literary Journal* 27 (Spring 1995): 74–85.

Augustine, Saint. *Confessions of Saint Augustine.* Trans. R. S. Pine-Coffin. New York: Penguin Books, 1994.

Beavers, Herman. *Wrestling Angels into Song: The Fictions of Ernest J. Gaines and James Alan McPherson.* Philadelphia: University of Pennsylvania Press, 1995.

Faulkner, William. *Absalom, Absalom!* 1936; rpt., New York: Vintage Books, 1990.

Gaines, Ernest J. *The Autobiography of Miss Jane Pittman.* New York: Bantam Books, 1971.

———. *A Gathering of Old Men.* 1983; rpt., New York: Vintage Books, 1994.

———. "Just Like a Tree." In *Bloodline.* New York: W. W. Norton, 1968. 221–49.

———. *In My Father's House.* 1978; rpt., New York: W. W. Norton, 1992.

———. *A Lesson before Dying.* New York: Vintage Books, 1993.

———. *Of Love and Dust.* New York: W. W. Norton, 1967.

Hobson, Fred. *The Southern Writer in the Postmodern World.* Athens: University of Georgia Press, 1991.

Joyce, James. "Ivy Day in the Committee Room." In *Dubliners.* 1916; rpt., New York: Penguin, 1982. 118–35.

Levin, Samuel. "Allegorical Language." In *Allegory, Myth, and Symbol.* Ed. Morton Bloomfield. Cambridge, Mass.: Harvard University Press, 1981. 23–38.

Madsen, Deborah. *Rereading Allegory: A Narrative Approach to Genre.* New York: St. Martin's Press, 1994.

May, John R. "Myth and Parable in American Fiction." *Thought* 57.224 (March 1982): 51–61.

Proehl, Geoffrey S. *Coming Home Again: American Family Drama and the Figure of the Prodigal.* Cranbury, N.J.: Associated University Presses, 1997.

Robbins, Jill. "Prodigal Son and Elder Brother: The Example of Augustine's *Confessions.*" *Genre* 16.4 (Winter 1983): 317–33.

Shaw, Bernard. *Pygmalion.* 1913; rpt., New York: Penguin Books, 1957.

Teskey, Gordon. *Allegory and Violence.* Ithaca, N.Y.: Cornell University Press, 1995.

Werner, Craig. *Playing the Changes: From Afro-Modernism to the Jazz Impulse.* Urbana: University of Illinois Press, 1994.

Whitt, Jan. *Allegory and the Modern Southern Novel.* Macon, Ga.: Mercer University Press, 1994.

8

Without a Cosmology: The Psychospiritual Condition of African-American Men in Brent Wade's *Company Man* and Melvin Dixon's *Trouble the Water*

MELVIN B. RAHMING

You hearers, seers, imaginers, thinkers, rememberers, you prophets called to communicate truths of the living way to a people fascinated unto death, you called to link memory with forelistening, to join the unaccountable seasons of our flowing to unknown tomorrows even more numerous, communicators doomed to pass on truths of our origins to a people rushing deathward, grown contemptuous in our ignorance of our source, prejudiced against our own survival, how shall your vocation's utterance be heard?
—Ayi Kwei Armah, *Two Thousand Seasons*

When Karla F. C. Holloway declares in *Moorings and Metaphors: Figures of Culture and Gender in Black Women's Literature* (1992) that texts by contemporary black males, unlike those of black women writers, "often isolate the word, circumscribe its territory, and subordinate its voice to expressive behaviors" (7), she is subsuming a gender-based difference of authorial perspective as well as authorial intent. When she further declares that "Black male writers' texts claim the power of creative authorship but do not seem to share the word with the reader, or among the characters, or within

narrative structures of the text," this difference assumes the face of an indictment, for it unmasks these writers' well-guarded and self-serving exclu-
sivity. When, going beyond the more obvious links to cultural constructions
of gender, she attributes this difference to the absence of spiritual history in
the texts of the black male writers—"the depth of spiritual history is absent from [these novels]" (8)—her findings take on an even sterner and more
focused visage, one that appropriately displays a serious concern for the
object of its focus. However, although Holloway takes a brief but penetrating glance at several African and African-American texts to illustrate the
absence of this spiritual history, her concern gathers most of its momentum
and urgency from her extrapolation of spiritual history within the thematic and aesthetic structures of texts written by African and African-American women, whose works she meticulously scrutinizes.

There is still a need, therefore, for this absence of spiritual history in texts
by black men to be ascertained and critiqued against the backdrop of a
spiritual, not merely a literary, tradition. Indeed, in a coherent culture all
traditions must eventually be examined from a spiritual perspective—valued,
that is, for the degree to which they assist the highest manifestation of the
human spirit. What constitutes this "highest manifestation" is, of course,
the crucial question, the answer to which is approached by different cultures
in different ways. Still, my point is that spiritual history as manifested in or
related to an African-American literary product must ultimately be explored
in the context of African-American spiritual history itself, not merely against
the spiritual aspects reflected in literary works. In this connection, it is crucial to remember that African-American spiritual history has been traced
to precolonial Africa, as far back as Kemet (ancient Egypt), for in this tradition "spirit" admits of no gendered dichotomy; rather, orientations to
gender have to be governed by the exigencies of spirit.[1]

Holloway's indictment raises complex questions concerning spirituality and
its relationship to cultural/artistic transmission. What, for example, is this
phenomenon called spirit? How does it influence cultural orientation? How
does it assist the process of cultural transmission? Is there a qualitative difference between the ways men and women manifest spirituality? How does
spirit affect the artistic impulse? Should spirit be prefigured into constructions of critical theory and, if so, how? How is the voice of spirit recognized
within or among other voices in a text? While my intention is not to formu-
late discursive answers to these questions, I do contend that any such answers must necessarily involve fundamental assumptions about the nature
of reality and the nature of human experience. The degree to which these

assumptions are perpetuated or tested by a people is the degree to which a culture is transmitted from one generation to another. For African-American people the means—political, linguistic, religious, and economic—by which these assumptions were validated and tested have been obscured and, in some cases, obliterated because of the cataclysmic epoch of slavery, the result being the tragic disruption of cultural perpetuity. Given this historical context and faced with the ever-looming threat of complete cultural annihilation, many African-American writers, mainly female, have artistically cultivated the need, on the one hand, to recover lost aspects of their African past and, on the other hand, to allow what remains of their inherent Africanity to impress itself on their Western geophysical present in culturally distinctive ways. But, as Gale Jackson reminds us, for African-American people recovery is possible only through "an act of spiritual memory" (21).

Appropriately, both Holloway and Jackson identify spirit (notwithstanding the problematic considerations that it brings to critical discourse) as the matrix of a distinctly African-American literary aesthetic, and for both the frame for African-American spiritual reference is precolonial and contemporary West Africa. What neither undertakes in their related research or in their exploration of the literary works, however, is the identification of Kemetic cosmological tenets, which were the basis of a unified civilization and a fully achieved understanding of the essential harmony and potential oneness of human and cosmic consciousness. It was also the cosmology that sustained the African apprehension of spirit (and the civilization it engendered) for nearly four thousand years (Amen 12). From this ancient African perspective, the individuated spirit that is not anchored to this kind of cosmology is regarded as shapeless, decentered, and devitalized because it is cut off from its cosmic source of empowerment. Today, because of the historical decline of this cosmological tradition, spiritual detachment is as evident in contemporary Africa as it is in African-America and in other parts of the planet. It would seem, then, that the threads of spiritual history that Holloway locates in texts of African-American women writers suggest these writers' attempt to recover a coherent cosmology and that the absence of spiritual history in texts by African-American male writers suggests, correspondingly, the writers' vulnerability to forms of spiritual deracination and decrepitude.

Therefore, this absence of spiritual history in texts by African-American men needs to be associated with a larger loss, the loss of the cosmological map from which a culture gets the bearings and the "moorings" for its spirit. As Wade W. Nobles explains, one of the basic principles of ancient African cosmology—and, I hasten to add, the mooring point for this discussion—is that "the African belief system understood that the nature of all things in the universe was the Ka of God or 'force,' or 'spirit'" (114). By "spirit," then, I mean that part of the God-force (or cosmic force) that constitutes the essence of every individual and every thing. Accordingly, by "spirituality" I mean the extent to which one consciously utilizes and cultivates one's spirit by adopting values, beliefs, rituals, and behaviors that reflect or promote one's essential connection to all people and things in the universe and to God. Following logically from this definition of "spirit" (and "spirituality") is another tenet of Kemetic cosmology: everything that exists is "characterized by a cosmological 'participation in the Supreme Force'" (114). Two other tenets (of this richly complex worldview) that will help to frame my discussion of novels by African-American men are (1) that ancestors are revered and (2) that rituals play a vital role in the cultivation of the individual and communal spirit.[2]

Arguably, the loss of this spirit-based apprehension of reality would affect the quality and direction of not only a culture's imaginative literature but also the literary criticism it spawns. It is the importance of this spirit-centered cosmology to both of these literary categories that I attempt to assert in this study, for I have come to suspect the worth of all literature and schools of critical theory that do not derive explicitly or implicitly from such a cosmology or do not assist the reader's attempt to discern the work's or the author's cosmological world. I have come to suspect, also, that most African-American male novelists either have not accepted a coherent cosmology as a force that should drive their fictive endeavors or, worse, that these novelists have no coherent cosmology to accept. The result is an ever-emerging canon that, except for a relatively few contemporary writers, reflects a world where individuals and communities do not operate from an awareness of their inextricable connection to each other and to the spirit of the cosmos and, consequently, do not consciously adopt values, rituals, beliefs, and behaviors that affirm this connection. In such a despiritualized ethos, the protagonists' behaviors, goals, and ideologies are usually guided by personal, political, and social exigencies, not by a sense of, or search for, a harmonious interrelationship of self, others, and environment. Similarly, the despiritualized worlds of these novels reflect the authors' failure to allow an apprehension of a cosmic interrelationship to drive their fictive concerns. Their artistic visions, then, attest to random and decentered epistemologies and ontologies, not to a cosmology that asserts a dialectic between human beings and the environment. Without such a cosmology, their works cannot suggest a conceptual and ritualistic framework for the integration of African-American consciousness.

My suspicion, at its core, is spiritual, growing out of my search for the meaning inherent in my life, my involvement with literature being a scintillating part of that search. Because of this ongoing quest, I am no longer content to leave, or to try to leave, consciously or not, my spirit out of the works that I read. Put another way, I see no compelling reason to perform on myself, especially while wearing the critical hat, the kind of spiritual and cultural amputation that is often disguised as aesthetic distance or as objectivity. As Marimba Ani points out, this attempt at objectivity inherently has more to do with objectification; the "cognitive modality which designates everything other than the 'self' as object . . . mandates a despiritualized, isolated ego and facilitates the use of knowledge as control and power over other" (xxvii). Indeed, the ancient African view of the human does not allow for this objectification:

> The emotional-spiritual and the rational-material are inextricably bound to each other, and if anything it is a human being's spirituality that defines [that person] as human, providing the context within which he or she is able to create art as well as technology. Such a view leads to a very different emphasis in artistic expression. The emotional identification with, and participation in, the art form by the person and the community are primary values that help to determine its shape. In this way the form itself becomes less of an "object." (203)

Ani buttresses my contention that there is an unavoidable relationship between criticism and spirituality. This contention is at the core of my response to the representation of African-American men in such canonized novels as Richard Wright's *Native Son* (1940), Ralph Ellison's *Invisible Man* (1952), and James Baldwin's *Go Tell It on the Mountain* (1953), and in lesser known, more contemporary ones such as Melvin Dixon's *Trouble the Water* (1989) and Brent Wade's *Company Man* (1992).

In my suspicion regarding these novels, I am bolstered by the findings of Afrocentric theorists (Naaim Akbar, Wade W. Nobles, Gale Jackson, Cedric X, and Joseph Baldwin) who "have embraced a line of reasoning which views the behavior of African Americans as having as its antecedents ancient African thought and philosophy" (Nobles 113). Because, of all the contemporary critical models, Afrocentricity is the only one that privileges the spirit-centered cosmology of ancient Africa in its theoretical constructs; because, consequently, it seeks to return consciousness to its cosmological nexus; because, furthermore, it recognizes that "as a people, our most cher-

ished and valuable achievements are the achievements of spirit" (Asante 43).
Hence, my approach to the texts which I discuss is Afrocentric. Let me point
out, however, that the tremendous complexity of the ancient African worldview means that Afrocentric theorists cannot always be expected to agree
about the extent to which a particular individual or communal system, practice, value, or attitude privileges spirit. In fact, as I will illustrate later, there
may be occasions when, caught up in the momentum of a discursive approach, an Afrocentric theorist unwittingly fails to privilege spirit. However, because it is, relatively speaking, still in its nascent stages, especially with
regard to its literary application, Afrocentricity can be expected to continue its methodological development (as a spirit-centered critical theory) as
its theorists find better ways of articulating and demonstrating its relationship to the various disciplines. Meanwhile, the virtual absence of Afrocentric literary analyses from contemporary critical discourse constitutes a spiritual handicap, especially to members of the African Diaspora.

⊡ ⊞ ⊟

If we accept George E. Kent's observation that "the novels of black male
writers have been dominated by the theme of asserting, retaining or recovering a virility that is usually threatened in a racist society" (138), we can
see how far we are from any cosmological concerns in novels by African-
American men. Mind you, virility does have its cosmological correspon-
dences; but a life dominated by the need to assert, retain, or recover virility
is a life that has less potential for empowerment than it does for impotence.
Moreover, this kind of preoccupation with the dictates of virility is, ironically, most unmanly. I am not suggesting that such a theme is unimportant;
to do so would be to trivialize the prodigious accomplishments of such
writers as Wright, Ellison, Baldwin, John Oliver Killens, John A. Williams,
Ernest J. Gaines, Ishmael Reed, and others. To be sure, the preoccupation
with virility might well be one of the excrescent tendencies of a culture forced
constantly to wage psychological war against institutionalized forms of
castration. What I am suggesting, however, is that the African-American
male needs—and our writers and critics must assist in supplying—something
even more vital and far more revolutionary: in fiction and in life, the African-American male needs a perception of himself that engenders not only
his virility but also his aesthetics, his ideology, and his mode of being. He
needs a perception of himself that locates his values, principles, and behaviors within what Ra Un Nefer Amen calls "the blue-print which guides his

steps to the fulfillment of his mission on earth" (46). He needs, in short, an authentic and ritualized cosmology.

For the most part, in the novels written by African-American men, this need remains unmet. Instead, the moods and actions of the major male figures in these works often derive from attitudes, ideologies, and values that make a cult out of protest, status, or individualism. Lacking any practical sense of their place within the cosmic scheme of being and seemingly oblivious to the possibility of developing such a sense, they fall prey to pursuits that decelerate the process of their spiritual flowering and, consequently, prevent them from transcending the limitations of personality and gender. This indictment holds true for prominent and time-honored novels as well as for more recent, lesser known ones. Generally speaking, however, novels authored by African-American men, while evidencing noteworthy forms of cultural commitment and defining moments of creative grace, attest at the same time to the deracinating repercussions of consciousness when it is not shaped by a ritualized cosmology. As such, they evince little or no authorial interest in the totality of the protagonist's spiritual history—that is, in the protagonist's connection to ancient African cosmology. Understandably, then, whenever I read or reread some of these works, I undergo contradictory responses.

I applaud, for example, the struggle of Wright's Bigger Thomas against the juggernaut-like assaults on his sensibilities, and I gratefully accept that the rendering of his struggle reflects my own sense of outrage at a society seeking to drown Bigger in a surging sea of bigotry. However, I abhor the theology of impotence that suffuses the novel and allows Bigger to accept his Christ-like death without even the consolation—the grace—of an imagined resurrection. And I take vehement objection not to the teeming evidence of Wright's naturalistic associations but rather to the screaming silence in which Wright enshrouds the history of Bigger's consciousness, in a manner that leaves the reader to suppose that the seed of Bigger's death germinated and flowered at the very moment of his conception. In *Native Son* Wright seems oblivious to the fact that neither the holocaust of the Middle Passage nor the vast torture chamber that was the American South could annihilate what John Russwurm has called "the principle of liberty . . . implanted in [the human] breast" (190). In Bigger's case, this annihilation is not only accomplished, it is consciously accepted, and—most terrifyingly—Bigger's experience, including his acceptance of his sociopolitical situation, is relegated to realms of allegory.

As with *Native Son,* so with another deservedly famous novel, Ellison's

Invisible Man. Joyfully, I recognize the protagonist's voyage from naivete to endarkenment (Molefe Asante's term) as paradigmatic; and I am elated to discover that the authorial craft on which this celebrated voyage takes place is fashioned from the material that fashioned me, the material of my own history and that of oppressed people everywhere. But I think Ellison should have taken his portrait of Ras the Exhorter more seriously, for Ras's ideology, had Ellison dared to free it from the satirically angry and diseased consciousness in which it is housed, could have at least awakened in the protagonist the potential for a discovery of the Afrocentric genius sleeping within him (I suspect that Ellison would fume at this suggestion). I also reject the existential limbo that characterizes the protagonist's final level of becoming (in the novel). Ironically, it is a psychospiritual disposition that pinpoints his need for something regenerative or transcendent in his consciousness and that makes regrettable Ellison's failure, like Wright's, even to hint symbolically at the historical direction in which his hero can look for the spiritual source of his anticipated empowerment. Such an undertaking would not undermine the artistic vision that insists, like Ellison's, on the presentation of historical, social, and political reality as it operates on and negotiates individual consciousness because the seed for individual and cultural affirmation is inherently a part of any societal reality, especially an oppressive one. The writer (in this case, Ellison) needs no crystal ball to hint at such a source; but he does need something perhaps much more challenging, the fictive acknowledgment of a pervasive spirituality, which not only "asserts one's ability to relate to the metaphysical levels of experience" but also "unites thought and feeling and thereby allows for intuitive understanding" (Ani xxviii).

And how about that other literary giant, Baldwin, whose language has the exhilarating power to fix me, Prufrock-like, "in a formulated phrase"? My problem with Baldwin concerns the conception of his male characters: though each courageously bears the cross of his own individual human predicament, he never gets a chance to imagine, much less to wear, a crown—unless, of course, the crown is worn, paradoxically, in the act of bearing the cross, a notion that undermines the Christian theology that engenders it. And if, as it seems, Baldwin wants us to accept the Pauline notion that the crown is worn only after physical death, then it becomes poignantly clear that Baldwin, despite his well-known disenchantment with the religion of his youth, is still trapped by the same dangerous and claustrophobic theology he rejected.

To be sure, the lives of all of Baldwin's African-American male characters operate within this yes-cross/no-crown dialectic. Such is the case with the Grimes men in *Go Tell It on the Mountain,* with Leo Proudhammer in *Tell Me How Long the Train's Been Gone* (1968), with Fonny Hunt in *If Beale Street Could Talk* (1974), and certainly with the men in *Just Above My Head* (1978). For the most part, the message of Baldwin's men, should they tell it on the mountain, will proclaim the absolute necessity of personal struggle and the unfathomable glory of cultural survival. Quite an important message it is. Still, struggle and survival, although unquestionably vital to our state of being and to our process of becoming, do not even begin to exhaust the infinite possibilities of the human spirit when it is cosmologically aligned, when, that is, it has developed a way of tapping into the inexhaustible source of power available, because of this cosmological alliance, to itself. And, as Kariamu Welsh observes, "Maintenance and survival are no longer adequate terminology to pass on to the next generation. Our presence in the future is undisputed, but maintenance nor survival will insure our propriety or prominence" (viii). Baldwin's male protagonists seem unaware (and seem not to have been conceived within an authorial matrix that accepts) that the struggle for humanity is not an end in itself and that the most worthwhile struggle is the attempt to attain our highest spiritual cultivation, the struggle to find the cosmological alignment that our ancient ancestors once averred. This struggle gives meaning and direction to all other forms of struggle and leads, as it once led Kemetic priests, to the manifestation of our God-like potential in the here and now, a psychospiritual condition where everything is possible—including liberation from individualized and institutionalized forms of oppression—and without which nothing is transcendent.

Collectively, Wright, Ellison, and Baldwin have had a powerful influence on the fiction by African-American men. For the most part this influence has advanced the status of this body of literature as an artistically dynamic and culturally resonant product. And although, as Bernard W. Bell correctly states, contemporary writers "achieve their *distinctive* voices simultaneously within and against a narrative tradition of continuity and change" (284; emphasis added), I conclude that with few exceptions—most notably Dixon's *Trouble the Water*—these writers' fidelity to Wright's, Ellison's, and Baldwin's conceptualization of male characters constitutes one proof of their narrative continuity. Continuity of this narrative tradition is also seen, correspondingly, in some contemporary writers' allegiance to the fictive reflection of an historical tradition that ignores its spiritual ties to ancient African (Kemetic) cosmology. One finds this allegiance to historical tradition in contemporary novels such as Wade's *Company Man*. In this novel, one finds an awareness, on the part of both protagonist and author, of the need for the African-American male to actualize his connection to black history but no demonstrated or implied awareness of his need to recognize and actualize his connection to the ancient spiritual or cosmological features of that history. Thus my critical response to this novel is characterized by the same kind of ambivalence evoked by the venerable literary giants to whom I have been referring.

To reiterate my central claim, a preponderance of the novels by African-American men bear witness to these authors' participation in the spiritually truncated world of Wright, Ellison, and Baldwin. Although these novels take the readers into a world where the protagonists are conceptually doomed to spiritual detachment, it must simultaneously be noted that there are nascent signs—most notably in Dixon's *Trouble the Water* and less so in Wade's *Company Man*—that the genre is being enriched by characters' yearnings for an experiential connection to their black communities and to their cultural history. Whereas *Trouble the Water* is conceptually allied to Kemetic cosmology, in *Company Man* the protagonist's concept of spiritual history does not embrace the spirit-centered autonomy of the ancient Kemetic worldview. Thus, his desired reconnection with his cultural history lacks the range and specificity necessary to label it cosmological (in the Kemetic sense). While Wade is definitely interested in the quality of his character's spirit, and while this interest in spiritual health urgently informs his narrative process, *Company Man* does not translate this interest in spirit into an interest in spirituality, the character's conscious adoption or creation of personal and communal behaviors and rituals designed to cultivate a spirit-centered existence. The result is a work that, though intended to dramatize the protagonist's ascent to a discovery of a life-improving vision of self, still leaves him disengaged from a spirit-centered cosmology.

⊡ ⊡ ⊡

Company Man is a stark and terrifying rendering of what happens to a black man's consciousness when, disconnected from his cosmological moorings (to continue with Holloway's metaphor) and having, consequently, no sense of spiritual or historical purpose, he conforms to the corporate dictates of white America. He develops a many-sided, many-leveled impotence; in fact, sexual impotence is the novel's central metaphor. Not only does the protagonist, Billy Covington, become increasingly sexually dysfunctional as he climbs the white corporate ladder, but his whole psychological and emotional infrastructure begins to disintegrate. Only when he realizes that, despite his glamorous title and despite the carefully manicured relationships that he maintained with white associates, he has no real power in that world; only after a series of bizarre events transpires in his corporate workplace and in his own psyche; only after these bizarre events prompt him to quit his job and to come to terms with his psychocultural needs by living a culturally grounded life—only then is he finally able to make love to his wife, Paula. But when, minutes later, he puts a gun to his head in a failed suicide attempt, we suspect that it was only his penis, not his spirit, that had been raised. And since by this time we know that Wade has linked Billy's sexual problem not only to the vampire-like demands of Varitech Industries but also to his lifelong retreat from cultural identity and responsibility, we are forced to accept the sexual dysfunction as symptomatic of a larger incapacity, a larger loss of power.

There is other evidence of this larger incapacity. Much of his psychospiritual deformity is communicated through the novel's form—a diary Billy is writing from his hospital bed to his former homeboy Paul in an attempt to explain to Paul (and to himself) the events that led to his attempted suicide. That the diary should be addressed to Paul becomes a curious bit of information, for the reader learns early on that Billy had discontinued all communication with him after Paul confessed that he was homosexual. This information, combined with Billy's marriage to a woman named *Paula* and his attempt to take his own life a few hours after making love to her after several months of impotence, leads one to suspect that Billy's self-imposed estrangement from Paul is in some profound way connected to his suicide attempt. Put another way, his rejection of Paul evinces his abjuration of an important spiritual (hence emotional and psychic) part of himself, which he had unconsciously been trying to reembrace through Paula. By the end of the novel the reader's suspicion—that Billy's cure necessitates his reconstruction of his relationship with Paul and, consequently, with himself—is confirmed, for the diary/novel itself concludes with the strong suggestion that the narrator's physical and spiritual health is predicated on his reconciling with Paul. Although the hospital-bound Billy anticipates a satisfying relationship with his wife and the joys and challenges of fatherhood (Paula is pregnant), he comes to believe that his blackness, masculinity, and emotional well-being depend on his ability not only to accept Paul but, more importantly, to accept that ungendered, spiritual part of himself that is capable of transcending differences based on gender and sexual orientation. His last words in the novel substantiate this prognosis:

Talking to you [Paul] like this has shown me some new possibilities. . . . I won't write to you about it [what I have in mind] now, but expect a letter from me in a few months. I'll only say that I realized that I have something I need to return, something you and I gave to each other a long time ago. It'll be a demanding project, but that's my own fault. I forgot for a while that it was unfinished and now I'm way overdue. . . . It involves travel and exotic places, and exploring ancient ruins others would just as soon leave alone. Does that sound like something you would be interested in? (219)

My point is not that Billy has been running away from an aspect of his sexuality—although that is a distinct possibility—but that his constricting notions of manhood precluded a friendship with an openly gay man. Billy's homophobic response to his friend suggests that his socially constructed definition of manhood was too limited to include the Pauls of the world. Ironically, this limitation means that the cramped space he allowed for his own manhood could not contain the fullness of who and what he was— hence the partial self-rejection. The fact that, except for his relationship with Paula, not one of Billy's adult relationships can even loosely be described as a friendship makes plausible the notion that unless he is able to integrate the ungendered, spiritual part of himself, the rest of his life is doomed to social impotence. However varied or complex the reasons for Billy's homophobia, it is certain that, given the thematic terms of the novel, homophobia is one of the agents of his spiritual decline. It is also certain that one of the indicators of his movement toward spiritual—and thereby psychic and emotional—health is his willingness to rebuild his relationship with Paul and relinquish his hackneyed notions of masculinity.

Wade's inscription of homophobia as symptomatic of black men's psychic malaise allows me to address one of those moments, alluded to earlier, when an Afrocentric theorist fails to uphold the spirit-centered nature of his or her argument. In *Afrocentricity* (1988), Asante argues that homosexuality is "a deviation from Afrocentric thought because it makes the person evaluate his own physical needs above the teachings of national consciousness"; that it "can and must be tolerated until such time as our families and schools engage in Afrocentric instructions for males"; and that it must ultimately be subordinated to the "collective will of our people" (57). But this argument cannot be regarded as Afrocentric because it is not spirit-centered. Contrarily, it is framed within a nationalist (and masculinist), rather than a spiritual, context. I would contend that the Afrocentric privileging of the community over the individual presupposes the community's embodiment of and allegiance to principles that promote the community's harmonious interaction with the cosmos. When this is not the case, the community, like the decentered individual, loses its way. Appropriately, in an Afrocentric vision national consciousness is valued not for its own sake but rather for its right relationship to spirit. It follows, then, that the argument that homosexuality should be regarded as a "deviation" must be based, first and foremost, on homosexuality's effect on the individual, communal, and national *spirit* if it is to be considered Afrocentric. Indeed, at a given moment, the national or diasporic consciousness—which is not expected or even desired to be static—may not be aligned with cosmic spirit, for some of the factors shaping the national consciousness may be inimical to the exigencies of cosmic consciousness. As far as *Company Man* is concerned, Billy's spiritual growth fosters not merely a tolerance of Paul's homosexuality but an endearing camaraderie of personality and spirit. Whether such camaraderie bodes ill for the national alignment to cosmic spirit is a question that Asante's position begs.[3] Meanwhile, *Company Man* points to the potential of Billy's spirit for simultaneously negotiating, accepting, and transcending such parochial constructions of male sexuality.

I find it commendable that Wade, unlike icons such as Wright, Baldwin, and Ellison, suggests both the cause of the protagonist's multileveled ailment and the direction for its possible cure without being clairvoyant and without vitiating the artistic integrity of the novel. In *Company Man* this dual function is embodied in the figure of Nathaniel Bond, Billy's father-in-law. An admirer and student of ancient African history, Dr. Bond attempts to share this important part of himself with Billy by giving him an annotated tour of his library. While it is clear that this library, a paean to the accomplishments of ancient Africa, is Dr. Bond's way of repudiating "that substrative belief that the black man had not contributed anything useful to mankind" (25) and of resisting his perpetual marginalization in America, it is also clear that Billy's reflections about the library and its owner evince his utter dismissal of a possibly viable relationship between African-American life and ancient African history: "his library of orphaned history—it was all a testament to cultural estrangement. His wealth had given him the opportunity to explore what for most of us is an unarticulated musing, the anomie of a stranded people. But having faced it, he disguised it as some new cosmology he was trying to create" (27). Billy's problem, then, is not that he rejects Dr. Bond's efforts as romantic, eccentric, and self-serving but rather that he is too myopic, too dazzled and disoriented by the glimmer of white corporate values to see that Dr. Bond's obvious need for cosmological grounding mirrors his own. That Billy had been socialized without such a cosmology is the root of his problems.

Billy's attitude toward his father-in-law becomes even more revealing when compared to his attitude toward the other authority figure in his life—his self-hating and culturally sycophantic grandmother. She "had come to see blackness as that mildew that slowly devours the paint on fine picket fences" and, consequently, did her forceful best to transform Billy into "a Generic, a man devoid of any cultural affiliation" (12). Clearly, she represents the major visual and mnemonic force that propels Billy away from his ancestral self. In fact, his grandmother's tug on his consciousness is so forceful that Billy continues to hear her voice even after she is dead. This voice, becoming more and more authoritative as it urges Billy along the path of cultural suicide, eventually assumes a disembodied presence that becomes so intrusive and so profoundly toxic that Billy's attempt to kill himself is best understood as his attempt to obliterate his grandmother's presence:

> And then I didn't want to hear it [my grandmother's] voice any more. . . . I held the gun up and she laughed. . . .
> *You might as well, you just another nigga now.* It was her I wanted to get rid of. I didn't want to hear her anymore. And I agreed with myself. I put my hand over mine and squeezed [the trigger] and then I heard the snap and felt the sting. (217)

As far as Billy is concerned, his grandmother and Dr. Bond represent two extreme and extremely dangerous cultural responses to white hegemony—on the one hand, the translation of personal and cultural history into a new cosmology and, on the other hand, the abnegation of the personal and cultural history of the self for the dream of otherness. In assessing his grandmother, Billy is forced to allow for a sense of mystery not only because he shares a lifelong, even haunting bond with her, but also because he feels certain that, despite her hatred of blackness, she loves him. However, in his evaluation of his father-in-law, with whom he shares no visceral "bond," he allows for no such inconclusiveness: "[One of the histories that Dr. Bond had given himself] was the one of his people and it stretched further back than the written word would allow. It was all an attempt to put distance between what he was trying to be and what he knew he still was. As if . . . every trip into his library took him further and further from where he began, from where he was, from where he had never really strayed" (27).

What complicates our reading of Billy's cultural detachment is his sophisticated awareness of the historical prejudices and privileges of whiteness in America, both of which he has to make daily attempts to negotiate, a process to which he devotes himself completely. The white mask that he wears in the presence of his associates, however, increasingly loses shape and contour until it fades to a placid anonymity; and his misreading of Dr. Bond's passionate pride in his ancestral heritage augurs that the face behind the mask is also amorphous and anonymous, there being no structured background against which it can project form and definition. Such is not the case with Dr. Bond, for his library constitutes the symbolic backdrop against which his image assumes distinctive shape and texture. Given the frames for Billy's spiritual and emotional reference—his grandmother and Paul, respectively—Billy's sense of self is without a definitive context.

Although Billy's polarized assessments of Dr. Bond and his grandmother represent his final attitude toward the two elders in his life, the fact is that he has no spiritual, cultural, or historical base from which to judge either. If he had—or even if he had been able to invent such a base for himself—he might have seen the limitations inherent in his conclusions: he might have known, with the autotelic certainty that comes with a shared ontological history, that Dr. Bond was responding to an ancestral call, however limited that response might have been; and he might also have intuited that somewhere along her journey to her highest spiritual cultivation his grandmother had lost her way, a loss that made highly suspect the subsequent principles by which she lived, including her "love" for him. Viewed from an African-centered spiritual perspective, that which teaches us to dissociate ourselves from cultural, ancestral history cannot be termed "love." Because Billy is ignorant of these culturally related zones of knowledge and because there is no person or institution in his life that offers him an empowering sense of cultural identity, his appointment with profound disillusionment is almost a foregone conclusion.

Like many male-authored texts, *Company Man* invites comparison with *Invisible Man*, a novel whose influence is indisputable. This comparison eventually uncovers a prescription for wholeness that hints at the protagonist's connection to spiritual history, though not at his realization of a need for a cosmology. In both *Company Man* and *Invisible Man* the circular structure establishes the dual perspective that allows for the works' mounting tension. Like Ellison's unnamed hero speaking from his underground room of hibernation, Billy Covington speaks (through a diary he is composing for his childhood friend Paul) from a hospital room, where he is undergoing a physical and emotional convalescence that is also a kind of hibernation.

While Ellison's prologue reveals to us a consciousness caught up in an existential meditation on its own reality, which the rest of the novel accounts for and anticipates, Wade's hospital room is an ever-present point of reference for the novel's events. Their significance is determined not by their organic relationship to each other but by the nature of their perceived contribution to Billy's (and the reader's) understanding of the factors contributing to his breakdown, the nature of his prognosis, and the prescription for his healing. Thus the narrative voice in Wade's novel resonates on two levels: the voice of reflection and analysis (the voice of the convalescing narrator) and the voice of the protagonist as he heads toward his breakdown. Each voice is therefore a double of the other, a construct that allows for a shared resonance and a similar frequency. Despite this subtle but informative difference between Ellison's and Wade's narrative structure, the place of fictive departure and return in each novel—the underground room in *Invisible Man* and the hospital room in *Company Man*—functions as a womb for the gestation of an embryonic consciousness.

Although both Ellison's and Wade's novels assume autobiographical postures, the pattern of movement differs in a manner that makes Wade's more conducive to the tenets of an Afrocentric ontology. Despite the circular structure of *Invisible Man,* that novel's construction of time is linear. Only in its retrospective modality (as indicated in the prologue and the epilogue) does the novel achieve its circularity. Conversely, the construction of time in *Company Man* is simultaneously linear and circular, a contradiction that is allowed not because, like Ellison's novel, the first-person narrator begins at the end and ends at the beginning, but because *Company Man's* narrative movement is associative. That is, the events are triggered, even shaped, by mnemonic incidents in the narrator's changing consciousness, incidents that frequently snap the narrator out of his chronological reconstruction of past events, zoom him back to his convalescing present (where he narrates events and situations relating to the ministrations of his doctor and nurse and the visits of his wife), and, eventually, back again to a more or less distant past. These mnemonic incidents also allow the quality of his hospitalized consciousness to affect the quality and texture of past events in a manner that is not true of Ellison's novel, so that the narrative thread of a particular event may be broken before the event is complete, to be continued again according to the dictates of the narrator's often-triggered memory. Consequently, the past is always revisited within the psychic dictates of the present and, paradoxically, the present is extended and heightened through the narrator's mnemonic gateways to the past. The result is a narrative ethos that approximates, more closely than Ellison's novel, the circularity of the African concept of time.

⊟   ⊟   ⊟

Interestingly enough, a grandmother exerts an equally powerful and disruptive presence in Melvin Dixon's *Trouble the Water*, a novel that warrants attention here because it is one of the relatively few contemporary novels by African-American men that unequivocally reflects an evocative and powerfully resonant concern with ancient African cosmology. As such, it is proof that a fidelity to this cosmology is no necessary impediment to the contemporary artistic imagination. To the contrary, *Trouble the Water* demonstrates that such fidelity can fecundate the imagination's potential for driving contemporary consciousness toward the manifestation of its ancient possibilities—toward, that is, cosmic realignment.

Furthermore, *Trouble the Water* vivifies each of the Kemetic cosmological tenets I identified earlier. The text achieves this by portraying characters' connection to and interaction with environmental consciousness. Dixon attempts not only to capture the role of ritual in specific characters' lives but also to translate ritual into a narrative aesthetic. He masterfully narrativizes the ubiquity of spirit in the world, using a discussion of the ancestral ties between grandmother and grandson to amplify this point. Although each of these facets of the novel can be illustrated by reference to the thematic and stylistic structures of the text, it suffices here to focus on the last one—that is, on the grandmother-grandson relationship—for several reasons. Not only is it the emotional center of the novel, but the spiritual nature of this relationship emblematizes the thematic and aesthetic structures of the novel as a whole, for these structures are also informed by Dixon's interest in the world of spirit. An exploration of this relationship, especially when juxtaposed with the grandmother-grandson relationship in *Company Man*, uncovers an authorial conception of male subjectivity that differs substantively from Wade's (as well as from that of Wright, Ellison, and Baldwin). Furthermore, and most importantly, Dixon's presentation of this grandmother-grandson relationship suggests how an interest in spiritual history may imaginatively influence the outcome of a spiritually moribund existence.

The title itself—an allusion to a well-known African-American spiritual ("Wade in de water / . . . God's gonna trouble de water")—locates the novel squarely within a cultural tradition of spirit. Mother Harriet, the matriarch of a small rural community in North Carolina, nurtures a relationship with her grandson, Jordan, that desecrates traditional African spiritual values. The impetus for her spiritually decrepit state is her hatred for Jordan's father, Jake—a hatred so overwhelming that her single reason for living is to plant and nourish in her grandson the seed of patricide. Although this hatred is her response to Jake's emotional abuse of her daughter Chloe (Jordan's mother whom Jake seduced, impregnated, and then abandoned), the grandmother's willingness to devote her entire life (and Jordan's) to his killing of his own father without any concern for the emotionally, psychologically, and spiritually destructive repercussions reveals a malignant, bereft spirit. On her psyche this capitulation, at once stark and consummate, exerts the force of a religion.

The thematic centrality of the grandmother-grandson relationship in *Company Man* and *Trouble the Water* invites other parallels. In both novels the protagonist's cultural identity and psychospiritual well-being depend, among other things, on his ability to rid his psyche of the ancestral call to self-destruction. Both characters are driven to real or symbolic killings of the grandmother—the adult Jordan dreams that he intentionally shoots his grandmother with the gun that she provides for him to use on his father; and, as has already been mentioned, Billy's attempt to kill himself (also with a gun) is also a deranged attempt to kill his grandmother. In both novels the ancestral spirit, embodied in the grandmother, typifies the kind of spiritual detachment that characterizes those African Americans (and people in general) who, already committed to destructive personal agendas, use their influence to poison the psyches of their progeny. That both grandmothers are blind to the spiritually crippling influence they exert on their grandsons signals a cultural disruption of generational proportions.

In both novels, the grandmothers' destructive machinations have serious spiritual implications, for they debase the role of the ancestors in traditional spirit-centered societies, a fact of which both authors are obviously aware and that both novels thematically reject. In *Company Man,* rather than becoming an ancestral spirit on whom Billy can ritualistically call for help in his attempt to locate himself culturally and historically, the grandmother becomes a "dark deceased," an earth-bound spirit who, having wasted its opportunities for spiritual cultivation during its human stage, is inclined to exert divisive or destructive influences on the living[4] and who, in this case, wishes to obstruct Billy's path to his highest spiritual cultivation by trapping him in a similar spiritual vortex. In *Trouble the Water,* Jordan, whose belief system, unlike Billy's, embraces traditional African ideas concerning the role of ritual and the power of ancestral spirits, feels certain, even before Mother Harriet's death, that she was on her way to becoming one of the dark deceased. When Jordan, after decades of self-imposed separation from Mother Harriet, finally confronts her on her deathbed, the narrative voice probes this aspect of Jordan's consciousness and in the process uncovers strategic facets of ancient African cosmology, facets that are neither suggested nor implied in Wade's novel:

> Jordan stood like a soldier and Mother Harriet studied him. To Jordan she could command life and death over him with the same easy effort she used to command it over herself. *Jordan was certain that even if she had died long ago her spirit would have lingered eternally between the river and the house at the top of the hill, moving its tedious way into the lives of her family, those living and those dead. . . . Jordan, the sole inheritor, the guardian, when she was gone, of her future in the other world; Jordan, the connection between her departed spirit and the voice of the living.* (220; emphasis added)

This passage references the Kemetic notion of the dark deceased as well as the Kemetic belief that the individual is a conduit to the ancestral spirit and the human world. However, the most compelling proof of the spirit-centered resolution of the grandmother-grandson relationship in Dixon's novel is the fact that before this scene concludes, Jordan, with the help of his wife Phyllis and his father Jake, rescues the spirit of the dying woman and saves her from the fate of the dark deceased. Having at last found the courage to confront and overcome his fear of his grandmother—thanks to a series of tension-packed events that had transpired in the hours immediately preceding this bedside visit—he comes to realize the symbiotic nature of his spiritual relationship to her and that this tortured relationship has impeded his spiritual growth. Jordan is finally ready to help her to lay down the heavy burden of her hatred for Jake and to free her grandson from the equally heavy burden of her patricidal expectations. And Jordan knows that if the hate can be exorcised, then his grandmother will be able to die, even as for the first time he will be ready to live, with the grace that comes from personal and spiritual reconciliation. Motivated not only by his awareness of Mother Harriet's imminent spiritual tragedy—she is about to become a dark deceased—but also by his own need for release from his emotional and spiritual bondage to her, Jordan leads the family in a ritual of spiritual intervention and renewal in a scene that is one of the most spiritually charged in all of African-American fiction.

Ritual is the force that drives the spiritual intensity of this scene: Mother Harriet, aware that she is dying, wants to ensure her memory in this world through a physical touch from Jordan: "now touch me, let me feel you close, so I'll know I'll be remembered" (224). However, Jordan knows that this final touch would symbolize to Mother Harriet his approval of her all-consuming hatred for Jake and his affirmation of her need for revenge. To Jordan himself such a touch would emblematize his acquiescence to Harriet's spiritual turpitude. Therefore, that touch does not happen until Jordan (aided by his wife and father) persuades Harriet to renounce her hatred through an act of forgiveness. When the touch does finally come, it is an inclusive gesture, involving not only Jordan but also his wife and father as well. The narrative description of this touching suggests the spiritual power of ritual and makes palpable the ancient African belief that the ancestor can continue to exercise cultural agency:

> And they held onto Mother Harriet tight. Phyllis's hands circled the woman's leathery stomach, Jordan held her hands, and Jake touched her wrinkled feet. Mother Harriet grabbed Phyllis's hand and led it from her stomach to her belly and to the dry hollow between her legs. *Heat from the dying flesh crawled into Phyllis and into Jordan and into Jake.*
>
> "Yes," said Mother Harriet, almost crooning. "Yes, yes," softly, then loud, "yesyesyesyesyes" until the word was a musical note between them, a note of song and ease and relief, a note against pain, *sealing her bond with them forever.* (225–26; emphasis added)

Thus, what begins as an attempt to wrest from Jordan a final seal of approval for a crippling hatred is transformed, by the power of forgiveness, into a ritualized act of empowerment that fosters community. In the process, the dying woman is able to pass on (literally) elements of her spirit to the people at her bedside. In this way, and in keeping with ancient African cultural tradition, she ensures her personal and cultural perpetuity in this world even after her physical death.

The deathbed scene is also significant because it affords the reader a chance, rare in novels by African-American men, to witness the initial stages of the psychic healing of a major male character, Jordan's father, Jake, through the application of aspects of his spiritual history. None of the other male characters discussed earlier locates African spiritual history as his healing source, and none of them connects his potential for healing to the condition of another member of the community as, for example, Jordan connects his potential for healing with that of Mother Harriet. Whereas the male characters of Wright, Ellison, Baldwin, and Wade approach personal pain and potential healing in existential isolation, Dixon conceptualizes and inscribes both pain and healing as communally based. Thus, all three of the individuals who gather at Mother Harriet's deathbed have for years been part of each other's pain, and the touching ritual not only redeems the dying grandmother but begins the healing process in Jordan, Phyllis, and Jake, each of whose lives had reached emotional and spiritual stasis.

Billy's and Jordan's response to their grandmothers' evil manipulations constitutes a symbolic allusion to the fact that one's psychospiritual health sometimes mandates the rejection of parts of one's personal history that obstruct spiritual well-being and, by extension, the spiritual health of the community. Thus, in adherence to the ancient African tradition of ancestral reverence, the privileged place of the elders and ancestors in the community does not automatically imply obedience or acquiescence in situations where the elders' or ancestors' spiritually corrosive values and behaviors debase the spirit of their progeny.

▣ ▣ ▣

Of the novels mentioned in this discussion, only Melvin Dixon's *Trouble the Water* presents a male character whose arrested spirituality is eventually redirected by the character's willingness to probe for its source, the liberating properties of a ritualized cosmology. Although the protagonist of Brent Wade's *Company Man* eventually confronts his need to negotiate the history, weight, and obligations of his blackness, the terms of that intended negotiation are unknown. What is certain about Wade's novel, however—and what I regard as its most important accomplishment—is its unequivocal insistence that Eurocentric values, as represented by white corporate America, can offer nothing of spiritual value to African-American men. Billy, for all his insights into the operation of that corporate enterprise, could not see that it issued from a European apprehension of a desacralized and despiritualized ethos, from a conception of human beings and the universe as separate entities. In his Anglicized universe, a universe objectified and knowable only by way of a trenchant rationalism, the human being is imprisoned by rampant individualism. Because Billy is alienated from this history of self and simultaneously isolated in a spiritually barren world, his journey, the novel's disturbing ending notwithstanding, signifies with the force and substance of a parable.

Nevertheless, if the psychospiritual condition of Billy and the other male characters discussed in this essay reflects, collectively, a general truth about the African-American male, then, it seems to me, African-American male writers and critics have a huge task, one that they share with all the other cultural entities—social, educational, political, and religious. From an Afro-centric or spirit-centered perspective, writers must assist the culture's attempt to link all of its agents to the common base of spirit. It is true, of course, that a novel that presents only spiritually destitute characters, communities, or worlds may still serve this purpose, inasmuch as the dramatizations of problems inherently raise the question of possible solutions—the raising of such questions may well be the author's intention. However, what constitutes a problem depends ultimately on the culture's worldview. In any case, novels that are not concerned with a cosmological matrix (or in which such a matrix cannot be identified) lose the power to propel the culture's movement toward individual and communal wholeness. As this reading of the psychocultural situation of contemporary male characters suggests, the only hope for the spiritually/culturally bereft Bigger Thomases, Invisible Men, and Billy Covingtons of this world is at best a limited physical survival and a commitment to persevere. As readers we can extrapolate from literature some degree of cultural enrichment and some contribution, however limited, to the process of becoming our highest/deepest selves—but is this all we require? I think not. Not giving up is not enough. Our humanity—our historically proclaimed divinity—is better served if more characters are conceived within the creative constraints of a spirit-centered cosmology.

There may be another dimension to the problem of African-American cultural representation in novels by African-American men—namely, the degree to which the Western modalities of realism, surrealism, naturalism, modernism, and postmodernism (the main aesthetic and philosophical parameters of our male writers) lend themselves to the treatment of African-American consciousness. It may well be that these modalities, issuing as they do out of a superficial understanding of the nature of reality, are too limited in scope to explore the psychospiritual plight of the African-American male as well as female, especially that aspect of the African-American psyche that is rendered distinctive and dynamic by its participation in the spiritual energies of community. Refreshingly and innovatively, some of our contemporary male writers—most notably Ishmael Reed and Randall Kenan—are experimenting with new forms and modalities in an attempt not only to capture the distinctness and dynamism of the African-American psyche but also to push that psyche to new levels of awareness, so that we may lessen the gap between our sociopolitical realities and the destiny that is configured on the pages of our spiritual history. Towards this end, our writers must attain and sustain the conceptual and artistic security to look deeply within African-American culture itself, especially within the African spiritual component of that culture, for the artistic and critical modalities through which they represent and signify.

Notes

1. For a discussion of the spirit-based nature of the Kemetic worldview, see Wade W. Nobles, "Ancient Egyptian Thought and the Development of African (Black) Psychology."

2. For the most comprehensive treatment of Kemetic cosmogony and cosmology, see Ra Un Nefer Amen, *Metu Neter: The Great Oracle of Tehuti and the Egyptian System of Spiritual Cultivation.* See also Malidoma Patrice Some, *Ritual: Power, Healing, and Community,* for a detailed discussion of the nature and purpose of ritual.

3. Since the publication of this edition of *Afrocentricity* in 1988, Asante has publicly qualified his position with regard to the Afrocentric attitude toward homosexuals.

4. For a fuller discussion of the "dark deceased" and their possible influence on the living, see Amen's *Metu Neter.*

Works Cited

Amen, Ra Un Nefer. *Metu Neter: The Great Oracle of Tehuti and the Egyptian System of Spiritual Cultivation.* New York: Khamit Corp., 1990.

Ani, Marimba. *Yurugu: An African-Centered Critique of European Cultural Thought and Behavior.* Trenton, N.J.: Africa World, 1994.

Asante, Molefi Kete. *Afrocentricity.* Rev. ed. Trenton, N.J.: Africa World, 1988.

Bell, Bernard W. *The Afro-American Novel and Its Tradition.* Amherst: University of Massachusetts Press, 1987.

Dixon, Melvin. *Trouble the Water.* Boulder: University of Colorado Press, 1989.

Holloway, Karla F. C. *Moorings and Metaphors: Figures of Culture and Gender in Black Women's Literature.* New Brunswick, N.J.: Rutgers University Press, 1992.

Jackson, Gale. "The Way We Do: A Preliminary Investigation of the African Roots of African American Performance." *Black American Literature Forum* 25 (1991): 11–22.

Kent, George E. "Afro-American Literature: Its Interpretation and Creation Today in Light of Historical Considerations." In *The Next Decade: Theoretical and Research Issues in Africana Studies.* Ed. Joseph Turner. Ithaca, N.Y.: Africana Studies and Research Center, Cornell University, 1984. 121–40.

Nobles, Wade W. "Ancient Egyptian Thought and the Development of African (Black) Psychology." In *Kemet and the African Worldview.* Ed. Maulana Karenga and Jacob Carruthers. Los Angeles: University of Sankore, 1986. 100–118.

Russwurm, John. "The Conditions and Prospects of Haiti." In *Black Literature in*

America: A Comprehensive Anthology. Ed. Richard Barksdale and Keneth Kinnamon. New York: Macmillan, 1972. 190–91.

Some, Malidoma Patrice. *Ritual: Power, Healing, and Community.* Portland, Ore.: Swan Raven and Co., 1993.

Wade, Brent. *Company Man.* Chapel Hill, N.C.: Algonquin, 1992.

Welsh, Kariamu. "Foreword." In *Afrocentricity,* by Molefi Kete Asante. Trenton, N.J.: Africa World, 1988. vii–viii.

9

Are Love and Literature Political?
Black Homopoetics in the 1990s

KENYATTA DOREY GRAVES

> One of the most serious challenges facing black gay intellectu-
> als is the development of a progressive view of homosexuality
> in the African American community. Such a perspective is
> needed to assist the larger African American community's
> struggle for self-determination by freeing it from the limita-
> tions of homophobia, as well as to liberate and self-actualize
> black gay genius.
> —Ron Simmons, "Some Thoughts on the Challenges Facing Black
>   Gay Intellectuals"

Eldridge Cleaver's *Soul on Ice* (1968) includes a scathing indictment of James Baldwin in particular and black homosexuals in general. Cleaver writes: "The white man has deprived
him [the black male homosexual] of his masculinity, castrated him in the center of his burning skull, and when he sub-
mits to this change and takes the white man for his lover as
well as Big Daddy, he focuses on 'whiteness' all the love in his
pent up soul and turns the razor edge of hatred against 'blackness'—upon himself, what he is, and all those who look like
him, remind him of himself. He may even hate the darkness
of night" (101). More than thirty years later, many in the black
community share Cleaver's dis-ease and discomfort with the
way the gay community is *raced*. Some black folk want it stated unabashedly that there is a difference between concrete
oppression based on race, a (generally) unconcealable identity, and *alleged* oppression based upon sexual orientation, an

identity that can (generally) remain hidden. These folk resent the manner in which the gay community appropriates the rhetoric, strategies, and gains of the civil rights movement. This argument assumes that either all the gay people are white or all the gay people are white and minority "sell-outs." Clearly, the political relationship between black folk and lesbian and gay folk beckons for a deeper investigation.[1]

Using these issues as a framework, I want to suggest that the late 1980s and 1990s constitute a third renaissance in black literature. Although many consider the Black Arts movement of the 1960s the "second" black renaissance, I build my argument on the late poet and theorist Essex Hemphill's suggestion that the second renaissance doesn't appear until the 1970s and 1980s, when black women's writing takes creative and critical center stage.[2] Extending Hemphill's thoughts, I posit that the third renaissance marks an open and deliberate engagement of sexual orientation in the literature as never before. This renaissance exists in the production of texts by black gay-, lesbian-, and bisexual-identified writers, images and characterizations of black people of diverse sexual expression in literature and other arts, and the emergence of an identifiable SGL (same-gender-loving)[3] aesthetic in black literature. The evidence of this renaissance appears in the emergence of several works during this period: anthologies edited by Adrian Stanford (*Black and Queer,* 1977), Joseph Beam (*In the Life: A Black Gay Anthology,* 1986), Essex Hemphill, (*Brother to Brother: New Writings by Black Gay Men,* 1991), Shawn Stewart Ruff (*Go the Way Your Blood Beats,* 1996), and Bruce Morrow and Charles H. Rowell (*Shade: An Anthology of Fiction by Gay Men of African Descent,* 1996); novels by Randall Kenan (*A Visitation of Spirits,* 1989), Melvin Dixon (*Vanishing Rooms,* 1990), and Darieck Scott (*Traitor to the Race,* 1995); and films by Marlon Riggs (*Tongues Untied,* 1985), and Isaac Julien (*Looking for Langston,* 1989).[4] The 1990s also witnessed the establishment of nationally recognized black gay pride celebrations and the National Black Lesbian and Gay Leadership Conference, among others.

I will explore sexuality in black literature and culture generally and literature by black SGL men in particular. I will also provide a departure point for a more focused black SGL critical approach to literature and examine the ways black and gay critical discourses and communities coalesce and diverge. Further, I will interpret specific essays, poems, and short stories published in 1990s through a black SGL critical prism and provide possibilities for a more thorough exploration of literary representations of black gay men.

▣ ▣ ▣

The term and identity "SGL" has gained momentum and currency over the last fifteen years; it has been recognized nationally through the work of Cleo Manago, a black SGL California-based activist and the founder of the AMASSI Cultural Center, a space for black affirmation and support for all sexual orientations. SGL connotes that one embraces the expression of his or her same-gender affections and love as a person of color. To call oneself same-gender-loving is a calculated act, clearly continuing the African-American tradition of self-naming and recalling the important distinction between *womanist* and *feminist* ideologies articulated by the novelist Alice Walker.[5] The SGL identity has gained particular favor with Africentrists and those who develop affectional relationships with both women and men. Moreover, the SGL movement offers an affirming and nurturing homespace for black homosexuals who have discovered that the identities gay and lesbian are often synonymous with whiteness and hegemonic institutions.[6] Similarly, popular culture and the advancement of political agendas by the gay community at large leave many heterosexual people of color with the impression that to be gay is to be white; claiming an SGL identity allows one to announce to one's native black community that one fully situates herself or himself within that community. Moreover, SGL places the spirit of love at the forefront of conversation about those who so identify. Often the first thing that comes to mind when one mentions gay or lesbian is behavior— sexual behavior specifically.[7] SGL suggests that sexual orientation is about whom one may have the capacity to love, just like those who identify as heterosexual. And finally, as a black-identified conception of sexuality, SGL provides an opportunity for identification by those who might be hesitant to otherwise identify with their birth orientation. In order to fully appreciate the bold and necessary statement that this identity envisions, let me suggest some issues for discussion, by way of foundation.

In his article "Some Glances at the Black Fag: Race, Same-Sex Desire, and Cultural Belonging," Marlon B. Ross trudges through the manner in which gay communities adopted strategies of political advancement employed by black communities and the impact of racism on interactions between the two. Ross argues that up until the 1960s and 1970s black SGL folk lived within black communities at large with a high degree of tolerance: everyone knew who "the children"[8] were and, for the most part, left "all of that" alone. During the 1950s and 1960s, white homosexuals began to populate urban areas in clearly defined gay neighborhoods or communities. Running to escape the homophobia and hatred of their white communities at large, they were pushed into urban ghettos in the cities. Well, guess who came to dinner?

By the mid 1960s, white gay enclaves had been clearly established and began to flourish next door to historically black communities. These white homosexual communities immediately noticed the manner in which black SGL people were living within their home communities relatively unbothered. Of course, exceptions existed then and they exist now; strains of black nationalist thought, for example, have persistently vilified black SGL men in an attempt to uplift the black male and rescue his masculinity from years of literal and metaphorical castration.[9] And in the late 1990s religious right organizations (traditionally white and caustically conservative) have attempted to build coalitions with black church congregations in efforts to oppose gay rights ballot issues, specifically gay marriage and the addition of sexual orientation as a basis for prosecuting hate crimes under existing legislation.

Ross shows how white homosexuals, who viewed black communities as a ripe site for them to "test their avant-garde status," began to model the minority consciousness of their neighbors. Most importantly, these white homosexuals noticed the way black communities massaged the margin as a liminal space with possibilities. Indeed, white gay communities learned from their black neighbors that to be cast to the edge is not to be tossed over it. In particular, the gay community noticed that black SGL people were not packing their bags and fleeing their home communities and that these communities clearly understood that within the ranks there are no expendable people, regardless of their sexual orientation. However, Ross questions,

> If a black homosexual were to be ostracized from his community, where on earth could he go? This dramatic difference in social, economic, and historical conditions between the black and white homosexual necessarily has led to *a different conception of sexual orientation and coming out.* . . . Integrating same-sex desire within the self meant finding a way to remain integrated within the home community while remaining true to one's desire. . . . For the black homosexual, same-sex desire was a matter of finding a way to reaffirm continuity, rather than a matter of breaking with a dominant culture. . . . After all, how could black gays break with dominant culture, since they were never part of it? (202; emphasis added)

White homosexuals were a different story completely. Though they moved physically, they did not separate from middle-class white ideologies or distance themselves from the racism entrenched in a dominant culture. White exploitation and the promulgation of supremacist ideology often defined the relationship between many white gay and black communities. Some white lesbians and gay men, raised to believe in the right of their privilege and ownership, resented being the sexual "niggers" of their community and made it clear to black communities that mutual oppression based on sexuality did not make them equals. This tension remains just as potent today, as many black SGL people question the need to endorse publicly gay political planks such as the right to marry, while white homosexuals and gay organizations remain silent as affirmative action programs are dismantled. In any event, as white gay communities continued to take notes on how to resist oppression from their black neighbors, gay rights have gained wider acceptance. Ross notes in the close of his analysis: "How ironic that the segregation of gay culture as an autonomous identity which occurred with the emergence of the gay rights movement should lead both to greater freedom and tolerance for homosexual expression in the larger society and to great segregation and intolerance within the African American community" (218). A clear example of Ross's analysis is evident in the fight against the spread of HIV and AIDS. During the 1980s, under the conservative administrations of Ronald Reagan and George Bush, the (white) gay community learned that a focused and continuous lobbying effort would be needed to secure funding for treatment, education, and prevention programs. While African-American organizations and institutions (certainly black churches) have continued to dismiss and ignore AIDS as a white, gay disease—and therefore irrelevant to the black community—the lobbying efforts of the gay community have resulted in a decrease in the spread of the disease within that community. Meanwhile, community-based organizations devoted exclusively to stemming the epidemic in black communities continue to struggle to secure financial resources without the political backing of mainstream political organizations within the black community such as the NAACP or Urban League.

▣ ▣ ▣

As a child I would go to sleep wishing that when I awoke I would be white.
I am no longer a child, but that child has not died. And so I write.
—Reginald Shepherd, "On Not Being White"

With this vortex of political, sexual, and racial questions as my starting point, I would like to turn my attention toward black gay writing during the third renaissance that does *not* center blackness. I'm arguing that the third renaissance is a period in which two phenomena are occurring simultaneously—the first being the emergence of an identifiable SGL aesthetic and the second being the flourishing of writing by black, gay men that privileges the experience of the larger white, gay community. I will begin my literary interpretations by exploring two black gay writers, Reginald Shepherd and Darieck Scott, who have engaged the dynamic of black/white coupling as it relates to identity politics off the page and on the page in essays and fiction.

I'm interested here in the manner in which white men and whiteness enter homosexual politics in black literature. As I have argued earlier and Marlon Ross has shown, whiteness must be engaged because so many African Americans equate it with gayness. Moreover, because there is a long history in the United States of black men suffering physical violence or murder for even the insinuation of an interracial sexual encounter, the topic typically draws strong opinions in black communities. I am suggesting here that part of what fuels tension in black communities over sexual orientation is the intersection of black folks' collective memory of this history of violence against black men with the association of gayness with whiteness.[10] Interracial relationships, therefore, are a logical place to begin an exploration of identity politics, where the two identities, black and gay, meet—or collide. In literature, this collision marks a kind of double consciousness W. E. B. Du Bois may have never imagined. Many texts examine racial politics through fictional interracial relationships, such as Dixon's *Vanishing Rooms* or Kenan's novel *A Visitation of Spirits* and short story collection *Let the Dead Bury Their Dead* (1992); others, such as Reginald Shepherd, opt for a more personalized route.

When I first opened Joseph Beam's *In the Life: A Black Gay Anthology,* I was immediately taken by the title of one of the nonfiction pieces. With one eyebrow raised, I turned to Shepherd's essay "On Not Being White." From the title alone, I expected that someone would disturb the peace; I was not disappointed. Shepherd's essay—a confessional, really—presents for our inspection a narrative on the manner in which he has fingered identity and the seminal role whiteness plays in the development of his identity as a black man and as a gay man. Shepherd shares autobiographical information about a poverty-ladened upbringing (which he equates with blackness), an early understanding of being different, and his entrance into private schools as an escape from blackness. It is when Shepherd turns his attention to his identity as a gay man that his engagement with whiteness seems most problematic. For Shepherd, the embodiment of desire is everything that he wishes to be and cannot. And the sum of those wishes is encased in whiteness. He notes: "And of course if I in particular am seen with a beautiful man, whiteness being intrinsic to my definition of beauty, then in my own mind and in the minds of those around me, around *us,* I am thereby one worthy of whiteness. By being seen with him, I am made an honorary white man for so long as I am with him. Suddenly I am a part of the community. So by being with him I have him and by being seen with him I manage almost to be him" (54). To be sure, the author seems most concerned with the gaze of those who see him with white men and thereby connect him with whiteness; he would thereby be granted the first-class citizenship such a fraternity confers. More than his physical proximity to white men, the closeness of his body to that of a white man is, for Shepherd, a movement towards society's center—the attendant abandonment of what he considers a marginalizing black life becomes the price he's willing to pay to enter the hallowed white gay milieu.

Shepherd's short story "Summertime, and the Living is Easy . . ." reads as if it were a fictive transcription of the anxiety of blackness he reveals in "On Not Being White." The story's protagonist, a young gay, black high school boarding student, spends a languorous summer living the good life at the home of his gay friend, Marshall. Marshall is rich, white, beautiful—everything that the protagonist (and Shepherd) desires. Throughout the summer, he moves from the bedroom to the pool and back to the bedroom, contemplating nothing more than Marshall's beauty as well as his current and former partners (all white). During this "white summer," the protagonist manages to avoid completely anything black, borne out by his erasure of the many black servants, cooks, and groundskeepers employed in maintaining his summer of leisure; he knows they exist, he knows they are black, but he simply does not see them.

Thirteen years after "On Not Being White," Shepherd shares that his fascination with finding an escape from blackness remains the cornerstone of his identity and work. "An Interview with Reginald Shepherd" appeared in the spring 1998 issue of *Callaloo* (the second of companion volumes devoted to "Emerging Male Writers"). Shepherd remains asthmatic over not being white, calls himself a "snow queen,"[11] reduces the majority of black and black gay poetry to political-identity cheerleading, and charts for himself an aesthetic ancestry that only he and the classic poet Carl Phillips remain talented enough to perpetuate.[12] Apparently, the *Callaloo* interview prompted Shepherd to ruminate further on identity; he published "Coloring Outside the Lines: An Essay at Definition" in the winter 1999 issue,

reaching conclusions without any significant degree of difference from his
1986 essay:

> For a white middle-class man, as central by birthright as can be, homosexual-
> ity is a displacement into a degree (and only into a degree) of marginality. But
> for a poor black boy from the Bronx projects . . . occupying the opposite place
> or lack of place in the social spectrum . . . homosexuality, conceived by people
> black and white alike as both a white and a middle-class phenomenon, can
> appear as an opportunity to displace displacement, to move toward the center.
> Gayness appears as a space outside of blackness, identity as utopia: my nowhere.
> (136)

What Shepherd finds in the gay community is an attempt to escape margin-
ality. Unequivocally and unapologetically, both the final destination of that
escape and the vehicle by which he must travel is white(ness). Therefore, I
locate Shepherd as an example of a gay, black writer who decidedly decenters
blackness as a prerequisite for entering homosexuality artistically, critically, and actually—the very pathology Cleaver wrongfully attributed to Baldwin. I find Shepherd's leave-taking of blackness to be more than a personal
choice and fair game for examination; he does, after all, open the door for
the interpretation of what others who see him think, and he gives consider-
able weight to that line of sight. In effect, it is the public viewing of him with
the object of his attraction that moves Shepherd into the space he desires.
In the third renaissance, the art of writers like Shepherd and the manner in
which he constructs desire for himself, his characters, and his poetic voice
reifies the common perception of gay as Anglo-specific.

Although Darieck Scott, in the fourth section of his essay "Jungle Fever:
Black Gay Identity, White Dick, and The Utopian Bedroom," shares that
he, too, is partnered with a white man, there is no hint that his coupling
results from some burning-as-if-his-very-soul-depended-upon-it need to be
so paired. Unlike Shepherd, who seems strangely unaware of an antiblack
perspective (as I read it, at least) in the matriculation of his desire, Scott's
effort is to ensure that our discourse on interracial relationships includes at
least two significant issues: an affirmation that neither identity nor desire is
fixed; and a disruption of the binary that intraracial relationships are pure,
compulsory, and essential to black liberation politics, while interracial relationships inhere the very definition of sexual domination and self-hatred.

I find more disagreement with the second of Scott's issues, which he engages in the example of Joseph Beam's oft quoted affirmation that "Black
men loving black men will be the revolutionary act of the 1980s."[13] While

he is encouraged by the idea of black men loving each other in a universal sense, Scott is troubled by the mandate he hears embedded within the affirmation. Particularly problematic to him is the way the filmmaker Marlon Riggs invokes it; Riggs's documentary *Tongues Untied* gives audiovisual bite to Beam's call to action and extends it beyond the decade to announce that "Black men loving Black men is *the* revolutionary act." As Scott observes:

> Beam's words . . . have frequently been reduced, in unstructured interactions between black gay men, in organization meetings as well as in print and artistic performance, to a directive against interracial dating. The various meanings we could ascribe to "black men loving black men" have been condensed to a single image, that of the black gay male romantic couple, the potency and appeal of which has sometimes had the effect of emphasizing romantic relationships between black men while devaluing the possibility of other kinds of relationships. ("Jungle Fever" 304)

Clearly, that Beam's proclamation is so often seized upon suggests that it might well represent a sort of healing balm the community needs to apply. Both Beam's initial proclamation and Riggs's reiteration of it appeared in black communities in the late 1980s and early 1990s, a time when a new emphasis on black SGL people further amplified the absence of black faces at the forefront of the gay rights struggle. As an expression adopted by masses of black SGL people, this "revolutionary act," or at least the call for it, responds to that absence and seeks to interrupt the popular notion of the essential whiteness of the gay community. Clearly, Beam's essay and Riggs's film are directed toward black communities. This affirmation, therefore, enters a conversation within black communities and wants to unearth the ordinariness of black SGL relationships there. Although Scott sees potential in the idea of black men loving each other, he cautions that demonizing the opposite construction, the black/white romantic relationship, dilutes the potency of such a balm.

Central to Scott's critique of the romanticized black male couple is the understanding of the fluidity of identity and desire. Scott destabilizes the integrity of gay and black as single identities by asserting the destructive potential of avowing an essential experience for either. He rightly points out the irony of positing a single black experience by gay men who have traditionally been excluded from conceptualizations of black because of their sexuality or from the domain of gayness because of their race. Moreover, since desire often concerns one's conceptualization of two bodies (oneself and one other), each with multiple identities (black, gay, male, southern, American), it must also be understood as a shifting, inexact phenomenon:

> The question remains whether the usefulness of traditional identity politics means that its approach is therefore *always* necessary. That is, positions *between* essentialized identities might also be said to occupy a space of dynamism—and, to be sure, of peril. . . . To stake out positions *between* is to foreground the strategic quality of identity, indeed of all political positions; between as choice, which is not the same as neither but is closer to both or all, prescribes constant shift, even if only in a limited way in the case of black gay identity, which (in its initial conception, at least) rocks between just two poles rather than swaying among many. (306–7)

Scott and I part company in his application of this theoretical construction. True, desire does not remain constant, and identities are discursively constructed; they are, however, real. Shifting desire and destabilized identities are wonderful fodder for journal engagements, but down here on the ground race is lived, touched, oppressed, and murdered. One does not simply trip and fall into an interracial relationship—at least, not here in the racially mapped United States, where desire has historically been racially determined. Therefore, to suggest that black men loving each other is a revolutionary act and to mean just that, with all the negative connotations of the opposite intact, is to choose black deliberately as a primary (if not sole) identity. Desire may be influenced, but it certainly is not out of the realm of individual control, at least as it pertains to race.[14] And while standing at the crossroads may offer choice (i.e., black or gay), standing between and claiming neither offers no power, no voice, and no direction.

Scott's contribution to *Shade*, "This City of Men," is far more complicated in its examination of what he has argued are the blurred intersections of race and desire. Unlike the protagonist of "Summertime," Scott's black protagonist Julius (or Jules, as he is nicknamed in the story), concerns himself with the pursuit of another black man. "This City of Men" is a letter of confession from Jules to Danielle, whom we assume to be his current girlfriend. The reader discovers, with Danielle, that Jules remains in Kansas long after he has finished hearing depositions because he has become sexually and intellectually drawn to Eric, a former high school friend who has been incarcerated in Fort Leavenworth for raping a young white boy. Jules retells Eric's story, the manner in which he allowed the young white boy to seduce him over time until the final act, which, of course, "he wanted." Slowly, Jules becomes sexually attracted to Eric and everything that Eric represents for him.

Still, what seethes beneath this taut exploration of Jules's desire is the pursuit of whiteness, although the engagements are subtly rendered. Jules describes Eric thusly: "About his color I can say more, I fear. His skin was (and is) very dark, poised just at the edge of ebony, finely dusky and suede-smooth even to the eye. . . . There is a compelling sensuality to the color, a physicality. A sexual potency" (124). Quickly, it becomes clear that Jules is as much fascinated with Eric as the latter was obsessed with his rape victim. His pursuit of what we have come to know as the big, thick, black buck image places him in the position of wanting to be the one who had been raped. The more Jules hears about the pursuit and the final rape, the more titillated he becomes. Subsequently, we learn that Eric knows exactly what Jules is doing, culminating in him telling Jules, "'I could do it to you, too. Would you like that?'" (138).

In "This City of Men" Scott explores the ways in which "black men who sleep with black men live with the burden of history, too, however differently that history might operate from the way it does in an interracial couple" ("Jungle Fever" 308). Scott foregrounds the way in which a racialized sexuality gets internalized for black, gay men. The only way for Jules to experience Eric sexually is to trade places (if only in his fantasies) with the white boy Eric violates. Scott provides a fascinating twist by imagining a character who, like Shepherd, seeks to enter the body of a white man—this time for the hunt of blackness. He purposefully relies upon stereotypical constructions—namely, Eric's physical description and the binary of Eric's vernacular speech against the polished, stilted language Jules employs even in the letter he composes to Danielle. Here Scott illuminates an internalized racism that leaves Jules so caught up in the pursuit of Eric, the stereotypically hypersexualized black man, that he is willing to alter the course of his life (he remains in Kansas despite having concluded his business, suggesting an uncertainty about the implications on his career). In the end, what we have is a black man, Jules, entering the gay community through the portal of attempting to trade places with whiteness, thereby distancing himself from his home community through the confession to Danielle. While Scott's problematizing of internalized racism in the construction of black gay desire is penetrating, ultimately "This City of Men" amplifies the *whiteness* of being gay. Such inscriptions, therefore, make all the more vital and essential the configuring of an SGL aesthetic to insinuate homosexuality into black literary discourse.

⊡ ⊡ ⊡

I chose this tribe
of warriors and outlaws.
—Essex Hemphill, *In the Life*

In articulating an SGL critical approach to black literature, I aim to delineate the nuances of same-sex desire to show how several texts contribute to the long and fertile history of black literary expression and tradition.
From my critical perspective, foregrounding the affiliation with the home
community is far more important than building political coalitions with the
larger gay community. As Marlon Ross reminds us, SGL black people tend
to live in black communities and attend black churches, block parties, June-
teenth celebrations, and historically black colleges and universities (and join
black fraternities and sororities at those schools). Privileging an affiliation
with blackness is simply an acknowledgment that being a black person is
the primary identity, ideologically and through everyday lived experiences,
for the majority of the black community. The very foundation of naming
ourselves, of claiming our own identity, is key to demonstrating a clear desire to be *black* gay men rather than *gay* black men. But the point is about
more than (mis)placing modifiers. Similarly, in a society where love and literature are political and everything is at stake, calling for a focus on SGL
issues in black literature can only strengthen the content and critical understanding of the literature generally.

In focusing on black SGL literature, I mean to suggest that gay readings
of black literature have brought some visibility to black homosexual writers but have largely privileged black gay male writers who partner with white
men or create characters who do (re: Baldwin's *Another Country*). Such
readings have also served to acknowledge that gay writers come from all
communities, once again borrowing on the strength of the African-American literary tradition, yet invoking this "we are the world" energy belies the
often supremacist ideologies of these same readings. The gay literature/queer
theory camp has illuminated little about black communities (except to con-
demn, unjustly, the black community and its presumed hyper-homophobia)
and has virtually ignored the possibility of a black SGL consciousness—that
is to say, a foregrounding of belonging to blackness.[15]

Further, I mean to show the complications and possibilities available when
black literature is opened and extended because of the critical attention
trained towards images of black SGL men, particularly those who struggle
to live openly and wholly within their own communities, and black SGL
writers. And although I'll be among the first to critique notions of black-

ness that do not include sexual diversity, I mean to accomplish this opening and expanding without further fractionalizing the community. By focusing on the love in black SGL relationships in a deliberate fashion, I mean to make it common knowledge to Intro to Black Lit students and British Lit Ph.D.s alike that black men have always loved and will always make love to each other and that these love relationships are not to be considered revolutionary except in the minds of those who find it difficult even to conceptualize such a thing, including those born with the same sexual orientation.

And by making more common the exploration of same-gender love in romantic literary relationships, I look forward to the natural inward direction such a discourse will inaugurate—for instance, a closer exploration of same-gender love in black male platonic and familial relationships. Surely we could use a refreshed notion of black masculinity and manhood that allows for a blared-eyes kind of gaze at intimacy between black men of all sexual orientations.

Often black SGL writers produce moving and accomplished texts that decenter whiteness, positioning it just outside the field of view. Consider the last section of Hemphill's poem "The Tomb of Sorrow," a name his former lover gives to Washington, D.C.'s Meridian Hill (according to Washington maps) or Malcolm X Park (according to black Washingtonians). During the first five sections, Hemphill establishes the type of pain that fills the ugly-beautiful park, including the open-air drug market the sidewalks become in the daytime and the open-air sexual trade available to men who step into the dark, grassy areas at night:

> These are meaningless kisses
> (aren't they?)
> that we pass back and forth
> like poppers and crack pipes,
> . . . .
> Gunshots ring out above our heads,
> a few of us are seeking romance,
> others a piece of ass,
> some—a stroke of dick.
> The rest of us are killing.
> The rest of us get killed. (76)

As in all of Hemphill's prose and poetry, the issues facing this poem's persona, clearly identified as a homosexual man, do not exist outside the boundaries of the black community (the infamous U Street area of northwest

Washington) in this poem. The love the voice of this poem wants is understood in the snap and fury of gusting activity, activity moored to community. What is fundamental to the voice is that he find some deeper love to come
into, while ensconced by his native black community, a homespace implod-
ing around him.

And although the economic and political realities that have transformed
Malcolm X Park into the "tomb of sorrow" are certainly vested in dominant culture, they are not in the field of view. That is to say that while racism and white supremacy pervade the economic realities of those who live
in this community, the face of whiteness itself is absent during the drug and
sex trade this speaker experiences. Had Hemphill opted to restrict the poem's sight to blackness (assumed to be heterosexual), the pursuit of love
would be unavailable to the voice of this poem. Similarly, a gay-sighted poem
would have ignored the harshness of the park environment and concerned
itself solely with copulation, race being the effaceable signifier.

Hemphill's poetry and prose clearly borrow from the protest tradition of
writers like Wright, Baldwin, Ellison, and Walker. His poetics are interwoven with an unquestioning assertion of an SGL consciousness into the truth
of black life. For Hemphill, understanding truth requires an examination
of the irony of a community that bears drug trade, drive-by shootings, and
dangerous sexual liaisons in a park renamed for an icon who preached communal self-preservation and advancement. By taking as the site of his poem
Malcolm X Park and making the gazer of his poem an SGL man, Hemphill
reinscribes a sense of black community that cannot possibly be dismissive
of sexual difference.

Within the discursive context of the race-sexual desire nexus, consider
Bennet Capers's affective and heartbreaking short story "Nobody Gets
Hurt." The story spans a mere twenty-four hours of linear time as the reader discovers two black men in their late teens, Paris and Roy, in personal crises. Paris is struggling to navigate his life after the death of his mother and
his three-week-old marriage to his mother's deathbed nurse, which fulfilled
his mother's dying wish that he marry. Recently laid off from his job and now
separated from his lover and best friend by way of a wedding band, Roy
attempts to convince Paris to help him rob a gas station. Paris refuses, sure
that Roy isn't serious, only to come home from work, turn on the television,
and discover that he misread Roy's desperation on a couple of levels:

> Before my mother got sick, Roy and me would come here almost every day,
> would spend hours sometimes just joking around, or watching TV, or getting

lit, not saying a word. This is my first time here since my mother got sick. What little furniture was here then is now gone, and looking at the emptiness, I know Roy's sold it all, electricity's probably been turned off too. Only his cot and his books are left, the books stacked in a corner by the window. *Native Son. Invisible Man. Giovanni's Room.* On the floor next to the books is a gun. I pick it up and run my fingers along its curve. It feels like something perfect, like a warm summer night—like six on a warm summer night. I open the cylinder, and look through six empty circles at Roy. He never even had bullets. I close the cylinder. Spin it round and round with my thumb. (26–27)

Capers provides a lucid and explosive moment of passion, history, and intimacy between two black men. His story calls to mind characters who love in the midst of ever-enclosing chaos—Sethe and Paul D or Janie and Tea Cake, for example. Capers, like Morrison and Hurston, gives us psychological insight into the turmoil of the pursuit of happiness when claiming ownership of that happiness is denied to the character based on his or her identity as black or female or SGL. In this scene, the formula of epiphany through violence that Bigger Thomas reaches or liberation through journey that the Invisible Man discovers is informed by and coalesces with the exploration of sexuality that Baldwin first engages in his groundbreaking openly gay-themed novel, *Giovanni's Room* (1956). The Baldwin reference is intertextual ancestor-calling; the tenderness available to Capers's reader in discovering that Roy would attempt to rob a gas station simply to get his lover's attention arrives at the price of a more subtle relationship between, say, Baldwin's John Grimes and that character's older teen-aged mentor, Elisha, in his autobiographical first novel, *Go Tell It on the Mountain* (1953). Such moments will become more and more available to us, seem less revolutionary, and feel more ordinary as more black writers weave same-gender-love into their protest, discovery, and survival thematics.

Other SGL writers like G. Winston James, the author of the short story "Church" (also in *Shade*), vehemently insert SGL into the discourse of black liberation in general. One of the most familiar sites of black liberation and community knowing is the black church. In his first-person narrative, James's protagonist has returned to his mother's home to await the end of his suffering from AIDS. It has been years since he attended the church of his youth, and the first half of the story is concerned with the familiar sounds, sights, scents, and soloists of the congregation. Everything about home returns to his spirit even before he settles into the pew. At the familiar point in the service where visitors are asked to stand and be welcomed, the pastor calls the protagonist to the front of the pulpit and questions him about his travels, his success as a writer, and his education. The "prodigal son" is filled with emotion and begins to speak to the congregation about living life fully until his mother is so overcome with passion that she shouts and weeps, "'Can't no AIDS just take my baby!'" (100). James writes: "I thought then that she was singing about more than God. Walking with my momma, and crying with my niece and nephew, I knew that she was singing about family. She was singing about the Church family. The Black family. Even in its weakness, it was stronger than tribulation" (101). The reverence bestowed upon the black church is immeasurable; often fulfilling cultural needs more than spiritual ones, worship in black communities has always been intertwined with the quest for freedom of the body. For example, enslaved African Americans crafted spirituals that became oral maps for navigating the Underground Railroad to self-ownership; many black churches doubled as schoolhouses during the Jim Crow era; and black church leaders often spearheaded efforts to desegregate American society during the 1950s and 1960s.[16] Therefore, as the protagonist of "Church" experiences the kinetic energy of the black church experience, James immerses the reader in a moment of *complete blackness*—what Ellison in *Invisible Man* deemed the "blackness of blackness." To insist that the protagonist bring his full self into his home church is to call forth the history of righteous struggle in black communities, to locate an SGL consciousness wholly within that history of struggle and a community knowing that is "stronger than tribulation." The close of the story is movement and power, as an SGL child is welcomed back into the center of the congregation, demonstrating the black community's potential to coalesce, reembrace, and change.

Writers like Hemphill, Capers, and James extend the boundaries of what has been thought to be *the* black experience in literature. In each case, they situate same-gender love within the midst of traditional depictions of black community. Consider, for a moment, the community that lives in and around Hemphill's "The Tomb of Sorrow," one that understands all of the myriad reasons why men seek trade in Malcolm X Park. Or imagine what breakfast conversation might be when Paris's neighbors in Capers's "Nobody Gets Hurt" open their morning paper and read about the two brother-lovers arrested for attempted armed robbery. And what sermon might the pastor of James's "Church" deliver following the protagonist's revelation? For each writer, same-gender love is not presented as a question to be resolved; whatever issues arise with respect to sexual orientation are generated by the representations of the communities in which the protagonists reside. The writers' insertion of same-gender-loving subjectivity into familiar landscape, lore, and literary tropes presents black communities an opportunity to envision the margin as what bell hooks has described as a place of "radical openness."[17] Similarly, an SGL critical approach to black literature suggests the possibilities for new interpretations of sexuality, sex roles, and family within the corpus of African-American literature.

Perhaps what is most encouraging about the charting of an SGL critical approach in the third renaissance of black literature is the ability to stand in a moment of change, fully conscious of the upheaval taking place. Essex Hemphill is the final author published in the *Norton Anthology of African American Literature;* I am encouraged by the signpost I read in the editors' decision to give Hemphill the final word and am heartened by Barbara Christian's assertion that Hemphill sought to "reestablish, *uncloseted,* his connection to the larger [black] community" (2608; emphasis added).[18] I take from Hemphill's creative lead my critical imperative in suggesting the existence of an uncloseted third renaissance and the fashioning of an SGL aesthetic, as a black-centered engagement of sexuality that militantly demands inclusivity in lieu of a myopic conceptualization of blackness, where same-gender love is too often peripheralized, demonized, or e-raced altogether.

Notes

1. In the summer of 1999 the New Press published *Dangerous Liaisons: Blacks, Gays, and the Struggle for Equality,* a collection of essays, edited by Eric Brandt, examining the intersection of political ideologies between African-American and gay communities.

2. See Essex Hemphill's "Introduction," in *Brother to Brother,* xxvii.

3. With all deference to the work of feminist theorists and others who, in examining the construction of sex roles, have suggested an important distinction between sex (male/female) and gender (masculine/feminine), the word "gender" in the term "same-gender-loving" connotes same-sex desire.

4. This paper is tailored to an analysis of writing by black men. The third renaissance of black literary art that I'm referencing is one in which the works of black SGL men *and* women gain prominence. Writings by Audre Lorde, Jacqueline Woodson, and Jewelle Gomez, as well as the Catherine E. McKinley and Joyce DeLaney anthology *Afrekete: An Anthology of Black Lesbian Writing* and the films of Cheryl Dunye and Michelle Parkerson represent the invaluable work of black lesbians during the third literary renaissance.

5. See Alice Walker's prose collection *In Search of Our Mothers' Gardens.*

6. Throughout the last thirty years, the face of the lesbian and gay rights move-

ment has been painted white in and by the media, although the modern gay rights movement began in New York, when black and Latino "drag queens" catalyzed the Stonewall rebellion in 1969.

7. For a cogent analysis of how sexuality, race, and behavior intersect, see Keith Boykin's chapter "Are Blacks and Gays the Same?" in *One More River to Cross,* particularly the section entitled "Comparing Behavior" (39–51).

8. "The children" is black SGL vernacular for members of black SGL community.

9. See Frances Cress Welsing's *The Isis Papers* for a relentlessly homophobic diatribe that argues that black men who are psychologically enervated by white supremacy "retreat" to homosexuality. Also see Molefi Kete Asante's 1988 pronouncement that "an Afrocentric perspective recognizes its existence but homosexuality cannot be condoned or accepted as good for the national development of a strong people" (57), which ensured that the burgeoning doctrine of Afrocentricity as a theoretical basis of scholarship included an antiprogressive notion of sexuality held over from 1960s black nationalist thought. Asante has since altered his position, granting that one need not be heterosexual to make valuable and lasting contributions to the betterment of black communities.

10. I am not granting the gay-equals-white misperception or reversing arguments I have attempted to advance so far in this essay. Instead, I'm suggesting that writing in the third renaissance practically and necessarily chooses not to ignore the dominant perception of a raced sexuality.

11. "Snow Queen" is black SGL vernacular—generally derogatory—for black gay men who date white men exclusively.

12. See Charles H. Rowell, "An Interview with Reginald Shepherd," 293.

13. See Joseph Beam, "Brother to Brother: Words from the Heart."

14. I want to be clear about my intentions here. I'm suggesting a less-than-romantic analysis of dating and relationships and arguing that decisions are made with respect to dating choices—a certain height is preferred to another, or educational background, or age, or eye color. Certainly, in the racially charged climate of the United States, it would be impossible for a black man to enter a relationship with a white man without considering the racial implications of that decision.

15. For example, Arthur Flannigan-Saint-Aubin performs a stereotypical misreading of the anthology *Brother to Brother: New Writings by Black Gay Men* in his article "'Black Gay Male' Discourse: Reading Race and Sexuality between the Lines." Throughout his analysis, he finds that the anthology is simply not "gay" enough, taking exception to an attempt to articulate black gay male desire (too much emphasis on black) or an engagement with a heterosexual audience (too little emphasis on gay). Finally, he questions, "is the intermixture of black and gay somehow sufficiently distinct from both categories to warrant an anthology that could not simply be a black or gay anthology?" (475–76). Because engagements with race in gay discourse have been marginal at best, Flannigan-Saint-Aubin meets with a high degree of difficulty in envisioning a black SGL consciousness that is about black-

ness complicated by sexuality. His prescription is clear: "I am suggesting here a black-gaymale entry into literary discourse that explicitly and presciently engages the white gay male reader by judiciously encoding him within the text" (488). Flannigan-Saint-Aubin's inability to imagine a literary space where black SGL men explore their interior lives within a wholly black sphere of thought demonstrates the urgency for an engagement of sexuality in black literature from an SGL perspective. Moreover, glancing through Henry Abelove et al.'s *Lesbian and Gay Studies Reader,* one may find articles that interrogate homophobia in black communities (e.g., Barbara Smith and Philip Brian Harper), but one will not find an interrogation of racism in gay communities.

16. For an innovative discussion of the interconnectedness of "heterosexual" sacred spaces and "homosexual" secular ones, see E. Patrick Johnson's article "Feeling the Spirit in the Dark: Expanding Notions of the Sacred in the African-American Gay Community."

17. In "Choosing the Margin as a Space of Radical Openness," hooks argues that those of us who are committed to "counter-hegemonic cultural practice" should seek the margin—standing away from those oppressive structures at the center—as the most fertile site of resistance, the space where distance provides an unobstructed sightline to re-vision our ideologies.

18. The volume lists Christian as the editor of the "Literature since 1970" section; therefore, I attribute the notes on Hemphill to her.

Works Cited

Abelove, Henry, Michèle Aina Barale, and David M. Halperin, eds. *Lesbian and Gay Studies Reader.* New York: Routledge, 1993.

Asante, Molefi Kete. *Afrocentricity.* Trenton, N.J.: Africa World Press, 1988.

Beam, Joseph. "Brother to Brother: Words from the Heart." In *In the Life: A Black Gay Anthology.* Ed. Joseph Beam. Boston: Alyson Publications, 1986. 230–42.

———, ed. *In the Life: A Black Gay Anthology.* Boston: Alyson Publications, 1986.

Boykin, Keith. *One More River to Cross: Black and Gay in America.* New York: Anchor Books, 1996.

Brandt, Eric, ed. *Dangerous Liaisons: Blacks, Gays, and the Struggle for Equality.* New York: The New Press, 1999.

Capers, Bennet. "Nobody Gets Hurt." In *Shade: An Anthology of Fiction by Gay Men of African Descent.* Ed. Bruce Morrow and Charles H. Rowell. New York: Avon Books, 1996. 14–28.

Christian, Barbara T. "Essex Hemphill." In *The Norton Anthology of African American Literature.* Ed. Henry Louis Gates Jr. and Nellie Y. McKay. New York: Norton, 1997. 2608–9.

Cleaver, Eldridge. *Soul on Ice.* New York: McGraw-Hill, 1968.

Dixon, Melvin. *Vanishing Rooms.* New York: Dutton, 1991.

Flannigan-Saint-Aubin, Arthur. "'Black Gay Male' Discourse: Reading Race and

Sexuality between the Lines." *Journal of the History of Sexuality* 3.3 (1993): 468–90.

Hemphill, Essex. "Introduction." In *Brother to Brother: New Writings by Black Gay Men*. Ed. Essex Hemphill. Boston: Alyson Publications, 1991. xv–xxxi.

———. "The Tomb of Sorrow." In *Brother to Brother: New Writings by Black Gay Men*. Ed. Essex Hemphill. Boston: Alyson Publications, 1991. 75–83.

———, ed. *Brother to Brother: New Writings by Black Gay Men*. Boston: Alyson Publications, 1991.

hooks, bell. "Choosing the Margin as a Space of Radical Openness." In *Yearning: Race, Gender, and Cultural Politics*. Boston: South End Press, 1990. 145–53.

James, G. Winston. "Church." In *Shade: An Anthology of Fiction by Gay Men of African Descent*. Ed. Bruce Morrow and Charles H. Rowell. New York: Avon Books, 1996. 91–102.

Johnson, E. Patrick. "Feeling the Spirit in the Dark: Expanding Notions of the Sacred in the African-American Gay Community." *Callaloo* 21.2 (Spring 1998): 399–416.

Julien, Isaac. *Looking for Langston*. New York: Third World Newsreel, 1989.

Kenan, Randall. *Let the Dead Bury Their Dead and Other Stories*. New York: Harcourt, Brace, and Co., 1992.

———. *A Visitation of Spirits*. New York: Grove Press, 1989.

McKinney, Catherine E., and L. Joyce Delaney, eds. *Afrekete: An Anthology of Black Lesbian Writing*. New York: Doubleday, 1995.

Morrow, Bruce, and Charles H. Rowell, eds. *Shade: An Anthology of Fiction by Gay Men of African Descent*. New York: Avon Books, 1996.

Riggs, Marlon T. *Tongues Untied*. San Francisco: Frameline, 1989.

Ross, Marlon B. "Some Glances at the Black Fag: Race, Same-Sex Desire, and Cultural Belonging." *Canadian Review of Comparative Literature* 21.1–2 (March–June 1994): 193–219.

Rowell, Charles H. "An Interview with Reginald Shepherd." *Callaloo* 21.2 (Spring 1998): 290–307.

Ruff, Shawn Stewart, ed. *Go the Way Your Blood Beats*. New York: Henry Holt and Co., 1996.

Scott, Darieck. "Jungle Fever: Black Gay Identity Politics, White Dick, and the Utopian Bedroom." *GLQ: A Journal of Lesbian and Gay Studies* 3 (1994): 299–321.

———. "This City of Men." In *Shade: An Anthology of Fiction by Gay Men of African Descent*. Ed. Bruce Morrow and Charles H. Rowell. New York: Avon Books, 1996. 117–40.

———. *Traitor to the Race*. New York: Dutton, 1995.

Shepherd, Reginald. "Coloring Outside the Lines: An Essay at Definition." *Callaloo* 22.1 (Winter 1999): 134–40.

———. "On Not Being White." In *In the Life: A Black Gay Anthology*. Ed. Joseph Beam. Boston: Alyson Publications, 1986. 46–57.

————. "Summertime, and the Living Is Easy . . ." In *Shade: An Anthology of Fiction by Gay Men of African Descent*. Ed. Bruce Morrow and Charles H. Rowell. New York: Avon Books, 1996. 65–75.

Stanford, Adrian. *Black and Queer*. Boston: Good Gay Poets, 1977.

Walker, Alice. *In Search of Our Mothers' Gardens: Womanist Prose*. New York: Harcourt, Brace, and Co., 1983.

Welsing, Frances Cress. *The Isis Papers*. Chicago: Third World Press, 1991.

10

Healing the Scars of Masculinity: Reflections on Baseball, Gunshots, and War Wounds in August Wilson's *Fences*

KEITH CLARK

And then the occasion arose when I had to meet the white man's eyes. An unfamiliar weight burdened me. The real world challenged my claims. In the white world the man of color encounters difficulties in the development of his bodily schema. Consciousness of the body is solely a negating activity. It is a third-person consciousness. The body is surrounded by an atmosphere of certain uncertainty.
—Frantz Fanon, *Black Skin, White Masks*

Sula was smiling. "I mean, I don't know what the fuss is about. I mean, everything in the world loves you [black men]. White men love you. They spend so much time worrying about your penis they forget their own. The only thing they want to do is cut off a nigger's privates. And if that ain't love I don't know what is. And white women? They chase you all to every corner of the earth, feel for you under every bed. I knew a white woman wouldn't leave the house after 6 o'clock for fear one of you would snatch her. Now ain't that love? They think rape soon's they see you, and if they don't get the rape they looking for, they scream it anyway just so the search won't be in vain. Colored women worry themselves into bad health just trying to hang on to your cuffs. Even little children—white and black, boys and girls—spend all their childhood eating their hearts out 'cause they think you don't love them. And

if that ain't enough, you love yourselves. Nothing in this world loves a black man more than another black man. You hear of solitary white men, but niggers? Can't stay away from one another a whole day. So it looks to me like you the envy of the world."
—Toni Morrison, *Sula*

I think in almost every play most of my male characters have scars.
—August Wilson

African-American men, whether discursive *subjects* or *subjugated* in contemporary social conflagrations, maintain a tenuous place in the American consciousness. The black male body serves an array of conflicting social and cultural functions: the infamous Willie Hortonization of black bodies, in which they are vilified as sexual predators while simultaneously providing grist for presidential campaign mills; the Michael Jordanization of the body, where the athleticized black corpus generates billions of dollars for disparate nonblack conglomerations ("Be Like Mike" and *Space Jam* being two of the myriad commercial ventures that emblazoned the basketball legend into the popular imagination); the criminalization of black bodies, evidenced by a prison industrial complex that conjures images of the southern plantation and the deluge of televised cautionary tales warning viewers about the feral black and brown menace and the white men in blue committed to its eradication (e.g., *Cops*). Inexorably, American culture has trafficked in the black male body. Alternatively objectified, sexualized, and demonized, such corporeal blaxploitation renders the words of Morrison's Sula Mae Peace incontrovertible: it must be love.

The primary impetus for my exploration of deformed images of masculinity in August Wilson's *Fences* stems from what I've observed as his commitment to dramatizing the physical and psychological manifestations of pain in black men. As his epigraphic quote evinces, scarring is a salient metaphor in his works: consider Levee in *Ma Rainey's Black Bottom* (1985), who was wounded during the racially motivated rape of his mother, or Hambone in *Two Trains Running* (1992), whose corpse is carved with scars "all on his back, his chest . . . his legs" (the origins of which are never revealed). I am interested in the link between psychic and physical pain—how physical wounds and scars allow us to enter into black men's interior lives to explore the sources of their omnipresent despair. Though many of Wilson's characters experience crushing racialized violence, I'm more concerned with the psychic-physical pain nexus and possible interventions in a culture consistently devoted to denying black men the emotional space to express and experience hurt (but not the experiences that engender such pain). Before turning my critical attention to *Fences,* I will discuss some contemporary instances of how society persistently fails to grant black men the room to express and experience pain in nonviolent and nonconfrontational ways.

Bigger's Homies at the Millennium: Psychocultural Erasure and the Black Male Body

Incontestably, horrific cultural events like the brutal assassinations of Emmit Till and Medgar Evers—their mangled corpses forever stamped into the collective African-American psyche—and the 1998 lynching of James Byrd in Jasper, Texas, grimly attest to our cancerous racial past and present. Moreover, other tragedies such as the murder of Ennis Cosby have compelled me to meditate on pain and violation in a slightly different context. Immediately following his son's murder by a white Russian emigrant, the 1980s' paterfamilias Bill Cosby found himself at the eye of a media storm not about his crushing personal loss but about an alleged "love child," a daughter purportedly sired during an adulterous relationship. Though this story was eventually proven false, that the press reported it as incontrovertible fact at a time when the comedian was undergoing immense personal suffering exposed America's parochial conceptualization of black men. Indeed, the image of black men in personal, psychic pain gainsays the more commonly and comfortably held fiction of their genetically inherent criminality and pathology, which bell hooks summarizes eloquently: "Images of black men as rapists, as dangerous menaces to society, have been sensational cultural currency for some time. The obsessive media focus on these representations is political. The role it plays in the maintenance of racist domination is to convince the public that black men are a dangerous threat who must be controlled by any means necessary, including annihilation" (61). Because this perverse belief has lodged itself within the marrow of our tradition and collective consciousness, reimagining black men in any other way might be considered heretical. Thus, the Cosbys, father and son, were eviscerated on several fronts—physical, personal, emotional. In America's deformed and deforming perspective, black men are denied an interiority, an emotional and psychic complexity that undermines their presumed bestiality. Never can they be pitiable victims of random violence perpetrated by whites; concomitantly, they are not allowed to mourn murdered sons. Acknowledging the inner life—the noncorporeal, noncriminal, nonathletic life—of African-American men ultimately contradicts a sacrosanct, patriotically correct narrative that deems them either implacable victimizers or parasitic victims like Richard Wright's *über-nigger,* Bigger Thomas, an amalgamation of both and undeserving of sympathy and compassion.

Hortense Spillers's discussion of the African body's seizure and objectification in Western culture provides a theoretical model that buttresses contemporary cultural narratives that reduce black men to purely corporeal entities devoid of psychological/emotional complexity. She posits that

> 1) The captive body becomes the source of an irresistible, destructive sensuality; 2) at the same time—in stunning contradiction—the captive body reduces to a thing, becoming being for the captor; 3) in this absence from a subject position, the captured sexualities provide a physical and biological expression of "otherness"; 4) as a category of "otherness," the captive body translates into a potential for pornotroping and embodies sheer physical powerlessness that slides into a more general "powerlessness," resonating through various centers of human and social meaning. (67)

What complicates Spillers's categorizations in contemporary cultural discourse are the practices of some "captivated" bodies, specifically black men who appropriate and validate the very abnegating fictions that render them spiritually and intellectually captive and bereft. Witness, for instance, the perpetuation of archetypes such as the ba-ad nigger (Stagolee, Shaft, Tupac, et al.) or the corrosive hypermasculinity and attendant misogyny that pervade too many male rap artists' toasts and boasts. Still, because Western culture has traditionally withheld "subject positions" from "captive" black bodies, literature has served as a vehicle for interrogating the pain of native sons trying to situate themselves within the confining discourses of Anglo-American male subjectivity—the Biggers and Invisible Men who experience a socially gnawing American hunger. As artistic intervention, then, Wilson's dramatic corpus lays bare and dissects a pain that goes beyond racial and economic injustices: *Fences,* especially, chronicles the catastrophic consequences of black men's obliviousness to their psychic malaise as well as the curative responses some men fashion to resist it.

Within and against this framework, I will explore how *Fences* offers alternative models for subjectivity for subjugated men who are consistently deprived of outlets for expressing pain or who express it in self- or community-annihilating ways. Innovatively, Wilson uses as his thematic and structural scaffolding institutions such as war, sports, and prison—all archetypally male-oriented events and venues—to register the pain black men endure when adhering to gender constructs that are anathema to personal and familial well-being. Avoiding the pitfalls of portraying black men as infallible victims, Wilson's protagonists often inculcate notoriously hegemonic constructions of masculinity that short-circuit their own emotional emancipation. Not merely fixed by the white gaze in the Fanonian sense (re: the first epigraph), figures such as Troy Maxson misguidedly valorize the very configurations of gender that deny their multisubjectivity and lend currency to the same cultural fictions that preclude their ability to feel and express pain. However, the black male mosaic Wilson embroiders in *Fences* contains numerous countervoices as well, for he simultaneously proffers black men who resist obdurate, deformative gender constructions. In a culture that refuses to acknowledge black men's interior selves, and given black men's complicity through their adherence to a "cult of manhood," the dramatist redefines the terms of subjectivity, linking them to the repositioning of the self within a communal/familial context that allows pain to be shared and destabilized. Thus, Wilson imaginatively employs tropes such as physical mutilation and sports to expose black men's misguided acceptance of deforming patriarchal masculinity, but also to inaugurate a consideration of black men's psychic and spiritual pain and the array of alternative and potentially regenerative responses to it.

Of Kith and Ki(l)n: Wilsonian Counteraesthetics

Unlike the dominant sociohistorical discourse that deems black men psychopathic and bestial, Wilson's dramatic oeuvre reflects his commitment to negating such pernicious cultural narratives. While his connection to American realist and naturalist drama is unmistakable, the political and historical trajectory of Wilson's plays is equally undeniable. To be sure, the playwright unashamedly delineates the 1960s as his artistic matrix: "But the Black Power movement of the '60s was a reality; it was the kiln in which I was fired, and has much to do with the person I am today and the ideas and attitudes that I carry as part of my consciousness" (Wilson, "Ground" 50–51). By identifying such a volatile cultural moment as his creative source, Wilson has undergone intense scrutiny on the basis of gender representation—a byproduct of the indefensible and pervasive sexism (and homophobia) that saturated 1960s black nationalism.

Carla J. McDonough's assessment of Wilson's connection to his Anglo-American dramatic forefathers and his inscriptions of black men is simultaneously valid and knotty:

Wilson's work is affected by and responds to a broad theatrical tradition: it encompasses the white fathers of American drama and the dramatic predecessors who helped to establish a theatrical tradition for African American dramatists. These two traditions have some similarities to the staging of masculinity that Wilson offers. For instance, Wilson's staging of masculinity reflects traditional American concepts of masculinity that tend to confuse "male" with "universal" and to overlook gender issues for men. (140)

The second point made here is particularly vexing though not surprising. Another critic, Kim Marra, underscores and expands upon McDonough's critique more vociferously: "Like most of his canonized predecessors, Wilson writes in a predominately realistic mode whose narrative structure posits a male protagonist and constructs female characters as Other. . . . However, the high profile and intellectual genealogy which may *insulate Wilson from feminist criticism also mandates a rigorous gender analysis of his work*" (123–24; emphasis added). While I might concur with these critics' observations on how Anglo-American dramatic traditions inform Wilson's dramatic design, I find their assertions about the author's gender inscriptions perplexing and problem-ridden.

To extrapolate that intersections between Wilson's aesthetics and those of a Eugene O'Neill or an Arthur Miller automatically make him a proponent of white patriarchal dramatic principles is at least a bizarre trivializing of complex questions regarding gender and race. At most, it represents an insidious form of inverted racialized chauvinism, where the black male dramatist is alternatively castigated for not centering women and accused of having benefited from some sort of critical immunity (Marra candidly identifies herself as a "middle-class white feminist critic" [123]). Indeed, the assumption underlying these criticisms is that a play by a black man that foregrounds black men's relationships to each other is automatically and unequivocally gynophobic and/or phallocentric—that drama centering black men must by definition promulgate misogynistic values. The calumnious reduction of Wilson's multifaceted vision to "patriarchy" is a byproduct of the pejorative narratives regarding black maleness I detailed at the outset. Black male authors, like their popular and more celebrated counterparts (e.g., Bill Cosby), are not allowed the artistic space to record black men's interiority and to articulate how these men address and negotiate different forms of pain and erasure.[1]

Given the binary foundations of most Western cultural and critical discourse, these critics' comments are unremarkable. However, a more fruitful investigation of Wilson's gender representations might address the specific formal and thematic nuances involved in his dramatizations of black American men; this line of inquiry does not immediately presuppose that the playwright elides questions related to black women. The basis of my exploration of Wilson's plays is precisely that they are indisputably counterhegemonic *and* counterpatriarchal. Indeed, he exactingly problematizes the sanctioned maleness articulated by canonical white male writers, where anachronistic constructions of masculinity often are deemed normative and unimpeachable (e.g., Stanley Kowalski's primordial animalism obliterates the "transgendered" Blanche DuBois's challenge to debilitating conventions governing the role of white women/gay men, concretized by her institutionalization at the end of *A Streetcar Named Desire*). By depicting black men in disparate social configurations—black men as fathers, artists, soldiers, athletes—Wilson enters and contests representations that have been decidedly monodimensional. Instead of black men constantly decrying their inability to "be men" in the most parochial sense of Anglo-American masculinity, Wilson delves into the "asymmetries"[2] of gender. Thus, he complexifies not only the same realist/naturalist American dramatic discourses that evince themselves in his plays, but he counters post-1950s black American dramatic figurations of black men (e.g., Hansberry, Baraka, Bullins) as perpetual victims who lack agency or outlets to relieve personal and social pain.

"This Is Men Talk, Woman"? *Fences* and the Re(en)gendering of the Male Dramatic Subject

Though Wilson ostensibly appropriates the prescribed conventions of American domestic drama, *Fences* ultimately reflects the playwright's "oppositional aesthetic directions,"[3] his calculated subverting and restitching of familiar dramatic fabric. While he frequently invokes familiar masculinist tropes—sports and war specifically in *Fences*—he assiduously displays how these institutions are potentially deforming and anathema to psychospiritual liberation. Indeed, Wilson delves into the interstices of masculinity by demonstrating that black men are capable of identifying and enacting alternative means to *re(en)gender* themselves—different ways to be gendered subjects that abandon confining and destructive vehicles for male subjectivity.

Like many male authors, Wilson invokes sports and war to explore black male dis-ease and deformation. Certainly, he is not the first black writer to do so; as Gerald Early has accurately observed, the Battle Royal in *Invisible Man* remains "one of the most famous fictional boxing depictions in all of

American culture" (25). The significance of the battlefield and ballpark as sites where "masculinity" can be performed and affirmed can be traced to the end of the nineteenth century. As E. Anthony Rotundo posits, "In a cultural setting where war and athletics were equated and war was thought to breed a new, forceful manhood, people readily came to the position that athletics, too, fostered the new form of manhood" (240–41). Traditionally, these two institutions are embedded in our cultural ethos as vehicles for sanctioned, untrammeled male behavior—competition, pugilism, annihilation.

However, Wilson refrains from romanticizing war or athletics as hallowed rituals of acceptable, homosocial activity (as in Hemingway, for example). Contrarily, he exposes how these institutions prevent black men from attaining subject status, primarily because they mandate a destructive hypermasculinity, which precludes intimacy among themselves and requires them to objectify both women and each other. By countering the prototypical black-male-as-long-suffering-victim archetype and instead foregrounding an array of black men in *Fences,* Wilson captures black men's polysubjectivity— the multiple vehicles for subject formation available when they look beyond and abjure confining constructions of Western/American masculinity.

Though he dominates the play in terms of voice and dramatic space, Troy Maxson is far from being Wilson's surrogate or mouthpiece. Troy upholds Wilson's axiomatic belief that "the blues are important primarily because they contain the cultural responses of blacks in America to the situation that they find themselves in. Contained in the blues is a philosophical system at work" (Moyers 168). To be sure, Troy possesses a reservoir of maxims, his blues-hued life bearing witness to black men's ability to, as he aphoristically recites, "take the crooked with the straights" (135). In effect the dramatist utilizes him to demonstrate the conundrum that is black male identity. Indeed, Troy's life reflects an amalgam of conflicted attempts to garner subject status, to negotiate a dizzying multitude of "straits." The genesis of Troy's perpetual consternation and anguish is his inability to play Major League baseball; segregation relegates him to the Negro Leagues. We further learn that Troy's interest in baseball evolved from his incarceration, the result of his attempted robbery of another man; during this violent encounter, Troy is shot in the chest before he kills his potential victim. Though he provides materially for his wife Rose (whom he met after his incarceration) and adolescent son Cory, Troy is dogged by what he sees as America's failure to grant him the rights and privileges that should accrue to native sons. His physical wound becomes an insignia—a tangible reminder of the fusillade of social and bodily blows fired at him.

Rather than depicting Troy as his spokesman or black male *Everyvictim* (think of Clay Williams or Walter Lee Younger), Wilson's characterization exposes the inherent flaw in fixating on racism as well as some black men's misguided desire to conform to a socially sanctioned script of maleness. The playwright launches this critique at the drama's outset in the quotidian drinking ritual between Troy and his best friend and fellow garbage man, Jim Bono; in other words, the dialogue itself telegraphs to the reader/viewer what will amount to Wilson's sustained critique of Troy's phallocentric mindset. The play opens in medias res, with the men lamenting racist practices on their job: Troy has filed a complaint asking why his boss "got the white men's driving [the garbage trucks] and the colored lifting?" (106). Without transition, the men engage a new topic: Troy's recent "eyeing" of Alberta:

> Troy: I eye all the women. I don't miss nothing. Don't never let nobody tell you Troy Maxson don't eye the women.
> Bono: You been doing more than eyeing her. You done bought her a drink or two.
> Troy: Hell yeah, I bought her a drink! What that mean? I bought you one, too. What that mean cause I buy her a drink? I'm just being polite.
> Bono: It's alright to buy her one drink. That's what you call being polite. But when you wanna be buying two or three . . . that's what you call eyeing her. (107)

Subsequently, Rose interrupts this discussion of Troy's impending affair by inquiring about the topic of conversation, which elicits this admonition: "Well, go on back in the house and let me and Bono finish what we was talking about. *This is men talk.* I got some talk for you later. You know what kind of talk I mean. You go on and powder it up" (109; emphasis added). Troy's rigid gender distinctions—his insistence that "men talk" remain a guardedly male endeavor and that women restrict themselves to the indoors, where they remain domesticated—demonstrate his acceptance of hegemonic conceptions of manhood, ones limited to the crude sexualizing of any contact between men and women. Clearly, Troy's behavior conforms to what Kaja Silverman calls the "dominant fiction" of masculinity, which "calls upon the male subject to see himself, and the female subject to recognize and desire him, only through the mediation of images of an unimpaired masculinity" (42). Importantly, Wilson uses Troy not to inscribe woman as Other but to question black men's allegiance to ineluctably jaundiced notions of men's and women's spaces and roles.

What is perhaps less obvious than Troy's unmitigated objectification of

Rose is how the ritualistic "men talk" does not necessarily foster communion but instead erects barriers between men. Wilson uses this opening scene to dramatize how black men are conditioned to circumscribe their own intragender relationships, limiting them to such potentially destructive behaviors as drinking and the objectifying of women. Indeed, Troy embodies how men de-emphasize their own interiority, the often unrecognized ground that has sown so much pain, in order to conform to dogmatic notions of gender. In other words, the opening dialogue demonstrates how men inhabit a linguistic and emotional prison-house of masculinity. In theorizing dramatic dialogue in the context of gender/masculinity, Robert Vorlicky posits a discursive framework that is particularly germane to my reading of the play's opening:

> Most characters in male-cast plays begin by engaging in social dialogue. They do so in an effort to situate themselves within the hegemonic patriarchy, which they presume to be supported by all the other participants in the talk exchanges. The characters use social dialogue because they want to confirm their common ground with each other. Moreover, social dialogue is safe; it guarantees cooperative communication. What we see and hear at this stage of the plays is an articulated *awareness* of their individual and collective power—political, economic, domestic, and sexual—as men within American Culture. . . . During the social dialogue that begins most male-cast plays, and with virtually no exceptions, the characters engage these topics explicitly. The topics are employment, consumerism, families, women, and their own active identification with the cultural ideal of male virility. (16)

While one might accurately interpret *Fences* as less a "male-cast" play and more a male-dominated one (five of its six main characters are men), the central point is that the very language governing men's interactions exacerbates their own emotional compartmentalizing and estrangement. Because they are so wedded to restrictive constructs and values, men such as Troy cannot envision an alternative form of subjectivity. Significantly, Wilson will use Bono and other male characters to counter Troy's unquestioning acceptance of what Vorlicky calls "hegemonic patriarchy."

In assessing Troy as representative of a flawed conceptualization of black selfhood, I think it important to scrutinize a cardinal moment in his blues experiences. During his ill-fated robbery attempt, he reveals that his potential victim "Shot me in the chest. It felt just like somebody had taken a hot branding iron and laid it on me" (150). This "branding" functions tropologically in the play, soldering the nexus between physical pain and the psychic price black men pay for permitting hegemonic institutions to dictate maleness and subjectivity. Significantly, Troy immediately ruminates that "They told me I killed him and they put me in the penitentiary and locked me up for fifteen years. That's where I met Bono. That's where I learned to play baseball." (150). Though these revelations may ostensibly be little more than hardships that might help explain Troy's current distemper, they also shape his destructive phallocentric impulses. Unabashedly, Troy subscribes to austere, prescribed gender roles emblematized not only by the gunshot—a literal marking of his manhood on his body—but also concretized by the very male-centered spaces that molded his identity.

Indeed, Troy's spatial confinement is an analogue to his inability to extricate himself from confining gender constructs. The subterranean prison milieu codifies an adherence to rigid though anachronistic gender roles as a space where men must continually exhibit such narrowly construed masculine traits of toughness, fierce individualism, competitiveness, and violence. This compulsory hypermasculinity is accentuated by Troy's introduction and devotion to sports. To be sure, I don't think that Wilson linked baseball and imprisonment coincidentally. Certainly, sports mirrors the implacably masculine ethos and hierarchies promulgated in prison, for it legitimizes the very traits our culture assigns as masculine. Moreover, that Wilson uses baseball specifically as the play's dominant trope is rhetorically and culturally salient.

In addition to Troy's copious anecdotes and stories that reference baseball and its lexicon (strikes, home runs, base stealing), the sport forms the matrix of Troy's conception of himself as a gendered subject. As Sandra G. Shannon observes, his "preoccupation with images associated with the traditionally masculine, extremely competitive sport robs him of the candor necessary to handle the delicate relationships in his life" (*Dramatic Vision* 110).[4] To be sure, our culture has venerated the "American pastime" as the bastion of a hallowed masculine ideal. Unlike other popular sports such as football and basketball, baseball remains the most sexually segregated—no cheerleaders as in basketball and football, no scantily clad, placard-bearing women announcing rounds as in boxing. Instead, women are relegated first and foremost to the role of spectator. The immutable gendered *fences* baseball erects are dramatized most clearly when Troy recounts his courtship of Rose, who had asked him where she ranked with respect to baseball among his priorities.[5] Answering her question about whether she or baseball comes first, Troy responds: "Baby, ain't no doubt it's baseball . . . but you stick and get old with me and we'll both outlive this baseball" (151).

For Troy, baseball, like his chest wound, tangibly demonstrates the extent to which a mythic masculine ideal is embedded into his conception of self—literally and metaphorically branded onto his body. Troy justifies his adultery by lamenting to Rose that it disrupted his prosaic, "safe" life by energizing him to "steal second" (164). Unequivocally, Wilson's thematizing of baseball substantiates the assertion that "The literature of baseball is continuously about male heterosexuality; its characters are straight men in the process of reinforcing their straightness" (Morris 4).

Indeed, Troy's conception of women as orifices through which he can enter the sacred though deforming realm of patriarchal masculinity is conveyed earlier, when he proclaims to Rose that he "fall[s] down on you to blast a hole into forever" (138) to relieve the pain he endures as provider and its attendant pressures. This visceral and violent image, where black women act as human balms for black men's pain, dovetails with Wilson's critique of hypersexuality and sports to underscore the psychological and familial price black men pay for adopting such imprisoning definitions of masculinity. Contrary to demonstrating "his cosmic role as progenitor in the recurring cycle of personal immortality" (Harrison 305), Troy's adulterous affair is symptomatic of the deformed constructions of masculinity corporealized in his bodily wound and codified by the bellicose language he employs (stealing, blasting) to articulate his interactions with women.

As a way to counter this provincial view of masculinity, Wilson foregrounds not merely pedestrian intergender conflicts (e.g., adultery), but intragender relationships as well. Imaginatively, Wilson interrupts American/African-American cultural praxes that pit men—both white and black—against each other in their quest for the esteemed yet malignant hegemonic masculinity. Most representative are the volatile male-on-male conflicts depicted in dramas such as Amiri Baraka's *The Slave* (1963) and *The Toilet* (1964) or Charles Fuller's *A Soldier's Play* (1981). Though *Fences* also foregrounds different forms of internecine gender conflict, Wilson categorically condemns such behavior while simultaneously depicting the possibility of alternative types of relationships between black men that are not predicated on competition and/or violence. Wilson exposes what might be considered "homosocial"[6] infidelity—the different ways black men undermine their relationships with each other—as central to the play's dramatic scope. Specifically, *Fences* characterizes how black men's inability to be "faithful" to one another constitutes another form of violation and thereby cements their status as deformed subjects. Though the most dramatic example of this might be Troy's quashing of his son Cory's opportunity to attend college on a football scholarship, more prominent examples include Troy's interactions with his best friend Bono and his brother, Gabriel.

Though most discourses, literary or social, have deemed black male intimacy taboo and alien, Wilson dismantles this shopworn precept by emphasizing not only Troy's objectification of women but also his willingness to forfeit relationships with other black men. Though Bono ostensibly functions as Troy's sycophantic alter ego, a one-man amen corner who ingests his stories whole and confers upon him the status of master storyteller ("I know you got some Uncle Remus in your blood" [115]), Bono ultimately represents the play's moral touchstone. While Troy sententiously justifies his adultery because it "sets right in my heart" (158), Bono's unmitigated admonition—"You's in control"—becomes a resounding counterpatriarchal declaration vis-à-vis the standard male narrative that equates sexual conquests with male subject status. Moreover, when Bono announces "I'm going home" (159), this is arguably the most critical moment in Wilson's contestation of degenerative notions of black male subjectivity. In effect, Bono deconstructs and reconfigures Troy's self-aggrandizing appropriation of baseball metaphors while asserting a radical new form of black male subjectivity.

I return momentarily to baseball's metaphorical function as a uniquely masculine endeavor, which Rotundo incisively iterates: "From the safety of 'home,' one individual after another attempted to enter a hostile territory and negotiate a safe arrival back home. The constant repetition of home leaving and return mirrored the daily journeys of men into the world and back again. Baseball embodied not just the competition of nineteenth-century manhood but also the organization of male life into zones of striving and safety" (244). In contradistinction to Troy's belief in risk taking and home-leaving—he complains to Rose that his cozy domestic life was emasculatingly "safe" and that he needed to "steal second" (164)—Bono's declaration marks the eternal return to the home-space, the "safe zone" traditionally encoded as feminine—or worse, antimasculine—in our cultural ethos. Through Troy's marital infidelity and Bono's sharp denunciation of it, Wilson dramatizes the former's willingness to jeopardize not only his heterosexual relationship but his homosocial ones as well. Crucially, the brotherhood the men forged in prison, along with their storytelling and drinking rituals, is terminated at this juncture.[7] Although Troy subsequently laments that he "Ain't got nobody to talk to" and begs Bono to "take a drink" (176–77), Troy's devotion to male prerogative and privilege destroys his relationships with black women and men alike. Thus, Troy's dual viola-

tions and Bono's condemnation demonstrate how Wilson *rescripts* black men's intragender relationships, where patriarchal masculinity is jettisoned, replaced by a view of manhood in which black men hold one another accountable for inculcating such debilitating constructions of maleness. In Wilson's allegorical design, the "good man" Bono embodies the new black man—one devoted to home and community and one who eschews anachronistically confining hallmarks of manhood. As well, *hom(m)e,* as suggested by its French homophone, becomes a site where a less chauvinistic, more sanguine form of masculinity can flower.

The Warrior's Marks: Suturing Psychic, Familial, and Bodily Wounds

By placing a cadre of black men at the center of his dramatic mise-en-scène, Wilson avoids the pitfalls of having one particular character's philosophy be interpreted as his own. Indeed, his multivalent view of black maleness, where characters such as Bono dispute Troy's corrosive attitudes about gender, is an artistic intervention, since monolithic portrayals of black men have been de rigueur. When explored in the context of Bono's antipatriarchal representation, Troy's brother Gabriel invites further scrutiny as another figure who incarnates black male bodily pain and the curative strategies to which black men may lay claim. Via his depiction, the dramatist further disputes and disrupts the culturally sanctioned notion that violence and/or sexual prowess are benchmarks for black men's sense of worth and selfhood.

Described as "injured in World War Two, with a metal plate in his head" (125), Gabriel might appear turgidly symbolic. Troy elaborates on Gabriel's physical maiming and alludes to how he has profited from it: "Man go over there and fight the war . . . messing around with them Japs, get his head blown off . . . and they give him a lousy three thousand dollars. And I had to swoop down on that" (128). Wilson himself has spelled out the ironic dramatic situation he strove to create by portraying Gabriel as having "suffered this wound fighting for a country in which his brother could not play baseball" (Shannon, "August Wilson" 225). Not to be lost is the cultural and historical impact and irony of Gabriel's wound. As Nat Brandt reports in *Harlem at War,* there were more than five hundred thousand blacks in the army but only seventy-nine thousand overseas because of segregation and the staunch belief that black soldiers would not perform as well as their white counterparts (111). As one of the few "chosen," like his archangel namesake, Gabriel suffers permanent mental and physical damage.

Quite astutely in terms of the play's construction and representations, Wilson devotes minimal space to discussions about Gabriel's plight; in fact Gabriel himself never mentions his crippling injury. Like Toni Morrison, Wilson invites the reader/spectator to fill in the gaps, thereby making the artistic production an organic and inclusive endeavor. One reason for the relative silence regarding Gabriel's physical debility may be found in Elaine Scarry's assertion that "precisely because it [pain] takes no object . . . it, more than any other phenomenon, resists objectification in language" (5). Incontrovertibly, war stands as the ultimate incursion of the black male body and psyche: not only does it occasion one's physical and emotional disembodiment, but it unequivocally objectifies the black self as expendable fodder for America's defense of "democratic ideals" that have historically been withheld from blacks regardless of gender. Thus, giving voice to Gabriel's psychic or physical impairment would reduce catastrophic events (his induction into the armed forces *and* his physical injury) to a language ill equipped to express the enormity of such assaults on his personhood.

In terms of the play's thematic and structural schematizations, Gabriel, who cannot or refuses to articulate his physical pain, diametrically opposes Troy, who as "Uncle Remus" almost obsessively tries to render or camouflage his own pain linguistically through innumerable stories and anecdotes. Because he attempts to garner a sort of linguistic subjectivity, however, Troy becomes imprisoned in a web of baseball metaphors and racial victimization narratives that rationalizes spousal and fraternal infidelity. That Gabriel simply lives his life almost prelinguistically frees him of the burden of conforming to the culturally esteemed hypermasculine aesthetic. Because speaking one's pain might involve the risk of being subsumed and prostrated by it, Gabriel embodies the ontological power available to black men by simply *being*— communing with those with whom they share common emotional and psychic space; this in and of itself becomes sustaining and affirming. As Wilson has said of him, Gabriel is irrepressibly "self-sufficient" (Shannon, "August Wilson" 225).

To be sure, Wilson's characterization of Gabriel eloquently speaks to the alternative modes of male subjectivity available to black men. The agency Gabriel exercises in the context of oppression marks a creative and constructive response to cultural erasure as well as his sibling's attempts to confine him. Incontestably, Gabriel is assaulted on several fronts, perhaps the most tragic being his own brother's institutionalizing of him; to be sure, his body becomes the site of attempted personal and sociohistorical evisceration. In another instance of homosocial violation (the first being his sullying of Bono's friendship by cheating on Rose), Troy "signs the paper" for Gabriel, thereby permitting the latter's confinement to a mental institution; as Rose tells Troy, the paper "say[s] the government send part of his check to the hospital and the other part to you" (168). In essence, Troy visits upon Gabriel the very abuses that derailed his own fulfillment: his confinement of Gabriel replicates his own spatial and psychic relegation to the Negro Leagues *and* the back of the garbage truck. Clearly, his mistreatment of Gabriel substantiates a dramatic praxis in which "a man's objectification of another man— or the male subject's construction of a male object—is most often located in the latter's difference from the former, which is usually determined by his race, ethnicity, class, religion, sexual orientation, or simply by his inadequate mirroring, or embodiment, of the gender codes of the (white) masculine ethos" (Vorlicky 10). In Troy's execrable reinforcement of phallocentric codes of conduct, Gabriel's mental difference and attendant inability to enact such codes render him expendable and exploitable—more Other than brother. Yet, in spite of Gabriel's myriad exploitative experiences—his corporeal and emotional mutilation in World War Two and Troy's physical internment of him—Wilson insists that black men can summon alternative responses to immeasurable and unspeakable pain, regardless of whether its genesis is consanguineous or sociocultural.

The playwright's own comments on Gabriel elucidate the character's centrality to the play's refiguration of black male subjectivity. Claiming that his mental deficiency makes him a "*spectacle* character" (Shannon, "August Wilson" 225; emphasis added), Wilson expatiates on this designation thusly: "Gabriel is one of those self-sufficient characters. He gets up and goes to work every day. He goes out and collects those discarded fruit [*sic*] and vegetables, but he's taking care of himself. He doesn't want Troy to take care of him. He moves out of Troy's house and lives down there and pays his rent to the extent that he is able" (225). These comments gainsay the belief that maleness is solely measured by one's ability to sire children, play baseball, or even earn a paycheck. Indeed, he exhibits an agency and authority that elude Troy. While the notion of spectacle often carries pejorative connotations, in Wilson's dramatic schema it becomes a restorative and regenerative space free of the debilitating sanctioned constructs of black manhood. To be sure, Gabriel's marginal, "spectacle" status becomes an emancipatory zone. Though ostensibly "mad" or psychically wounded, Gabriel is reminiscent of Toni Morrison's "madwomen" (e.g., Sula and Hanna Peace in *Sula*), whose "craziness" frees them from society's dictates that circumscribe the behavior of and outlets for black people.[8]

Wilson's designation of Gabriel as a "spectacle" figure summons compar-
isons to what the Russian formalist scholar Bakhtin labeled the "carnivalesque" features of Dostoevsky's novels: "Because carnivalistic life is
drawn out of its *usual* rut, it is to some extent 'life turned inside out,' the
reverse of the world (*'monde a l'envers'*)" (122).[9] Indisputably, Gabriel's
inverted, improvised modus vivendi provides an antipodal life-narrative to
Troy's, which upholds anachronistic notions of maleness—ones grounded
in hypersexuality and masculine privilege. Moreover, in terms of spectacle,
Bakhtin goes on to adduce:

> All *distance* between people is suspended, and a special carnival category goes
> into effect: *free and familiar contact among people.* This is a very important
> aspect of a carnival sense of the world. People who in life are separated by
> impenetrable hierarchical barriers enter into free familiar contact on the carni-
> val square. . . . Carnival is the place for working out, in a concretely sensuous,
> half-real and half-play-acted form, a *new mode of interrelationship between
> individuals,* counterposed to the all-powerful socio-hierarchical relationships
> of noncarnival life. The behavior, gesture, and discourse of a person are freed
> from authority of all hierarchical positions (social estate, rank, age, property)
> defining them totally in noncarnival life, and thus from the vantage point of
> noncarnival life become eccentric and inappropriate. (123)

A glance at Gabriel's familial interactions undergirds Wilson's inscription
of him as a "spectacle" figure who disrupts putative and culturally enshack-
ling notions about what constitutes maleness—the untrammeled sexualiza-
tion of women, male-on-male violence, and a fervent quest for economic
fulfillment being paramount.

Unequivocally, Troy's relationships with all of the play's characters are
mediated by his obsession with power and authority in the most corrosive
sense, which his actions bear out. He cheats on Rose; he sacrifices his friendship with Bono, who refuses to countenance his infidelity; he prevents Cory
from obtaining a college football scholarship; he confines Gabriel to a mental
asylum; and he berates his thirty-four-year-old son, Lyons, whom he deems
a worthless jazz musician who refuses to maintain a "real" job. These actions differ markedly from Gabriel's relationships with his sister-in-law and
nephews. At a pivotal moment in the play in which Troy confesses his infidelity to Rose, Gabriel enters and declares, "Hey Rose . . . I got a flower
for you. That's a rose. Same rose like you is" (161). This quasi courtship is
not mediated by sexual desire or a need to uphold a warped definition of
masculinity; Gabriel's behavior is determined by Rose's genuine concern for

his welfare and is free of parochial gender constructs that restrict heterosexual relationships to the sexual realm.

Clearly, Gabriel's ability to insinuate himself into the family at crucial and volatile moments threatens, albeit inadvertently, Troy's martinet-like power. Even seemingly benign acts such as Gabriel proclaiming Lyons "King of the Jungle" (145) take on especial significance. As he does with Rose, Gabriel assumes the power to name and rename, assigning his family endearing descriptors free of affectation or self-aggrandizement. Gabriel's associational relationship to language stands in stark contrast to Troy's blustery narratives about his past, his battle with "Death" (112–14), his sexual conquests, or his baseball pyrotechnics. In fact, Gabriel's declaration of Lyons's kingly status subverts his brother's presumed omnipotence—T/*roy* will devolve into the titular "king" whose solipsism abrogates his sovereignty. Gabriel's "decoded sense of male subjectivity" (Vorlicky 190) liberates him from culturally sanctioned but enervating fictions of "true manhood," narratives to which his brother subscribes with crushing consequences.

Gabriel's newly fashioned, counterpatriarchal form of maleness is reified in the play's concluding stage directions. Preparing to attend Troy's funeral, Gabriel performs a "dance, a slow, strange dance, eerie and life giving. A dance of atavistic signature and ritual" (192). This voiceless gesture metamorphoses the physically wounded Gabriel into what Arthur W. Frank calls the "wounded storyteller," whose "chaos narrative" "traces the edges of a wound that can only be told around. Words suggest its rawness, but that wound is so much of the body, its insults, agonies, and losses, that words necessarily fail" (98). Gabriel translates his pain into an art that transcends the very binding language of masculinity that consumes Troy. Moreover, Gabriel's willingness to engage a medium traditionally associated with female epistemology (think of the women dancers in Ntozake Shange's choreopoem *for colored girls who have considered suicide/when the rainbow is enuf*) renders him a transgendered subject, a man who transcends the entrapping fictions of masculinity that American culture promulgates.[10] To be sure, Gabriel's apoplectic dance becomes a de-coded act that propels him beyond the strictures of gender. Ultimately, his cathartic transgendered and translingual performance incarnates a radical form of resistance and perseverance, and, through him, Wilson contests the equation of black male subjectivity with hypersexuality, economic control, violence, and competition.

Far from sanctioning constructs of untrammeled masculinity, *Fences* painstakingly critiques blemished forms of maleness usually associated with black male dramatic subjects. In fact, the play's configuration buttresses this point. That Troy's death occurs offstage and unseen demonstrates yet another act of discursive reenvisioning, for the preponderance of plays foregrounding black men's experiences culminates in some form of ritualized violence and perpetuates the notion that black men's tragic fates are foreordained and inevitable. Whether it be Baraka's *Dutchman* in the 1960s or Fuller's *A Soldier's Play* in the 1980s, the primary dramaturgical convention in black men's drama has involved climactic inter- or intraracial gendered violence. While I'm not suggesting that Wilson altogether abandons this discursive template (see his 1984 play *Ma Rainey's Black Bottom*, which ends in paroxysmal violence), his relegation of Troy's death to the play's margins buttresses the playwright's alternative vision of black male subjectivity—a vision that doesn't center violence or death as the sine qua non in dramatic representations of black men's lives.

In the dramatic laying on of hands Wilson performs in *Fences*, deformed black men scarred by phallocentric institutions such as war and baseball can be healed and resuscitated. Indeed, Wilsonian counteraesthetics inaugurates new protocols for black masculinity, for his characters are more than the sum of their social experiences—men whose corporeal or social disembodiment does not yield spiritual decay or communal/familial estrangement. As adumbrated in Rose's remembrance of his death—"He swung that bat and then he just fell over" (188)—the great American pastime of reenacting rigid, destructive codes of masculinity that Troy upholds has indeed passed its time.

Notes

1. Scholars critical of various aspects of Wilson's plays (gender being only one issue that has drawn criticism) are by no means limited to women and/or feminists. In fact, his most stentorian critic has been Robert Brustein, the former dean of the Yale School of Drama. For representative commentary, see "Forum: Race, Art, and Inclusion" and "The Lesson of *The Piano Lesson*."

2. I borrow this term from Robert Vorlicky's trenchant study on masculinity in drama, *Act Like a Man*. He contends that several contemporary American playwrights are "embracing the notion that the asymmetries of gender affect the construction of male subjectivity, resulting in a varied range of male identities when dramatizing men alone together" (3). I would certainly include Wilson within this trend, for he has trumpeted black men's otherness—their existence as beings other than the victimizers or predators to which American culture has become accustomed.

3. bell hooks uses this phrase in discussing what she sees as the belabored representation of intergender conflicts in black literature, where relationships between men and women remain confined to jejune, heterosexist constructs: "Certainly the diverse inventive retelling of gender conflict between black women and men, though often

striking and deeply moving, rarely suggests oppositional aesthetic directions and possibilities. They are most often new takes on old themes, interesting in that they call attention to the need for visionary imaginative works that expand our notions of self and identity as they themselves do not. They point to the way our struggle for subjectivity has too long mired in heterosexism, a narrative of selfhood contained within a paradigm of coupled relationships" (18). I contend that Wilson appropriates traditional signifiers of sexual conflict—(in)fidelity—but only to problematize and reexamine relationships between the sexes and *among* men, especially.

4. Deeanne Westbrook offers a unique interpretation of baseball symbology in *Fences*. She melds Freudian-Lacanian psychoanalytic theory, Edenic myths, and Greek mythology to extrapolate Troy Maxson's Byzantine life-narrative.

5. For an insightful discussion of the play's commingling of baseball and gender, see Missy Dehn Kubitschek's "August Wilson's Gender Lesson," in which she examines how Troy's chosen metaphors persistently objectify the women in his life. In "Filling the Time: Reading History in the Drama of August Wilson," John Timpane provides a thorough historical backdrop for interpreting baseball's tropological function. He summarizes and interprets events that occurred in the major leagues during 1957 (the year in which *Fences* is set) to illumine their significance vis-à-vis the play's themes and structure.

6. I take this term from Eve Kosofsky Sedgwick. See the introduction in her study *Between Men: English Literature and Male Homosocial Desire*, where she distinguishes between "homosocial" and "homosexual" desire.

7. My reading of the Troy-Bono relationship echoes Michael Awkward's. He posits in "'The Crooked with the Straights': *Fences*, Race, and the Politics of Adaptation" that Troy's affair with Alberta "eventuates in the dissolution of the rituals of friendship with Bono in part because the grounds upon which the intensity of the latter's admiration of the protagonist is based—evidence of Troy's clear-sightedness, his ability to understand and not be tempted to overstep the boundaries with which his life presents him—have been undercut" (218).

8. Mark William Rocha's "Black Madness in August Wilson's 'Down the Line' Cycle" perceptively differentiates how mental illness functions in Anglo-European and African and African-American cultures and communities. He argues that one locates in Wilson's dramas "a consistent and explicit rejection of an Anglo-European consciousness that perceives human beings as commodities. . . . Wilson shows black madness to mean something different than the term 'madness' means in western culture" (191).

9. Carnivalesque discourse has provided unique and instructive frameworks for interpreting African-American literature. Houston A. Baker Jr. draws upon Bakhtin's and Julia Kristeva's theories of carnivalesque to (re)interpret the blues/vernacular underpinnings of Wright's *Black Boy*; see his *Blues, Ideology, and Afro-American Literature,* especially part four of the section "Reassessing (W)right: A Meditation on the Black (W)hole" (145–51).

10. In *Scars of Conquest/Masks of Resistance* Tejumola Olaniyan's innovative discussion of how dance and music function in Shange's *for colored girls* is apposite in considering these media's tropic significance in *Fences:* "Music and dance, as forms in perpetual motion—'pure solution'—have the potential to transgress institutionalized limits and open up zones of possibilities, which, even if not realized or realizable, are capable of luring the dominated into the subversive realm of the dream. . . . It is through the idioms of music and dance that the 'ladies' in *for colored girls* express and confront their fears, disappointments, frustrations, transforming them to hopes and determinations: music and dance as therapy" (124). In a similar vein, Gabriel's dance becomes personally cathartic and liberating, countering Troy's fixation on the constricting lexicon of baseball.

Works Cited

Awkward, Michael. "'The Crooked with the Straights': *Fences,* Race, and the Politics of Adaptation." In *May All Your Fences Have Gates: Essays on the Drama of August Wilson.* Ed. Alan Nadel. Iowa City: University of Iowa Press, 1994. 205–29.

Baker, Houston A., Jr. *Blues, Ideology, and Afro-American Literature: A Vernacular Theory.* Chicago: University of Chicago Press, 1984.

Bakhtin, Mikhail. *Problems of Dostoevsky's Poetics.* Ed. and Trans. Caryl Emerson. Minneapolis: University of Minnesota Press, 1984.

Brandt, Nat. *Harlem at War: The Black Experience in WWII.* Syracuse, N.Y.: Syracuse University Press, 1996.

Brustein, Robert. "Forum: Race, Art, and Inclusion." *American Theatre* 13.9 (November 1996): 62–63, 81–82.

———. "The Lesson of *The Piano Lesson.*" *New Republic,* 21 May 1990, 28–30.

Early, Gerald. *The Culture of Bruising: Essays on Prizefighting, Literature, and Modern American Culture.* Hopewell, N.J.: Echo Press, 1994.

Frank, Arthur W. *The Wounded Storyteller: Body, Illness, and Ethics.* Chicago: University of Chicago Press, 1995.

Harrison, Paul Carter. "August Wilson's Blues Poetics." In *Three Plays,* by August Wilson. Pittsburgh: University of Pittsburgh Press, 1991. 291–318.

hooks, bell. *Yearning: Race, Gender, and Cultural Politics.* Boston: South End Press, 1990.

Kubitschek, Missy Dehn. "August Wilson's Gender Lesson." In *May All Your Fences Have Gates: Essays on the Drama of August Wilson.* Ed. Alan Nadel. Iowa City: University of Iowa Press, 1994. 183–99.

Marra, Kim. "Ma Rainey and the Boyz: Gender Ideology in August Wilson's Broadway Canon." In *August Wilson: A Casebook.* Ed. Marilyn Elkins. New York: Garland, 1994. 123–60.

McDonough, Carla J. *Staging Masculinity: Male Identity in Contemporary American Drama.* Jefferson, N.C.: McFarland and Co., 1997.

Morris, Timothy. *Making the Team: The Cultural Work of Baseball Fiction.* Urbana: University of Illinois Press, 1997.

Moyers, Bill. "August Wilson, Playwright." In *A World of Ideas: Conversations with Thoughtful Men and Women about American Life Today and the Ideas Shaping Our Future.* Ed. Bill Moyers. New York: Doubleday, 1989. 167–80.

Olaniyan, Tejumola. *Scars of Conquest/Masks of Resistance: The Invention of Cultural Identities in African, African-American, and Caribbean Drama.* New York: Oxford University Press, 1995.

Rocha, Mark William. "Black Madness in August Wilson's 'Down the Line' Cycle." In *Madness in Drama.* Ed. James Redmond. Cambridge: Cambridge University Press, 1993. 191–201.

Rotundo, E. Anthony. *American Manhood: Transformations in Masculinity from the Revolution to the Modern Era.* New York: Basic Books, 1993.

Scarry, Elaine. *The Body in Pain: The Making and Unmaking of the World.* New York: Oxford University Press, 1985.

Sedgwick, Eve Kosofsky. *Between Men: English Literature and Male Homosocial Desire.* New York: Columbia University Press, 1985.

Shange, Ntozake. *for colored girls who have considered suicide/when the rainbow is enuf.* New York: Macmillan, 1977.

Shannon, Sandra G. "August Wilson Explains His Dramatic Vision: An Interview." In *The Dramatic Vision of August Wilson.* Washington, D.C.: Howard University Press, 1995. 201–35.

———. *The Dramatic Vision of August Wilson.* Washington, D.C.: Howard University Press, 1995.

Silverman, Kaja. *Male Subjectivity at the Margins.* New York: Routledge, 1992.

Spillers, Hortense. "Mama's Baby, Papa's Maybe: An American Grammar Book." *Diacritics* 17 (1987): 65–81.

Timpane, John. "Filling the Time: Reading History in the Drama of August Wilson." In *May All Your Fences Have Gates: Essays on the Drama of August Wilson.* Ed. Alan Nadel. Iowa City: University of Iowa Press, 1994. 67–85.

Vorlicky, Robert. *Act Like a Man: Challenging Masculinities in American Drama.* Ann Arbor: University of Michigan Press, 1995.

Westbrook, Deeanne. *Groundrules: Baseball and Myth.* Urbana: University of Illinois Press, 1996.

Wilson, August. *Fences.* In *Three Plays,* by August Wilson. Pittsburgh: University of Pittsburgh Press, 1991. 95–192.

———. "The Ground on Which I Stand." *American Theatre* 13.7 (September 1996): 50–52, 71–74.

———. *Ma Rainey's Black Bottom.* New York: Plume, 1985.

———. *Two Trains Running.* New York: Plume, 1992.

Selected Bibliography

Andrews, William L. "The Black Male in American Literature." In *The American Black Male: His Present Status and His Future*. Ed. Richard G. Majors and Jacob U. Gordon. Chicago: Nelson-Hall, 1994. 59–68.

Bell, Bernard W. *The Afro-American Novel and Its Tradition*. Amherst: University of Massachusetts Press, 1987.

Belton, Don, ed. *Speak My Name: Black Men on Masculinity and the American Dream*. Boston: Beacon Press, 1995.

Bigsby, C. W. E., ed. *The Black American Writer*. 2 vols. Baltimore: Penguin, 1969.

Blount, Marcellus, and George P. Cunningham, eds. *Representing Black Men*. New York: Routledge, 1996.

Boyd, Herb, and Robert L. Allen, eds. *Brotherman: The Odyssey of Black Men in America*. New York: Ballantine, 1996.

Bryant, Jerry H. *Victims and Heroes: Racial Violence in the African American Novel*. Amherst: University of Massachusetts Press, 1997.

Callahan, John F. *In the African-American Grain: The Pursuit of Voice in Twentieth-Century Black Fiction*. Urbana: University of Illinois Press, 1988.

Cooke, Michael G. *Afro-American Literature in the Twentieth Century: The Achievement of Intimacy*. New Haven, Conn.: Yale University Press, 1984.

"The Crisis of the Black Male." *The Black Scholar* 18 (May–June 1987).

Davis, Thadious M. "A Female Face; or, Masking the Masculine in African American Fiction before Richard Wright." In *Teaching African American Literature: Theory and Practice*. Ed. Maryemma Graham, Sharon Pineault-Burke, and Marianna White Davis. New York: Routledge, 1998. 98–131.

Dixon, Melvin. *Ride Out the Wilderness: Geography and Identity in Afro-American Literature*. Urbana: University of Illinois Press, 1987.

Dudley, David L. *My Father's Shadow: Intergenerational Conflicts in African American Men's Autobiography.* Philadelphia: University of Pennsylvania Press, 1991.

Ellis, Trey. "The New Black Aesthetic." *Callaloo* 12.1 (1989): 233–43.

"Emerging Male Writers." Special issue of *Callaloo* 21.1/21.2 (1998).

Franklin, H. Bruce. *Prison Literature in America.* New York: Oxford University Press, 1978.

Gary, Lawrence E., ed. *Black Men.* Beverly Hills, Calif.: Sage Publications, 1981.

Gates, Henry Louis, Jr. "The Black Man's Burden." In *Fear of a Queer Planet: Queer Politics and Social Theory.* Ed. Michael Warner. Minneapolis: University of Minnesota Press, 1993. 230–38.

———. *Thirteen Ways of Looking at a Black Man.* New York: Random House, 1997.

Gayle, Addison, Jr. *The Way of the New World: The Black Novel in America.* Garden City, N.Y.: Doubleday, 1975.

———, ed. *The Black Aesthetic.* Garden City, N.Y.: Doubleday, 1972.

Gibson, Donald B. *Five Black Writers.* New York: New York University Press, 1970.

———. *The Politics of Literary Expression: A Study of Major Black Writers.* Westport, Conn.: Greenwood Press, 1981.

Golden, Thelma, ed. *Black Male: Representations of Masculinity in Contemporary Art.* New York: Whitney Museum of American Art, 1994.

Harper, Phillip Brian. *Are We Not Men? Masculine Anxiety and the Problem of African-American Identity.* New York: Oxford University Press, 1996.

Harris, Trudier. *Exorcising Blackness: Historical and Literary Burning Rituals.* Bloomington: Indiana University Press, 1984.

Hemenway, Robert, ed. *The Black Novelist.* Columbus, Ohio: Charles E. Merrill, 1970.

Hogue, W. Lawrence. *Discourse and the Other: The Production of the Afro-American Text.* Durham, N.C.: Duke University Press, 1986.

hooks, bell. "Reconstructing Black Masculinity." In *Black Looks: Race and Representation.* Boston: South End Press, 1992. 87–113.

Johnson, Charles and John McCluskey, Jr., eds. *Black Men Speaking.* Bloomington: Indiana University Press, 1997.

Kent, George E. *Blackness and the Adventure of Western Culture.* Chicago: Third World Press, 1972.

Majors, Richard G., and Jacob U. Gordon, eds. *The American Black Male: His Present Status and His Future.* Chicago: Nelson-Hall, 1994.

Middleton, Peter. *The Inward Gaze: Masculinity and Subjectivity in Modern Culture.* London: Routledge, 1992.

Roberts, John W. *From Trickster to Badman: The Black Folk Hero in Slavery and Freedom.* Philadelphia: University of Pennsylvania Press, 1989.

Staples, Robert. *Black Masculinity: The Black Man's Role in American Society.* San Francisco: Black Scholar Press, 1982.

Stepto, Robert B. *From Behind the Veil: A Study of Afro-American Narrative.* 2d ed. Urbana: University of Illinois Press, 1979.

Thomas, Kendall. "'Ain't Nothin' Like the Real Thing': Black Masculinity, Gay Sexuality, and the Jargon of Authenticity." In *Representing Black Men.* Ed. Marcellus Blount and George P. Cunningham. New York: Routledge, 1996. 55–69.

Turner, Darwin T. "Visions of Love and Manliness in a Blackening World: Dramas of Black Life from 1953–1970." *Iowa Review* 6 (1975): 82–98.

Contributors

HERMAN BEAVERS, an associate professor of English and director of the Afro-American Studies Program at the University of Pennsylvania, is the author of *A Neighborhood of Feeling* (1986) and *Wrestling Angels into Song: The Fictions of Ernest J. Gaines and James Alan McPherson* (1994). He is working on a study on representations of masculinity in the twentieth century, tentatively titled *Prodigal Allegories,* and on a collection of poems entitled *Still Life with Guitar.*

KEITH CLARK teaches in the Department of English at George Mason University. He is the author of *Black Manhood in James Baldwin, Ernest Gaines, and August Wilson* and of articles on Baldwin, William Faulkner, Gaines, Lorraine Hansberry, and Ann Petry, which have appeared in journals such as *African American Review, Callaloo,* and *Faulkner Journal.*

JAMES W. COLEMAN teaches in the Department of English at the University of North Carolina at Chapel Hill. He is the author of *Blackness and Modernism: The Literary Career of John Edgar Wideman* (1989) and a forthcoming book on contemporary black male fiction.

KENYATTA DOREY GRAVES is a graduate student in the Department of English at the University of Maryland at College Park and a high school English teacher. The recipient of a Ford Foundation fellowship and the Zora Neale Hurston/Richard Wright Award for Fiction Writing, he has served as the national conference director for the National Black Graduate Association and the National Black Lesbian and Gay Leadership Forum. He is completing work on a novel.

TRUDIER HARRIS is J. Carlyle Sitterson Professor of English at the University of North Carolina at Chapel Hill. She is the author of a number of books, including *Exorcising Blackness: Historical and Literary Lynching and Burning Rituals* (1984), *Black Women in the Fiction of James Baldwin* (1985), and *The Power of the Porch: The Storyteller's Craft in Zora Neale Hurston, Gloria Naylor, and Randall Kenan* (1996); the editor of *New Essays on Baldwin's "Go Tell It on the Mountain"* (1996); and coeditor of *The Oxford Companion to African American Literature* (1997), *Call and Response: The Riverside Anthology of the African American Literary Tradition* (1998), and *The Literature of the American South: A Norton Anthology* (1998). During 1996–97 she was a resident fellow at the National Humanities Center, where she worked on her latest book, tentatively titled *This Disease Called Strength: Legend, Literature, and Black Female Character.*

RAYMOND E. JANIFER is an associate professor of English and director of the Ethnic Studies Program at Shippensburg University. He is the author of *The Black Arts Movement and the Early Fiction of John Edgar Wideman* (2000) as well as numerous nonfiction essays, journalism, short stories, and scholarly essays about African-American literature and culture.

SHEILA SMITH MCKOY is an assistant professor of English and African-American Studies at Vanderbilt University. Her areas of concentration include African, Afro-Caribbean, and African-American literary, cultural, and film studies. She is working on a literary and cultural study of race, riot, and the black body in the United State and South Africa, tentatively titled *When Whites Riot: Writing Race and Violence in American and South African Culture,* and a compilation of Charles Chesnutt's theoretical and practical writings on race in America.

WILLIAM R. NASH, an assistant professor of American literature and civilization at Middlebury College, has published several articles about and an interview with the novelist Charles Johnson, as well as essays on Gloria Naylor, Walter Mosley, Bob Marley, John A. Williams, Frances E. W. Harper, and African-American dialect poetry. He has also completed a book-length study of Johnson's fiction.

MELVIN B. RAHMING is a professor of English at Morehouse College, where he teaches courses in African-American and Caribbean literatures, and cofounder/codirector of the International Conference on Caribbean Literature. He is the author of *The Evolution of the West Indian's Image in the African American Novel* (1996) and has published articles in several scholarly journals, including *College Language Association Journal* and *Studies in the Literary Imagination*.

A. T. SPAULDING is an assistant professor of African-American literature and literary theory at the University of Delaware. He is working on a study of postmodern dimensions of neo-slave narratives by Ishmael Reed, Charles Johnson, Octavia Butler, and other writers.

Index

Abelove, Henry, 197n.15

Abrahams, Roger D., 105n.13

Absalom, Absalom! (Faulkner), 135, 140, 141

African American Review (journal), 3

African Americans. *See* black gay men; black male writers; black men; black women; black women writers

Afrocentricity (Asante), 55, 166, 177n.3

Afrocentrism: and homosexuality, 166–67, 196n.9; and SGL identity, 181; spirit-centered cosmology of, 159–60; in Wideman's Homewood Trilogy, 55, 68

ahimsa, 127

AIDS, 183, 193–94

Akbar, Naaim, 159

allegory, 150–51

All-Night Visitors (Major), 89–107; "Anita" section, 96; as black male text, 89, 99, 100; black phallic tricksterism in, 91–92, 93, 94, 95, 96, 98, 100–101, 103; black phallus as physical presence in, 100; Calibanic phallicism in, 93–94, 95, 96, 98; experimentation in, 89, 93; liminality in, 92–93; multifarious aims of, 8–9; resistance to appropriation in, 94–95; "Tammy" section, 95–96; traditional Western grounding of,

90; two sets of linguistic signs in, 93. *See also* Bolton, Eli

AMASSI Cultural Center, 181

Amen, Ra Un Nefer, 160–61

American Literature (journal), 3

Amistad mutiny, 118–19, 131n.6

Andrews, Raymond: *Baby Sweets*, 23, 26, 28, 39; black gay men portrayed by, 7, 23; Faulkner compared with, 7; Kenan contrasted with, 29; paucity of books devoted to, 3; *Rosiebelle Lee Wildcat Tennessee*, 26, 39; as southern writer, 26–27; storytelling emphasized over character development by, 48. See also *Appalachee Red*; Muskhogean County trilogy

Ani, Marimba, 159

Another Country (Baldwin): Eric's sexual coming of age in, 21; interracial relationships in, 21, 190; and Kenan's *Visitation of Spirits*, 19–23; rural South as locus of homoerotic desire in, 21; Rufus Scott, 17, 19; whiteness defining black gay relationships in, 17

Appalachee Red (Andrews): black gay men in, 23; disease of strength in, 7–8, 37–53; James Baldwin Prize for, 26, 35n.11; John Morgan, 40, 41, 43, 46; in Muskhogean County trilogy, 26, 39;

family events, 61–65; poetic license in, 56; *Sent for You Yesterday*, 54, 55

homophobia: in Africa and African Diaspora, 16–17, 179; in Afrocentricity, 166–67, 196n.9; of black nationalism, 2, 182, 204; in Kenan's "Clarence and the Dead," 29–31; white gays forming enclaves to escape, 182

homosexuality: characterized as outside African cultural experience, 16–17; fear associated with, 28, 29; whiteness associated with, 17. *See also* black gay men; homophobia

hooks, bell, 104n.3, 125, 195, 197n.17, 202, 218n.3

Horton, Willie, 201

Hughes, Langston, 1, 4, 5, 23, 57

Hurry Home (Wideman), 56, 61

Hurston, Zora Neale, 2, 52n.8, 63, 193

hypermasculinity, 2, 11, 203, 210, 211, 214

If Beale Street Could Talk (Baldwin), 163

If He Hollers Let Him Go (Himes), 38

In My Father's House (Gaines), 138

In the Life (Hemphill), 190

In the Life: A Black Gay Anthology (Beam), 180, 184

Invisible Man (Ellison): Andrews's *Appalachee Red* compared with, 45; Battle Royal in, 206–7; on "blackness of blackness," 194; black phallic duplicity in, 105n.10; black phallic tricksterism in, 92, 105n.10; existential limbo of, 162; protest in, 5; Ras the Exhorter, 162; social and metaphorical invisibility in, 2; Wade's *Company Man* compared with, 169–71

"Ivy Day in the Committee Room" (Joyce), 144

Jackson, Allan ("The Sorcerer's Apprentice"): and Allmuseri, 117; and Rubin Bailey, 113, 119; escapes trap that ensnared his father, 109; father unable to connect with, 115–16; finds his own way, 111, 116; transcends his father's limited views, 116; works the spell that heals and liberates his father, 113

Jackson, Gale, 157, 159

Jackson, Richard ("The Sorcerer's Apprentice"): broken by his experiences, 113, 115; racialized sense of self, 117; smashed thumb of, 113; unable to connect with his son, 115–16

Jacobs, Harriet, 49

Jaffe, Harold, 89

James, G. Winston, 193–94

James, Sherman, 37–38

James Baldwin (Kenan), 34n.3

Janifer, Raymond E., 8

Jefferson (*A Lesson before Dying*): "already dead," 142, 146; and Reverend Ambrose, 141, 146–48; and Paul Bonin, 151–52; and Christmas pageant, 146; death serves as catalyst for resistance, 146; diary of, 148–49; Grant Wiggins ushers to manhood, 135, 142, 150; Grant Wiggins visits in prison, 142; Miss Emma on, 140–41; reconciliation with Grant Wiggins, 138; redemption of, 138; referred to as hog, 140, 150; significance of his name, 152; trial of, 140; visited by schoolchildren, 148, 153n.3

John Henry syndrome, 37–39, 43, 46, 50, 51nn.1–2

Johnson, Charles: Allmuseri in works of, 117–21, 122, 126–27; *Being and Race*, 5, 54, 127, 128; and Black Arts movement, 109, 128, 132n.9; *Black Humor*, 132n.9; *Black Men Speaking*, 112; on black men's writing as same story recycled, 5; cartoonist aspiration of, 112, 125–26; divisive markers rejected by, 110; Ellison's influence on, 128; on experiences of blackness, 6; *Faith and the Good Thing*, 108, 112, 131n.5; fatherhood in fiction of, 108–34; finds his own voice, 111; and Gardner, 129, 130n.4; Hughes compared with, 4; liberates black text from protest literature, 5; limitations of text and discursive expressiveness as concern of, 106n.14; Melville as literary predecessor of, 131n.7; philosophical system of, 109, 130n.3; "The Second Front," 112, 125–26; studied by Wideman, 57; surrogate fathers in works of, 9, 116; thematic complexity and technical sophistication

Composed in 10/13 Sabon
with Sabon display
by Celia Shapland
for the University of Illinois Press
Manufactured by Thomson-Shore, Inc.

University of Illinois Press
1325 South Oak Street
Champaign, IL 61820-6903
www.press.uillinois.edu